MW00460548

PROJECT PLANNING AND SCHEDULING

USING

PRIMAVERA® P6™

For all industries including Version 4 to 7

Planning and Progressing Project Schedules

With and Without Roles and Resources

in an

Established Enterprise Environment

BY

PAUL EASTWOOD HARRIS

Primavera, P3, P3e, P3e/c, Primavera Enterprise, Contract Manager, Primavera Expedition, Primavera Contractor, Primavera Project Planner, Primavera TeamPlay, P6, Primavision, PrimeContract, SureTrak and myPrimavera are either registered trademarks or trademarks of Oracle Corporation in the United States and/or other countries.

Windows, Microsoft® Office Project Standard 2007, Microsoft® Office Project Professional 2007, Microsoft® Project Standard 2003, Microsoft® Project Professional 2003, Microsoft® Project Standard 2002, Microsoft® Project Professional 2002, Microsoft® Project 2000, Microsoft Project® 98 and Excel are registered trademarks of Microsoft Corporation.

Asta Powerproject is a registered trademark of Asta Developments plc.

Adobe® and Acrobat® are registered trademarks of Adobe Systems Incorporated.

All other company or product names may be trademarks of their respective owners.

Screen captures reprinted with authorization from Oracle Corporation.

This publication was created by Eastwood Harris Pty Ltd and is not a product of Oracle Corporation.

DISCLAIMER

AUTHOR AND PUBLISHER

Paul E Harris
Eastwood Harris Pty Ltd
PO Box 4032
Doncaster Heights 3109
Victoria, Australia

Email: harrispe@eh.com.au
Web: http://www.eh.com.au
Tel: +61 (0)4 1118 7701
Fax: +61 (0)3 9846 7700

Please send any comments on this publication to the author.

ISBN 978-1-921059-33-9 (1-921059-33-8) - B5 Paperback
ISBN 978-1-921059-34-6 (1-921059-34-6) - A4 Spiral

26 May 2010

INTRODUCTION

This publication is an upgrade of the *Project Planning & Control Using Primavera P6 For all industries including Versions 4 to 6* and has been written to enable new users to learn the planning and scheduling functions of Primavera Versions 3.5 to 7.

Many users will have prior experience with SureTrak, P3, Asta Powerproject or Microsoft Project and the author explains where there are differences in the products' functionality.

The author would appreciate any constructive comments on how this publication may be improved.

SUMMARY

The publication may be used as:
- ➤ A training manual for a three-day training course, or
- ➤ A self teach book, or
- ➤ A reference manual.

The screen shots for this publication are taken from both Primavera Version 6.0 and Version 7 but this publication may be used to learn Primavera Version 3.5, 4.1, 5.0, 6.0, 6.1, 6.2 or 7.

One, two or three-day training course may be run using this publication and it includes exercises for the students to complete at the end of each chapter. After the course students may use this publication as a reference book.

This publication is ideal for people who would like to quickly gain an understanding of how the software operates and explains how the software differs from Primavera P3, SureTrak and Microsoft Project, thus making it ideal for people who wish to convert from these products.

CUSTOMIZATION FOR TRAINING COURSES

Training organizations or companies that wish to conduct their own training may have this publication tailored to suit their requirements. This may be achieved removing, reordering or adding content to the publication and by writing their own exercises. Please contact the author to discuss this service.

AUTHOR'S COMMENT

As a project controls consultant I have used a number of planning and scheduling software packages for the management of a range of project types and sizes. The first publications I published were user guides/training manuals for Primavera SureTrak, P3 and Microsoft Project users. These were well received by professional project managers and schedulers, so I decided to turn my attention to Primavera Enterprise which is now called Primavera P6. This publication follows the same proven layout of my previous publications. I trust this publication will assist you in understanding how to use Primavera P6 on your projects.

APPRECIATION

I would like thank my daughter Samantha Harris, Andrew Dick and editor Susan Aaron for their assistance in the production of this book.

CURRENT BOOKS PUBLISHED BY EASTWOOD HARRIS

Planning and Control Using Microsoft® Office Project and PMBOK® Guide Fourth Edition
Including Microsoft Project 2000 to 2007 - B5 – Perfect
ISBN 978-1-921059-31-5 - B5 Paperback, ISBN 978-1-921059-32-2 - A4 Spiral

Planning and Scheduling Using Microsoft Office Project 2007
Including Microsoft Project 2000 to 2003 Revised 2009, published September 2009
ISBN 978-1-921059-27-8 - B5 Paperback, ISBN 978-1-921059-28-5 - A4 Spiral

Project Planning and Control Using Primavera® Contractor Version 6.1
For the Construction Industry, May 2009
ISBN 978-1-921059-25-4 - B5 Paperback, ISBN 978-1-921059-26-1 - A4 Spiral Bound

99 Tricks and Traps for Microsoft® Office Project
Including Microsoft® Project 2000 to 2007, published May 2007
ISBN 978-1-921059-19-3 - A5 - Paperback

PRINCE2™ Planning and Control Using Microsoft® Project
Updated for Microsoft® Office Project 2007, published March 2007
ISBN978-1-921059-17-9 - B5 Paperback

Planning Using Primavera® Project Planner P3® Version 3.1
Revised 2006, published March 2006
ISBN 1-921059-13-3 - A4 Spiral Bound

Planning Using Primavera® SureTrak Project Manager Version
3.0 Revised 2006, published June 2006
ISBN 1-921059-14-1- A4 Spiral Bound

SUPERSEDED BOOKS BY THE AUTHOR

Planning and Scheduling Using Microsoft® Project 2003
Planning and Scheduling Using Microsoft® Project 2002
Planning and Scheduling Using Microsoft® Project 2000
Project Planning and Scheduling Using Primavera® Contractor Version 4.1
PRINCE2 TM Planning and Control Using Microsoft® Project
Planning and Control Using Microsoft® Project and PMBOK® Guide Third Edition
Planning and Scheduling Using Primavera® Version 5.0 For Engineering and Construction
Planning and Scheduling Using Primavera® Version 5.0 For IT Project Office
Project Planning and Scheduling Using Primavera® Version 4.1 for IT Project
Project Planning and Scheduling Using Primavera® Version 4.1 or E&C
Project Planning and Scheduling Using Primavera® Enterprise - Team Play Version 3.5
Project Planning and Scheduling Using Primavera® Enterprise - P3e and P3e/c Version 3.5
Planning Using Primavera® Project Planner P3® Version 3.1
Planning Using Primavera® Project Planner P3® Version 3.0
Planning Using Primavera® Project Planner P3® Version 2.0
Planning Using Primavera SureTrak® Project Manager Version 3.0
Project Planning Using SureTrak® for Windows Version 2.0

1   INTRODUCTION

1.1   Purpose

The purpose of this book is to provide a method for planning, scheduling and controlling projects using Primavera Version 6.0 Version 7 and earlier versions within an established Enterprise Project database or a blank database up to an intermediate level.

The screen shots for Primavera P6 Version 6.2 and earlier were captured using and Windows XP and P6 Version 7 screen shots were captured using Windows 7. Users with other operating systems and personalized display themes may have their dialog boxes/forms formatted differently

.
This book covers the following topics:

- Understand the steps required to create a project plan and monitor a project's progress
- Understand the Primavera P6 environment
- Create a project and set up the preferences
- Define calendars
- Creating a Work Breakdown Structure and adding activities
- Format the display
- Add logic and constraints
- Use Filters, Group, Sort and Layouts
- Print reports
- Record and track progress of an unresourced schedule
- User and Administration Preferences and Scheduling Options
- Create and assign roles and resources
- Resource optimization including leveling
- Update a project containing resources
- Other methods of organizing data and Global Change
- Managing the enterprise environment including multiple project scheduling

The book is not intended to cover every aspect of Primavera P6, but it does cover the main features required to create and update a project schedule. It should provide you with a solid grounding, which will enable you to learn the other features of Primavera 6.0 by experimenting with the software, using the help files and reviewing other literature.

This book was written to minimize superfluous text, allowing the user to locate and understand the information contained within as quickly as possible. If at any time you are unable to understand a topic in this book, it is suggested that you use the Primavera Version 6.0 Help menu or User Manuals, which are available on the software CDs in pdf format, or the Oracle website to gain a further understanding of the subject.

Other versions of the software from Version 3.5 onwards are covered in this book and the "What's New" chapters identify the major changes in the software. If you are using this book with an older version, you may find some features do not exist, but I have tried to indicate in which version the new features were introduced and/or removed. Primavera Systems Inc. and the new owners Oracle Corporation continually releases Service Packs for the software and there may be instances where the software operates differently due to the loading of a Service Pack.

1.2   Required Background Knowledge

This book does not teach you how to use computers or to manage projects. The book is intended to teach you how to use Primavera in a project environment. Therefore, to be able to follow this book you should have the following background knowledge:

- The ability to use a personal computer and understand the fundamentals of the operating system.
- Experience using application software, such as Microsoft Office, which would have given you exposure to Windows menu systems and typical Windows functions such as copy and paste.
- An understanding of how projects are managed, such as the phases and processes that take place over the lifetime of a project.

1.3   Purpose of Planning

The ultimate purpose of planning is to build a model that enables you to predict which activities and resources are critical to the timely completion of the project. Strategies may then be implemented to ensure that these activities and resources are managed properly, thus ensuring that the project will be delivered both **On Time** and **Within Budget**.

Planning aims to:

- Identify the total scope of the project and plan to deliver it,
- Evaluate different project delivery methods,
- Identify Products/Deliverables required to deliver a project under a logical breakdown of the project,
- Identify and optimize the use of resources and evaluate if target dates may be met,
- Identify risks, plan to minimize them and set priorities,
- Provide a baseline plan against which progress is measured,
- Assist in stakeholders' communication, identifying what is to be done, when and by whom and
- Assist management to think ahead and make informed decisions.

Planning helps to avoid or assist in evaluating:

- Increased project costs or reduction in scope and/or quality,
- Additional changeover and/or operation costs,
- Extensions of time claims,
- Loss of your client's revenue,
- Contractual disputes and associated resolution costs,
- The loss of reputation of those involved in a project, and
- Loss of a facility or asset in the event of a total project failure.

1.4 Project Planning Metrics

The components that are normally measured and controlled using planning and scheduling software:

- Scope
- Time
- Resource Effort/Work (these are called Units in Primavera P6)
- Cost

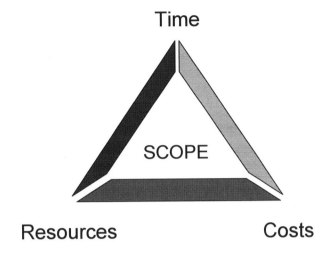

A change in any one of these components normally results in a change in one or more of the others.

Other project management functions that are not traditionally managed with planning and scheduling software but may have components reflected in the schedule include:

- Document Management and Control,
- Quality Management,
- Contract Management,
- Issue Management,
- Risk Management,
- Industrial Relations, and
- Accounting.

The development of Enterprise Project Management systems has resulted in the inclusion of many of these functions in project planning and scheduling software. Primavera includes modules for:

- Issue Management,
- Risk Management, and
- Document Management.

1.5   Planning Cycle

The planning cycle is an integral part of managing a project. A software package such as Primavera makes this activity much easier.

When the original plan is agreed to, the **Baseline** or **Target** is set. The **Baseline** is a copy of the original plan and is used to compare progress of an updated schedule. Earlier versions were limited 50 baselines but this restriction has been removed in later versions.

After project planning has ended and project execution has begun, the actual progress is monitored, recorded and compared to the **Baseline** dates.

The progress is then reported and evaluated against the Baseline.

The plan may be changed by adding or deleting activities and adjusting Remaining Durations, Logic or Resources. A revised plan is then published as progress continues. A revised Baseline may be set if the original Baseline becomes irrelevant due to the impact of project scope changes, a change in methodology or excessive delays.

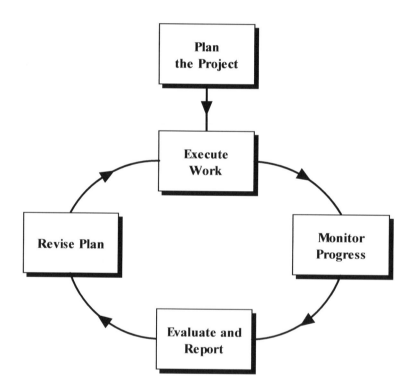

Updating a schedule assists in the management of a project by recording and displaying:

- Progress and the impact of project scope changes and delays as the project progresses,
- The revised completion date and final forecast of costs for the project,
- Historical data that may be used to support extension of time claims and dispute resolution, and
- Historical data that may be used in future projects of a similar nature.

1.6   Levels of Planning

Projects are often planned at a summary level and then at a later date detailed out before the work commences. Smaller projects may be scheduled in detail during project planning, but large or complex projects may require several iterations before the project plan is fully detailed out.

The main reasons for not detailing out a project early are that:

- There may not be enough information at that stage and

- Preparing detailed schedules wastes time as they may be made redundant by unforeseen changes.

The following planning techniques discussed in other well known project management books may be considered:

PMBOK® Guide Third Edition

The PMBOK® Guide Third Edition, which is a project management reference book published by the Project Management Institute, discusses the following techniques:

- The **Rolling Wave**. This technique involves adding more detail to the schedule as the work approaches. This is often possible, as more information is known about the scope of the project as work is executed. The initial planning could be completed at a high level in the **Work Breakdown Structure** (**WBS**). As the work approaches the planning may be completed at a **WBS Component** and then to a **Work Package** level planning.

- The use of **Sub-projects**. These are useful in larger projects where more than one person is working on the project schedule. This situation may exist when portions of projects are contracted out. A sub-project may be detailed out when the work is awarded to a contractor.

- The use of **Phases**. A Phase is different from a PRINCE2 Stage, as Phases may overlap in time and Stages do not. Phases may be defined, for example, as Design, Procure and Install. These Phases may overlap, as Procurement may commence before Design is complete. The Phase development of a schedule involves the detailing out of all the associated WBS elements prior to the commencement of that Phase.

- The PMBOK® Guide does not have strict definitions for levels of plans but assumes that this process is undertaken when decomposing the **Work Breakdown Structure** (**WBS**). There are some other models available that may be used as guidelines, such as the PMI "Practice Standard for Work Breakdown Structures."

PRINCE2 Plans

PRINCE2 is a project management methodology that was developed in the UK. This methodology defines the type of plans that a project team should consider.

Stages in PRINCE2 are defined as time-bound periods of a project, which do not overlap in time and are referred to as Management Stages. The end of a Stage may signify a major event, such as signing a major contract. Project Phases may overlap in time, but Stages do not. Under PRINCE2 a Project Plan is divided into Stages and a Stage plan is detailed out prior to its commencement. PRINCE2 defines the following levels of plans:

- **Programme Plan** – which may include Project Plans or one or more portfolios of multiple projects,

- **Project Plan** – this is mandatory and is updated through the duration of a project,

- **Stage Plan** – there are a minimum of two Stage Plans: an **Initiation Stage Plan** and **First Stage Plan**. There would usually be one Stage Plan for each Stage,

- **Exception Plan** – which is at the same level and detail as a Stage Plan and replaces a Stage Plan at the request of a Project Board when a Stage is forecast to exceed tolerances (contingent time), and

- **Team Plan** – which is optional and would be used on larger projects where Teams deliver Products that require detailed planning. A typical example is a contractor's plan, which would be submitted during the bid process.

Jelen's Cost and Optimization Engineering

This book defines the following levels of plans:

- Level 0: This is the total project and is, in effect, a single bar spanning the time from start to finish.

- Level 1: This schedules the project by its major components. For example, a level 1 schedule for a process plant may be broken into process area, storage and handling area, site and services, and utilities. It is shown in bar chart format.

- Level 2: Each of the level 1 components is further subdivided. For example, utility systems are broken into water, electrical, gas, sanitary, etc. In most cases, this schedule level can only be shown in bar chart format although a bar chart with key constraints may be possible.

- Level 3: The subdivision continues. This is probably the first level that a meaningful critical path network can be drawn. It is also a good level for the project's overall control schedule since it is neither too summarized nor too detailed.

- Levels 4–?: The subdivision continues to whatever level of detail is needed by the user. When operating at these more detailed levels, the planners generally work with less than the total schedule. In most cases these "look-ahead" schedules span periods of 30–180 days. The user may utilize either bar chart or CPM format for these schedules.

This paragraph was reproduced from Jelen's Cost and Optimization Engineering, author F. Jelen, copyright 1983, ISBN 0-07-053646-5, with the written permission from the publisher McGraw-Hill.

1.7   Monitoring and Controlling a Project

After a plan has been produced, it should be executed and the work authorized in accordance with the plan. If there is to be a change in the plan, then the plan should be formally changed. If necessary, the client should be informed and, if required by the contract, approval should be sought.

It may be difficult to obtain approval for extension of time claims when the plan is not followed then and furthermore this will make dispute resolution more difficult.

Monitoring a project ensures:

- The required deliverables/products are produced,

- The required quality is met,

- The deliverables/products are produced on time, with the planned resources and to budget, and

- Historical data is recorded for use in planning future projects.

Controlling a project provides the next level of management with information that enables them to manage a project and make informed decisions on problems:

- Ensure that the project is being executed according to the plan,

- Compare the project's progress with the original plan,

- Review options,

- Forecast problems as early as possible which enables corrective action to be taken as early as possible, and

- Obtain data required for preparing extension of time claims and for dispute resolution.

2   CREATING A PROJECT PLAN

The aim of this chapter is to give an understanding of what a plan is and some practical guidance on how a schedule may be created and updated during the life of a project.

2.1   Understanding Planning and Scheduling Software

Planning and scheduling software enables the user to:

- Enter the breakdown structure of the project deliverables or products into the software. This is often called a Work Breakdown Structure (WBS) or Product Breakdown Structure (PBS),
- Break a project down into the work required to create the deliverables and enter these into the software as Activities under the appropriate WBS,
- Assign durations, constraints, predecessors and successors of the activities and then calculate the start and finish date of all the activities,
- Assign resources and/or costs, which represent people, equipment or materials, to the activities and calculate the project resource requirements and/or cash flow,
- Optimize the project plan,
- Set Baseline Dates and Budgets to compare progress against,
- Use the plan to approve the commencement of work,
- Record the actual progress of activities and compare the progress against the Baseline and amend the plan when required, allowing for scope changes, etc.,
- Record the consumption of resources and/or costs and re-estimate the resources and/or costs required to finish the project, and
- Produce management reports.

There are four modes or levels in which planning and scheduling software may be used.

	Planning	Tracking
Without Resources	**LEVEL 1** Planning without Resources	**LEVEL 2** Tracking progress without Resources
With Resources	**LEVEL 3** Planning with Resources	**LEVEL 4** Tracking progress with Resources

As the level increases, the amount of information required to maintain the schedule will increase and, more importantly, your skill and knowledge in using the software will increase. This book is designed to take you from Level 1 to Level 4.

2.2   Enterprise Project Management

Primavera is an Enterprise Project Management software package that enables many projects to be managed in one database. These projects may be summarized under a hierarchical structure titled the Enterprise Project Structure (EPS). This function is similar to summarizing activities of a project under a Work Breakdown Structure (WBS).

An EPS is used for the following purposes:

- To manage user access to projects within the database.
- To manage activities over multiple projects that have a common interest, such as a critical resource.
- Top-down budgeting of projects and resources that may later be compared to the bottom-up or detailed project estimates.
- To allow standardized reporting of all projects in the database.

Individual projects must be created within an EPS database. Primavera has not been designed as a single project planning and scheduling software package and there is an administrative overhead in managing projects in an EPS database. You may wish to consider managing single projects using Primavera Contractor which does not have the overhead of managing an Enterprise database but has activity limits.

Primavera has a function titled Portfolios that enables a limited number of projects to be viewed at a time. For example, Portfolio would enable you to view projects in a physical area, or of a specific type or client.

2.3   Understanding Your Project

Before you start the process of creating a project plan, it is important to have an understanding of the project and how it will be executed. On large, complex projects, this information is usually available from the following types of documents:

- Project charter or business case
- Project scope or contract documentation
- Functional specification
- Requirements baseline
- Plans and drawings
- Project execution plan
- Contracting and purchasing plan
- Equipment lists
- Installation plan
- Testing plan

Many project managers conduct a **Stakeholder Analysis** at the start of a project. This process lists all the people and organizations with an interest in the project and their interests or desired outcomes.

- Key success factors may be identified from the interests of the influential stakeholders.
- It is important to use the stakeholder analysis to identify all the stakeholder activities and include them in the schedule.

It is imperative to gain a good understanding of how the project is to be executed before entering any data into the software. It is considered good practice to plan a project before creating a schedule in any planning and scheduling software. These documents are referred to by many terms such as Project Execution Plan or Project Methodology Statement. You should also understand what level of reporting the project team requires, as providing either too little or too much detail will often lead to a discarded schedule.

There are three processes required to create or maintain a plan at each of the four levels:

- Collecting the relevant project data,
- Entering and manipulating the data in software, and
- Distributing, reviewing and revising the plan.

The ability of the scheduler to collect the data is as important as the ability to enter and manipulate the information using the software. On larger projects, it may be necessary to write policies and procedures to ensure accurate collection of data from the various people, departments, stakeholders/companies, and sites.

2.4   Level 1 – Planning Without Resources

This is the simplest mode of planning.

2.4.1   Creating Projects

To create a project in a Primavera database, you will need the following information:

- An EPS Node, OBS Node in the database to assign the project,
- Project ID (a code assigned to the project) and the Project Name,
- The Project Start Date (and perhaps the Finish Date), and
- The Rate Type. Primavera has five rates per resource and this option enables you to select a rate as the default resources rate.

It would also be useful to know other information such as:

- Client name, and
- Project information such as location, project number and stakeholders.

2.4.2   Defining the Calendars

Before you start entering activities into your schedule, it is advisable to set up the calendars. These are used to model the working time for each activity in the project. For example, a 6-day calendar is created for those activities that will be worked for 6 days a week. The calendar should include any public holidays and any other exceptions to available working days, such as planned days off.

Primavera has three types of calendars:

- **Global** – which may be assigned to activities and resources in any project,
- **Project** – these are project-specific calendars assigned to activities, and
- **Resource** – that are assigned to resources.

Project and Resource calendars may be linked to Global calendars, enabling any changes to holidays made to a Global calendar to be inherited by the associated Project and Resource calendars.

2.4.3   Defining the Project Breakdown Structures

A project breakdown structure (PBS) is a way of categorizing the activities of a project into numerous codes that relate to the project. The codes act as tags or attributes of each activity.

During or after the activities are added to the schedule, they are assigned their PBSs so that they may be grouped, summarized, and filtered in or out of the display.

Primavera has two principal methods of assigning a PBS to your project:

- The Work Breakdown Structure (WBS) function, which is comparable to the P3 and SureTrak WBS functions.
- The Activity Code function that operates in a way similar to P3 and SureTrak.

Before creating a project, you should design your PBSs by asking the following questions:

- Which phases are involved in the project (e.g., Design, Procure, Install and Test)?
- Which disciplines are participating (e.g., Civil, Mechanical and Electrical)?
- Which departments are involved in the project (e.g., Sales, Procurement and Installation)?
- What work is expected to be contracted out and which contractors are to be used?
- How many sites or areas are there in the project?

Use the responses to these and other similar questions to create the PBSs.

2.4.4 Adding Activities

Activities must be defined before they are entered into the schedule. It is important that you carefully consider the following factors:

- What is the scope of the activity? (What is included and excluded?)
- How long is the activity going to take?
- Who is going to perform it?
- What are the deliverables or output for each activity?

The project estimate is usually a good place to start looking for a breakdown of the project into activities, resources, and costs. It may even provide an indication of how long the work will take.

Activities may have variable durations depending on the number of resources assigned. You may find that one activity that takes 4 days using 4 workers may take 2 days using 8 workers or 8 days using 2 workers.

Usually project reports are issued on a regular basis such as every week or every month. It is recommended that, if possible, an activity should not span more than two reporting periods. That way the activities should only be **In-Progress** for one report. Of course, it is not practical to do this on long duration activities, such as procurement and delivery activities, that may span many reporting periods.

Good practice recommends that you have a measurable finish point for each group of activities. These may be identified in the schedule by **Milestones** and are designated with zero duration. You may issue documentation to officially highlight the end of one activity and the start of another, thereby adding clarity to the schedule. Examples of typical documents that may be issued for clarity are:

- Issue of a drawing package
- Completion of a specification
- Placing of an order
- Receipt of materials (delivery logs or tickets or dockets)
- Completed testing certificates for equipment or systems

2.4.5 Adding the Logic Links

The logic is added to the schedule to provide the order in which the activities must be undertaken. The logic is designated by indicating the predecessors to, or the successors from, each activity. There are two methods that software uses to sequence activities:

- Precedence Diagramming Method (PDM), and
- Arrow Diagramming (ADM).

Most current project planning and scheduling software, including Primavera, uses PDM. You can create a PDM diagram using the Network Diagram function.

There are several types of dependencies that may be used:

1. **Mandatory dependencies**, also known as **Hard Logic** or **Primary Logic**, are relationships between activities that may not be broken. For example, a hole has to be dug before it is filled with concrete, or a computer delivered before software is loaded.

2. **Discretionary dependencies**, also known as **Sequencing Logic** or **Soft Logic** or **Secondary Logic** , are relationships between activities that may be changed when the plan is changed. For example, if there are five holes to be excavated and only one machine available, or five computers to be assembled and one person available to work on them, then the order of these activities could be set with sequencing logic yet changed at a later date.

   Both **Mandatory dependencies** and **Discretionary dependencies** are entered into Primavera as activity relationships or logic links. The software does not provide a method of identifying the type of relationship because notes or codes may not be attached to relationships. A **Note** may be added to either the predecessor or the successor activity to explain the relationship.

3. **External dependencies** are usually events outside the control of the project team that impact the schedule. An example would be the availability of a site to start work. This is usually represented in Primavera by a Milestone that has a constraint applied to it. This topic is discussed in more detail in the next section.

The software will calculate the start and finish dates for each activity. The end date of the project is calculated from the start date of the project, the logic amongst the activities, any **Leads** (often referred to as **Negative Lag**) or **Lags** applied to the logic and durations of the activities. The following picture shows the effect of a lag and a lead on the start of a successor activity:

An example of a **Finish to Start** with positive lag:

An example of a **Finish to Start** with negative lag:

It is good practice to create a **Closed Network** with the logic. In a **Closed Network**, all activities have one or more predecessors and one or more successors except:

- The project start milestone or first activity, which has no predecessors, and
- The finish milestone or finish activity, which has no successors.

NOTE: When a closed network is not established then the Critical Path, Total Float and Free Float will not calculate correctly.

The project's logic must not loop back on itself. Looping occurs if the logic states that A preceded B, B preceded C, and C preceded A. That is not a logical project situation and will cause the software to generate an error comment during network calculations.

Thus, when the logic is correctly applied, a delay to an activity will delay all its successor activities and delay the project end date when there is insufficient spare slippage time to accommodate the delay. This spare time is normally called **Float** but note that Microsoft Project uses the term **Slack** for **Float**.

2.4.6   Constraints

External dependencies are applied to a schedule using **Constraints** and these may model the impact of events outside the logical sequence of activities. A constraint would be imposed to specific dates such as the availability of a facility to start work or the required completion date of a project. Constraints should be cross-referenced to the supporting documentation, such as Milestone Dates from contract documentation, using the **Notebook Topics** function. Typical examples of constraints would be:

- **Start on or After** for the availability of a site to commence work, and
- **Finish on or Before** for the date that a total project must be delivered by, or handed over, to a client.

2.4.7   Risk Analysis

The process of planning a project may identify risks, so a formal risk analysis should be considered. A risk analysis may identify risk mitigation activities that should be added to the schedule before it is submitted for approval.

2.4.8   Contingent Time

The addition of contingent time should be considered when submitting a schedule for approval. Estimates usually have contingency and if this money is to be expended then an allowance for time to spend the contingent funds needs to be made. Contingent time may be added to a schedule in a number of ways:

- Insert one or more contingent time activities in the project. These would be adjusted in length as the project progresses to maintain the planned end date.
- Assign work days in the calendar nonwork days. For example, a building project could be scheduled on a 5-day per week basis, knowing that work will be undertaken on the Saturday.
- Increase the activity durations by a factor.
- Assign positive lags between activities, although this is not recommended by the author.

2.4.9   Scheduling the Project

The software calculates the shortest time in which the project may be completed, Activities are moved forward in time until they meet a Relationship or Constraint or a calendar nonwork time. Un-started activities without logic or constraints are scheduled to start at the Project Start Date or as permitted by calendar nonwork times.

Scheduling the project will identify the **Critical Path(s)** when there is a **Closed Network**. The Critical Path is the chain(s) of activities that takes the longest time to accomplish; a delay to any activity in the chain will delay the end date of the project. The calculated completion date depends on the critical activities starting and finishing on time. If any of them are delayed, the whole project will be delayed. The schedule in the following picture is on a 5-day per week calendar so there is no work on Saturday and Sunday. The Critical Path in the following picture runs from the "Start Milestone" to "Activity 1" to "Activity 2" to "Activity 3" and to the "Finish Milestone."

Activities that may be delayed without affecting the project end date have **Float**, which are "Activity 4" and "Activity 5" in the following picture.

- **Total Float** is the amount of time an activity may be delayed without extending the project end date. The delay of an activity with a positive Total Float value may delay other activities with positive Total Float, however will not delay the end date of the project unless the delay is greater than the float. The delay of any activity with a zero Total Float value (and is, therefore, on the Critical Path) will delay other subsequent activities with zero Total Float and extend the end date of the project. "Activity 5" has 8 days before it delays the end date and "Activity 4" has 11 days before it delays the end date. The Total Float is displayed by the thin horizontal line.

- **Free Float** is the amount of time an activity may be delayed without affecting the start date of any of its immediate successor activities. "Activity 4" following has 3 days Free Float before it delays "Activity 5" and "Activity 5" has 8 days Free Float before it delays the "Finish Milestone."

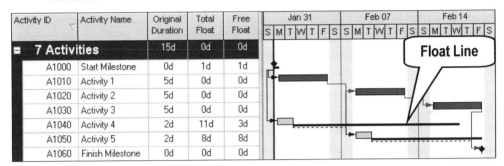

2.4.10 Formatting the Display – Layouts and Filters

There are tools to manipulate and display the activities to suit the project reporting requirements. These functions are covered in the **Group, Sort and Layouts and the Filters** chapters.

2.4.11 Printing and Reports

There are software features that enable you to present the information in a clear and concise manner to communicate the requirements to all project members. These functions are covered in the **Printing and Reports** chapter.

2.4.12 Issuing the Plan

All members of the project team should review the project plan in an attempt to:

- Optimize the process and methods employed, and
- Gain consensus among team members as to the project's logic, durations, and Project Breakdown Structures.

Team members should communicate frequently with each other about their expectations of the project while providing each with the opportunity to contribute to the schedule and further improve the outcome.

2.5   Level 2 – Monitoring Progress Without Resources

2.5.1   Setting the Baseline

The optimized and agreed-to plan is used as a baseline for measuring progress and monitoring change. The software may record the baseline dates of each activity for comparison against actual progress during the life of the project.

2.5.2   Tracking Progress

The schedule should be **Updated** (progressed) on a regular basis and progress recorded at that point. The date on which progress is reported is known by a number of different terms such as **Data Date**, **Update Date**, **Time Now** and **Status Date**. The **Data Date** is the field Primavera uses to record this date. The **Data Date** is **NOT** the date that the report is printed but rather the date that reflects when the update information was gathered.

Whatever the frequency chosen for updating, you will have to collect the following activity information in order to update a schedule:

- Completed activities
  - ➢ Actual Start date
  - ➢ Actual Finish dates
- In-progress activities
  - ➢ Actual Start date
  - ➢ Percentage Completed
  - ➢ Duration or Expected Finish Date of the Activity
- Un-started work
  - ➢ Any revisions to activities that have not started
  - ➢ New activities representing scope changes
  - ➢ Revisions to logic that represent changes to the plan

The schedule may be updated after this information has been collected. The recorded progress is compared to the **Baseline** dates, either graphically or by using columns of data, such as the **Baseline Finish Variance** column:

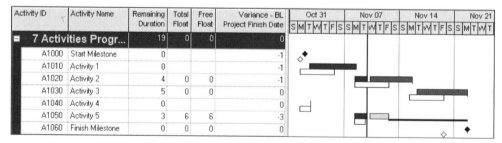

Activity ID	Activity Name	Remaining Duration	Total Float	Free Float	Variance - BL Project Finish Date	Oct 31	Nov 07	Nov 14	Nov 21
⊟	**7 Activities Progr...**	19	0	0	0				
A1000	Start Milestone	0			-1				
A1010	Activity 1	0			-1				
A1020	Activity 2	4	0	0	-1				
A1030	Activity 3	5	0	0	0				
A1040	Activity 4	0			0				
A1050	Activity 5	3	6	6	-3				
A1060	Finish Milestone	0	0	0	0				

2.5.3 Corrective Action

At this point it may be necessary to further optimize the schedule to bring the project back on track by discussing the schedule with the appropriate project team members. The possible options are:

- Reduce the contingent time allowance.

- Assign a negative lag on a Finish to Start relationship, which enables a successor to commence before a predecessor is completed.

- Change relationships to allow activities to be executed in parallel.

- Reduce the durations of activities. In a resourced schedule this could be achieved by increasing the number of resources assigned to an activity.

- Work longer hours per day or days per week by editing the calendars, or

- Reduce the scope and delete activities.

2.6 Level 3 – Scheduling With Resources, Roles and Budgets

2.6.1 Estimating or Planning for Control

There are two modes that the software may use at Level 3.

- **Estimating**. In this mode, the objective is to create a schedule with costs that are used only as an estimate. The schedule will never be updated. Activities may have many resources assigned to them to develop an accurate cost estimate and include many items that would never be updated in the process of updating a schedule.

- **Planning for Control**. In this mode, the intention is to assign actual units (hours) and costs to resources, then calculate units and costs to completion, and possibly conduct an Earned Value analysis. In this situation, it is important to ensure that the minimum number of resources are assigned to activities, and preferably only one resource assigned to each activity. The process of updating a schedule becomes extremely difficult and time consuming when a schedule has many resources per activity. The scheduler is then under threat of becoming a timekeeper and may lose sight of other important functions, such as calculating the forecast to complete and the project finish date.

2.6.2 The Balance Between the Number of Activities and Resources

When Planning for Control on large or complex schedules, it is important to maintain a balance between the number of activities and the number of resources that are planned and tracked. As a rule, the more activities a schedule has, the fewer resources should be created and assigned to activities.

When a schedule contains a large number of activities and a large number of resources assigned to each activity, the result may be that no members of the project team are able to understand the schedule and the scheduler is unable to maintain it.

Instead of assigning individual resources, such as people by name, consider using "Skills" or "Trades," and on very large projects use "Crews" or "Teams."

This technique is not so important when you use a schedule for estimating the direct cost of a project (by assigning costs to the resources) or if you are not using the schedule to track a project's progress (such as a schedule that is used to support written proposals).

Therefore, it is more important to minimize the number of resources in large schedules that will be updated regularly, because updating every resource assigned to each activity at each schedule update is very time consuming.

2.6.3 Creating and Using Resources

First, one would usually establish a resource pool by entering all the required project resources into a hierarchical table in the software. The required quantity of each resource is assigned to the activities. In an Enterprise environment these resources may already be defined for you.

Entering a cost rate for each resource enables you to conduct a resource cost analysis, such as comparing the cost of supplementing overloaded resources against the cost of extending the project deadline.

Estimates and time-phased cash flows may be produced from this resource/cost data.

2.6.4 Creating and Using Roles

Primavera has an additional function titled **Roles**, which is used for planning and managing resources.

- A Role is a skill or trade or job description and may be used as an alternative to resources during the planning period of a project.
- Roles are defined in a hierarchical structure and hold a **Proficiency Level**.
- Roles may be assigned to activities in a way similar to how resources are assigned. Roles can be replaced later by resources after it has been decided who is going to be assigned the work.
- Primavera Version 5.0 introduced a function allowing a Role to be assigned a rate.

2.6.5 The Relationship Between Resources and Roles

Primavera has the ability to define roles and associate them with resources. A role is a job title, trade or skill and may have many resources. A multi-skilled resource may have multiple roles. For example, a role may be a Clerical Assistant and there may be five clerical assistants in a company who would be assigned the Clerical Assistant Role. If one clerical assistant were also a data entry person, then this resource would be assigned two roles: Clerical Assistant and Data Entry.

2.6.6 Activity Type and Duration Type

Activities may be assigned an **Activity Type** and **Duration Type**, which affect how resources are calculated. Additional software features enable the user to more accurately model real-life situations. These features are covered in the **Assigning Roles, Resources and Expenses** chapter.

2.6.7 Budgets

The Budget function enables Top-Down Budgeting at a summary level against each EPS Node in an accounting style. Budgets may be compared to the detailed estimates calculated after resources have been assigned to Activities. The Budget function is not covered in detail in this book.

2.6.8   Resource Usage Profiles and Tables

These features enables the display and analysis of project resource requirements both in tables and graphs.

The data may be exported to Excel or reports run for further analysis and presentation.

2.6.9   Resource Optimization

The schedule may now have to be resource optimized to:

- Reduce peaks and smooth the resource requirements, or
- Reduce resource demand to the available number of resources, or
- Reduce demand to an available cash flow when a project is financed by a customer.

Leveling is defined as delaying activities until resources become available. There are several methods of delaying activities, and thus leveling a schedule, which are outlined in the **Resource Optimization** chapter.

2.7   Level 4 – Monitoring and Controlling a Resourced Schedule

2.7.1   Monitoring Projects with Resources

When you update a project with resources, you will need to collect some additional information:

- The quantities and/or costs spent to date per activity for each resource, and
- The quantities and/or costs required per resource to complete each activity.

You may then update a resourced schedule with this data.

After a schedule has been updated, then a review of the future resource requirements, project end date, and cash flows may be made.

Updating a resourced project is time consuming and requires experience and a good understanding of how the software calculates a schedule. Ideally this should only be attempted by experienced users or by a novice under the guidance of an experienced user.

2.7.2   Controlling a Project with Resources

At this point, it is possible to undertake a great deal of analysis and often Earned Value Performance Measurement techniques are used.

3   STARTING UP AND NAVIGATION

After clicking on the icon or menu item on your desktop to start Primavera, you will be presented with the **Login** form.

3.1   Logging In

Clicking on the ⬛ icon under **Database** will open the **Edit Database Connections** form where you may select an alternative database to open:

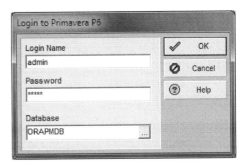

- Select the required database from the list of databases,

- Click the [✓ Select] icon,

- Enter your Login Name and Password, which are case sensitive, and then

- Click [✓ OK] to open the selected database.

To specify how you want the software to start, after the software has started, go to **Edit**, **User Preferences...** and click the **Application** tab.

3.2   Welcome Form

You may then be presented with the Welcome form.

- Select **Project Portfolio** which will display only those projects assigned to the selected portfolio; this is in effect a filter that operates on projects.

- [Create New...] takes you to the **Create a New Project** wizard; this topic is covered in the next chapter.

- [Open Existing...] will enable you to select a project from the selected portfolio.

- [▷ Open Last] will take you to the last opened project.

- [Open Global Data] will take you to the location specified in the **Application** tab specified in **Application Starts Up** in the **Edit**, **User Preferences...** form.

- Click on **Do not show this window again** and the next time you login you will be taken directly to the location nominated in the **User Preferences...**, **Application** tab.

 It is suggested that you select from the **User Preferences...**, **Application** tab either the **Projects** if you work on different projects all the time or the **Activities** option if you work on the same project all the time.

3.3   The Home Window

To open the **Home Window** click the [Home] button on the Navigation toolbar; a screen will be displayed titled **Home**. Select **View**, **Toolbars** from the menu. The option to hide or display the **Navigation** and **Directory** toolbars and the **Status Bar** is available as well as the options to hide or display the text associated with the toolbar buttons.

The tool bars are titled:

> ➤ Menu Bar
> ➤ Navigation Bar
> ➤ Directory Bar
> ➤ Status Bar

- The **Toolbar** menu may be displayed by right-clicking on either toolbar.

- Most toolbars and toolbar text may be hidden or displayed.

- Project related buttons on the **Directory Bar** will be inactive unless a project is opened.

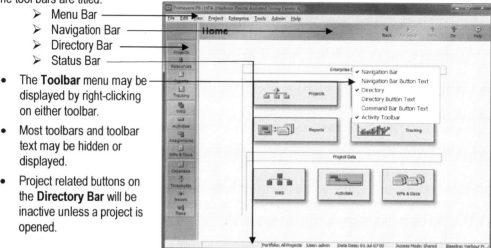

3.4   The Projects Window

The sample database supplied with Primavera will be used to demonstrate how to navigate around the screens. Click on the **Projects icon** to open the **Projects Window**.

3.4.1   Project Window Top Pane

The top window displays the **Enterprise Project Breakdown** structure (EPS):

- The [+] and [–] icons, to the left of the EPS names are used to display or hide levels of the EPS. The picture shows that the Health Care EPS Node has two projects.

> ➤ Harbor Pointe and
> ➤ Lincoln Hospital.

- Open the **Enterprise Project Structure (EPS)** form by selecting **Enterprise, Enterprise Project Structure...** from the menu.

- It is now clear which entries are EPS Nodes and which are Projects.

- The menu commands **View**, **Expand All**, **Collapse All** and **Collapse To...** will summarize the bands to the required level in the EPS.

3.4.2 Project Window Bottom Pane

The bottom window may be hidden and may be displayed by clicking on the ▣ button or selecting **View**, **Show on Bottom**, **Project Details**.

Information regarding an EPS Node or project assigned to an EPS Node is available at the bottom of the screen by selecting the EPS Node or Project and selecting tabs in the bottom window.

Many of the fields are grayed out which means they are calculated or summarized from other data or the project is not open and the data may not be edited.

Right-clicking on a tab name will display a menu and selecting **Customize Project Details** will open the **Project Details** form and you may select which tabs are displayed.

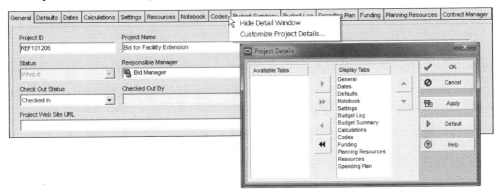

3.5 Opening One or More Projects

Enterprise and Project data may be accessed in the **Projects Window**. To access Project activity information, such as activities, resources and relationships, a project must be opened and the **Activities Window** displayed. One or more projects may be opened at the same time by selecting one or more projects and/or one or more EPS Nodes, then:

- Right-click and select **Open Project**,
- Selecting **Ctl+O**,
- Select **File**, **Open...** to open the **Open** form:

The **Open** form display the access options for opening a project are **Exclusive**, **Shared** or **Read Only**.

A single recently opened project may be opened from the **File** menu; a new function in Version 7.

Note: A project may only be opened as **Exclusive** (meaning that only the current user may edit it) by using the **File**, **Open** form. All other methods will result in the project being opened in the **Shared** mode and all users with access to the project may open and edit the project(s) at the same time. The **Shared** option may result in one user edits being over written by another users edits, depending on who save what and when. A project that is opened in the **Shared** mode by multiple users with different **User Preferences Time Units** will result in the users calculating different values for Activity, WBS Nodes and Project durations in days.

Note: If more than one project is to be opened at a time then it is **VERY IMPORTANT** that the **Multiple Project Scheduling** chapter is read and understood.

3.6   Opening a Portfolio

The **Portfolio** function reduces the number of Projects that are viewed in the **Projects Window**:

- To create a **Portfolio** select **Enterprise, Project Portfolios…** and open the **Portfolio** form.
- Create a portfolio and add projects using **the Portfolio** form. A **Portfolio** may be **Global** and all users have access or **User** and just available to that user.
- The **File, Open** (project) form also enables the selection of a **Portfolio** which reduces the number of projects that are displayed in the **Open** (project) form.
- After a **Portfolio** has been selected using **File, Select Project Portfolio…** only those projects in the Portfolio will be displayed in the **Projects Window**.

3.7   Navigating Around a Project

After a project is open, the **Activities** ion [Activities] on the **Directory** bar may need to be clicked on to open the **Activities Window**. The need to click this button differs with the industry version of the software. The following toolbars are now available:

- **Navigation** toolbar. The **Forward, Backward** and **Home** buttons are now functional as there are now three Windows available.

- **Activity** toolbar, below the Navigation toolbar.

- **Layout Options** bar.

- **Command** toolbar, on the right of the screen. The text may be hidden with the **Toolbar** menu.

- **Directory** toolbar, which will now have all options active.

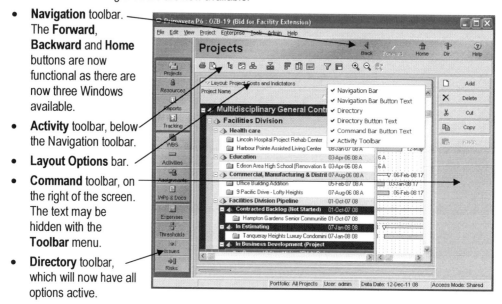

3.7.1   Command Toolbar

The Command toolbar may have the text hidden but may not be hidden completely and is used to operate on activities such as adding, copying, deleting, cutting and pasting and assigning Roles, Resources, Activity Codes and Relationships.

3.7.2   Activities Toolbar

The Activities toolbar is displayed with the **Activities Window** and may be hidden as well as used to hide, display or format the information on the screen.

3.7.3   Navigation Toolbar

When a button on the **Navigation** toolbar is clicked, an additional **Window** is opened. When a **Window** such as the **WBS** or **Activities** is opened, it remains active after the view is closed. The **Back** [Back] and **Forward** [Forward] buttons on the **Navigation** toolbar are used to scroll through the open **Windows**.

3.7.4 Directory Toolbar

The **Directory** toolbar is used to select and open additional Windows. After a project has been opened and a Window such as the **Project**, **WBS**, **Activities**, **Resources** and **Resource Assignments** has been opened, the ▣ and ▣ on the **Navigation** toolbar are used to return to previously opened Windows. All the Windows associated with a project are closed when a project is closed.

 It is recommended that the **Toolbar Text** is hidden after the icon pictures are understood as this releases more space for the schedule.

Toolbars may not be edited by adding or removing command buttons.

3.7.5 Top and Bottom Panes of Windows

Windows such as the **Project**, **WBS**, **Activities**, **Resources** and **Resource Assignments** have **Top** and **Bottom Panes**, some of which may be formatted to meet your requirements. The Bottom pane may also be hidden from view in most Windows. The following commands will enable you to hide and display the bottom panes, they are all the same as the **Projects Window** discussed earlier.

- Selecting **View**, **Show on Bottom**, **Activity Details** or

- Right-clicking with the mouse and selecting **Activity Details** from the menu will display the **Bottom** pane, or

- Clicking on the ▣ button on the **Activities** toolbar will hide or display the **Bottom** pane.

The following commands will enable you to format the top and bottom panes.

- Selecting **View**, **Show on Top** and **Show on Bottom** will show the display options.

- Some **Details** forms may be formatted to display only the tabs that are of use to the scheduler. To format the display right-click in the top of the details pane and select **Customize Activity Details...**, the arrows are used to hide and display tabs and reorder them.

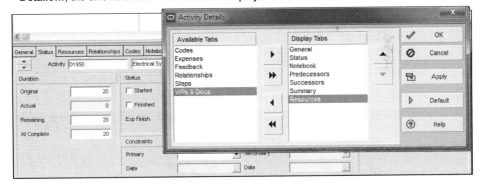

3.8 User Preferences – Time Units P6 Version 7

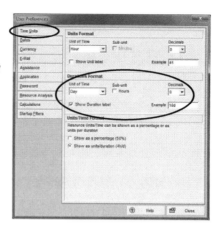

The **User Preferences enable** each user to select how some information is displayed or calculated.

- Select the **Time Units** tab:
  - ➤ The **Duration Format** section determines how the activity durations are displayed.

3.9 User Preferences – Time Units P6.2 and Earlier

The **User Preferences enable** each user to select how some information is displayed or calculated. These are covered in detail in The **User and Administration Preferences and Advanced Scheduling Options** chapter. To adjust how the date and time are displayed select **Edit**, **User Preferences…**, if you have been granted access:

- Select the **Time Units** tab:

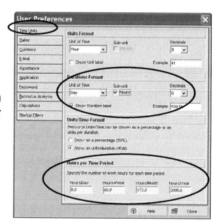

  - ➤ The **Duration Format** section determines how the activity durations are displayed.
  - ➤ Primavera P6.2 and earlier essentially calculates in hours and the **Hours per Time Period** options convert the duration in hours to Days, Weeks, Month and Years for all projects that the user has opened. This is a problem if activity calendars have different hours per day as some durations in days will be incorrect.
  - ➤ This field was removed in P6 Version 7 and now each calendar has its own values.

3.10 User Preferences – Date

- Select the **Dates** tab:
  - ➤ This is where you decide if the time is to be displayed,
  - ➤ How it is formatted, and
  - ➤ How the year is displayed.

  NOTE: It is strongly recommended that the time is always displayed so the user knows the time of Actual Dates and Constraints because the software will often select 00:00, first second of a day.

3.11   Right-clicking with the Mouse

It is important that you become used to using the right-click function of the mouse as this is often a quicker way of operating the software than using the menus. The right-click function will usually display a menu, which is often different depending on the displayed **View** and Active Pane selected. It is advised that you experiment with each view to become familiar with the menus.

3.12   Accessing Help

The help file may be accessed by:

- Pressing the F1 key,

- Selecting **Help**, **Contents...**

- Clicking on the ⊙ button in the top right side of the screen in the **Navigation** toolbar.

Selecting **View**, **Hint Help** will display information about a field when the mouse is moved over the field heading, as per the preceding picture. This is useful for understanding how the fields calculate.

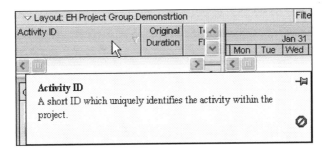

3.13   Application of Options within Forms

Primavera is consistent in the way the data in most forms may be Grouped, Sorted and Filtered. After the basics are understood, then as these principles may be applied to most forms you will find it easier to navigate around the software.

After the format or options have been selected within forms such as Bars, Filters and Group and Sort, click:

- The ✓ OK button to apply the format and close the form, or

- The Apply button to apply the format and leave the form open.

This is useful for checking if the option displays as required before closing the form.

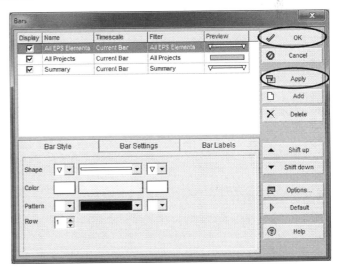

Often there is an arrow in a box and this indicates that there is a menu that may be opened by clicking on the arrow. Data in a form may be formatted and filtered from this menu.

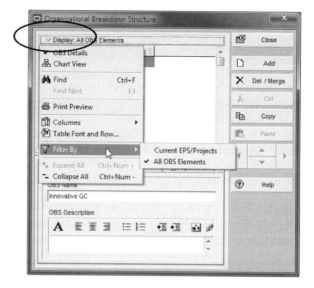

Sorting data within a forms such as Resources, OBS, may be achieved by clicking on the title above the first data item. Clicking on the **EPS ID** box will rotate the sort from Hierarchical, to Alphabetical to reverse Alphabetical.

If there is a filter applied, then this data may not sort.

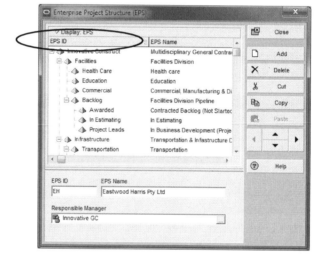

3.14 Closing Down

The closing down options are:

- Select **File**, **Close All** or **Ctrl+W** to close all **Projects** and **Windows** and return to the **Home Window**.

- Select **File**, **Exit** or click the ⊠ button in the top right side of the Primavera window to shut down all projects and close Primavera.

ⓘ If you close down the system leaving one or more projects open, then these projects will be open the next time you log in. Go to the **Edit**, **User Preferences**, **Application** tab and set the **Application Startup Window** to **Activities** so the software will open with your last project **Activities Window** displayed.

3.15 Terminology Differences between Industry Versions

Oracle Corporation different industry versions of the software and the functionality differs slightly between the versions. This book was written using the Construction and Engineering version. The main terminology differences are:

- The Duration of an Activity is titled:
  - ➢ **Original Duration** in "E&C," "Construction and Engineering" and "Power, Energy, and Process" versions, and
  - ➢ **Planned Duration** in the "IT," "Technology and Manufacturing" and "Public and A&D" versions.
- The total of the planned or budgeted costs or units is titled:
  - ➢ **Budgeted Costs and Units** in "Construction and Engineering," and "Power, Energy, and Process" versions, and
  - ➢ **Planned Costs and Units** in the "IT," "Technology and Manufacturing" and "Public and A&D" versions.

IT – Originally TeamPlay in Primavera Version 3.5

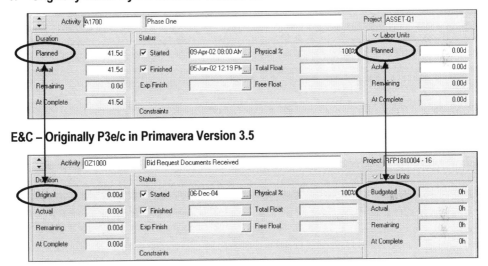

E&C – Originally P3e/c in Primavera Version 3.5

This book was originally written for those using P3e/c in Primavera Version 3.5, then upgraded to Primavera Version 4.1, then Version 5.0, Version 6.0 for Construction and Engineering and now Primavera for Engineering and Construction Contractors. Please inform me, the author Paul E Harris, if there are any other differences in the versions that I should include in later releases of this book.

3.16 Workshop 1 - Navigating Around the Windows

Background

To become familiar with Primavera you will open your database and navigate around the Windows.

Note: Your Window may look different from the one used in this publication which a demonstration database provided by Oracle Primavera.

Assignment

1. Open your database. If a project is open select **File**, **Close All** to close the project.
2. Display the **Home Window** by clicking on the ▨ button or select **View, Home**.
3. Select **Edit, User Preferences...** select the **Application** tab and select the **Application Startup Window** as **Projects**. This will ensure the database opens at the **Project Window** each time you start up Primavera.
4. Close the **User Preferences...** form.
5. From the **Home Window** hide and display the **Navigation** and **Directory** toolbars and **Button Text** by right-clicking on a tool bar and by using the **View, Toolbars** menu.
6. Leave all available Toolbars and Toolbar Button Text displayed.
7. Hide and display the **Status Bar** by using the **View, Toolbars** menu.
8. Click on the **Projects** button to open the **Projects Window**.
9. Expand and close the EPS using the ⊞ and ⊟ buttons to the left of the project descriptions.
10. Select a project you have access to and open the **Project Window** by right-clicking on the project and selecting **Open Project**. Click on the ▨ button to open the **Activities Window** if it does not open automatically.
11. Move back to the **Projects** and **Home Window** and then back to the **Activity Window** using the ◀, ▨ and ▨ buttons.
12. Display the **Activity Details** form in the Bottom pane by selecting **View, Show on Bottom, Activity Details**.
13. Hide and display the bottom pane by clicking on the ▨ button on the **Activity** toolbar.
14. Open the **Activity Details** form, right-click on a tab in the **Activity Details** form and select **Customize Activity Details...** then hide and display some tabs.
15. Close the project by selecting **File, Close All** and return to the **Project Window**. From the **Projects Window**, ensure some bars are displayed by double clicking in the bar area.
16. Open the **Bars** form by clicking on the ▨ button, uncheck all the bars in the **Display** column, click ▨ Apply and the bars will disappear without closing the form. Now check all the bars and click on the ✓ OK button and the bars will appear and the form will close.
17. Adjust the timescale using the ⊕ ⊖ buttons.
18. Select **Enterprise, Enterprise Project Structure...** and repeatedly click on the **EPS ID** button (this is the heading **EPS ID**) and notice how the **EPS** is sorted in three different ways. Leave it with the EPS displayed hierarchically.

Continued.....

19.   Close the **Enterprise Project Structure (EPS)** form.

20.   Select **Enterprise, OBS... to open the Organizational Breakdown** form and click the ▽ Display: and inspect the **Filter** options and select **All OBS Elements**.

21.   Click **OBS Name** repeatedly and notice how the **OBS** is sorted in three different ways.

22.   Close the **OBS** form.

23.   Open the **User Preferences** form by selecting **Edit, User Preferences** and select the method you wish to display the date from the **Dates** tab and set your options as per below showing the time in hours:

NOTE: It is strongly recommended that the time is always displayed as per the picture below so the user knows the time when Actual Starts, Actual Finish and Constraints are applied because the software will often select 00:00, first second of a day.

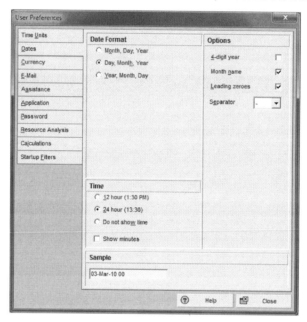

24.   Close the **User Preferences** form.

NOTES FOR TRAINING COURSE INSTRUCTORS AND/OR ADMINISTRATORS:

1.   Training course instructors and/or administrators may consider purchasing the instructors PowerPoint presentation from **www.eh.com.au**. This slide show is full editable and a sample in pdf format may be downloaded from this web site.

2.   If you are a training organization and you wish to train multiple users in one database please contact the author for a paper on how to set up your database.

3.   Completed workshops and layouts may be downloaded from **www.eh.com.au.**

4.   When multiple users are working in a single database the Database Administrator or Course Instructor should:

- Create an EPS Node for each student to work in,

- Assign a unique Project ID for each student to use,

- Create a unique Resource for each student to use and

- Assign a protocol for the students to create Resource IDs as all the student resources have to have a unique name.

4   CREATING A NEW PROJECT

There are several methods for creating a new project:

- Use the Project Architect wizard, or
- Import a project created from another Primavera database or created with another software program such as P3, SureTrak or Microsoft Project, or
- Copy an existing project and edit it.

Before discussing how to create a project, we will discuss the file types that Primavera operates with.

4.1   File Types

Different Versions of Primavera run on different databases including Oracle and Microsoft databases. Primavera will only operate with the database format with which it has been installed and set up with.

There are several Primavera propriety file formats that you need to be aware of:

- **XER** – A Primavera proprietary format used to exchange one or more projects between Primavera databases regardless of the database type in which it was created and exports all project data. Earlier versions of **XER** files may be imported into later version databases.
- **PLF** – A Primavera proprietary format used to exchange **Layouts** between Primavera databases regardless of the database type in which it was created.
- **ANP**– A Primavera proprietary format used to save the position of activities in an **Activity Network**.
- **ERP**– A Primavera proprietary format used to exchange **Reports** between Primavera databases regardless of the database type in which it was created.
- **XML** – A new **Primavera PM** format introduced with Primavera Version 6.0 which is used to import data from the Project Manager module.
- **PCF** – A Primavera proprietary format used to exchange **Global Changes** between Primavera databases regardless of the database type in which it was created.

Primavera will import and export to the following file types using the wizards found under the menu commands **File**, **Import...** and **File**, **Export...**:

- **Project (*.mpp)**. This is the default file format that Microsoft Project uses to create and save files. Microsoft Project 2007 is a different format to the 2000 – 2003 format.

 Primavera 6.0 and 6.1 will not import any mpp file when Microsoft Project 2007 is installed as MSP 2007 disables this function. This disabling was resolved with the release of 6.2, but P6.2 does not import a 2007 mpp file.

- **Project 2000 - 2003 (*.mpp)**. This is the default file format that Microsoft Project 2000, 2002 and 2003 uses to create and save files. Importing these files requires Microsoft Project to be installed on the PC.
- **Microsoft Project 98 (*.mpp)**. This is the format created by Microsoft Project 98.
- **MPX (*.mpx)**. This is a text format data file created by Microsoft Project 98 and earlier versions. MPX is a format that may be imported and exported by many other project scheduling software packages.
- Microsoft Project formats such as **Project Database (*.mpd)**, **Microsoft Access Database (*.mdb)** and **(*.mpt)** can be imported, however **Microsoft Project** is required to be installed on the computer. This function was new to Version 4.1 and removed in Version 6.2.

- Microsoft Project **XML** format is supported in Version 6.2 and later. This allows import of a file created by Microsoft Project 2007 or 2000 to 2003 XML without the installation of Microsoft Project 2007.

- **Primavera Project Planner P3** and **SureTrak** files saved in **P3** format. A SureTrak project in SureTrak format should be saved in Concentric (P3) format before importing.

- **XLS**. Primavera Version 5.0 has a new function allowing the import and export of data in Excel format.

4.2 Creating a Blank Project

You may create a new project at any point in time by selecting **File**, **New** from the menu. You will be guided through the **Create a New Project** wizard which will require the following information:

- The **EPS** Node the project is to be assigned to.

- The **Project ID**, a code to represent the project (a maximum of 20 characters), and **Project Name**.

- A **Planned Start** date, which is the earliest date any unstarted activity will be scheduled to commence and an optional **Project Must Finish By** date. When a **Project Must Finish By** date is set the project float will be calculated to this date and not to the latest activity finish.

- The **Responsible Manager** is selected from the OBS structure. If the OBS has not been defined or the responsibility not assigned then Enterprise may be selected as the Responsible Manager.

- The **Resource Rate Type**. Each resource may have five different rates. This is where the default rates are selected but may be changed after a resource has been assigned to an activity.

- At this point you may either create the project and start working or run the **Project Architect**. The **Project Architect** will enable you to access **Methodology Manager** when predefined templates may be used to build a project. **Project Architect** is not covered in detail in this publication but there are some notes in the following paragraph.

4.3 Setting Up a New Project

To review or modify some of the basic Project or EPS information entered when a project was created, ensure that the **Project Details** form is displayed in the bottom of the screen:

- Highlight a project or EPS Node,

- The project must be open to edit some project data.

- You must also have the appropriate access rights to edit data.

- Select **View**, **Show on Bottom**, **Project Details** and click on the **General** tab:

- The **Risk Level** may be used to sort and filter Projects and EPS Nodes.

- The **Project Leveling Priority** is used when leveling a project to reduce peaks in resource requirements. Value of 1 is the highest and 100 the lowest.

- **Check Out Status** enables the user to determine if the project is checked in or checked out. (New to Version 4.1) **Checked Out By** and **Date Checked Out** enables the user to establish if the project is currently checked out.

4.4   Project Architect Wizard and Methodology Manager

The Methodology Manager is a separate program for storing project methodologies and are represented by activities with WBS, OBS, Activity Codes, Roles, Resources, etc., which form the basis of a project template. The Methodology Manager has three types of Methodologies:

- **Base Methodologies** that may be used to create a total project, e.g. project start up and completion activities.
- **Plug-in Methodologies** which are sets of activities that may be used to develop a project created from a **Base Methodology**.
- **Activity libraries** are smaller sets of activities that may be used to develop a project.

Plug-in Methodologies and **Activity libraries** are similar but more powerful than the P3 **Fragnets**.

The Methodology Manager also has the following important functions that may be used when creating a new project:

- **Estimating Factors**, enable high and low values to be assigned to each Activity Duration and Resource in a Methodology. When a Methodology is imported into a project using the **Project Architect,** a **Project Complexity** between the value of 0 and 100 is specified and the values for the Activity Durations and Resources are proportioned between the low value (when a **Project Complexity** of 0 is assigned) and the high value (when a **Project Complexity** of 100 is assigned).
- **Estimation Weights** may be assigned to Activities and WBS Nodes. After a Methodology has been imported the **Estimation Weight** may be used to apportion the total estimated labor and non-labor resource quantities to Activities in a process termed **Top-Down Estimating** using the **Tools, Top-Down Estimation** function.

4.5   Importing a Project

You may be required to import a project that has been created in another program supplied by someone from within or outside your organization. Primavera is equipped with a set of tools for importing projects from other sources. Files may be imported from:

- Another Primavera Version, irrespective of the database it was created in, using the **XER** or **XER** file format.
- Primavera Project Planner P3 and SureTrak in **P3** format.
- Microsoft Project **(*.mpp)**, **(*.mpd)**, **(*.mbd)** and **(*.mpt)** files when you have Microsoft Project installed on your computer. P6 Version 7 will import a Microsoft Project 2007 mpp file when Microsoft Project 2007 is installed.
- Other scheduling software using **(*.mpx)** file formats.
- Data in Excel format **(*.xls)**.
- Primavera PM – (XML) a format introduced with Primavera Version 6.0 which imports data from the Project Manager module.

Select **File, Import...** to open a wizard that will guide you through the process of importing projects into your schedule.

It is the author's experience that the database may be filled with a large amount of unwanted data such as a calendar for each resource and many duplicate resources when importing from other projects if the process is not fully understood. A trial import with a couple of activities and resources should be considered before importing a large amount of data, or you may wish to consider importing via Excel.

When importing with Excel, the data items such as Activity Codes and Resources must exist before the import and may not be imported in the same way as in P3.

Activity Codes may be imported by loading the Software Developers Kit (SDK) and using a spreadsheet available from the Primavera Knowledgebase which was listed at the time of writing this publication under Solution ID prim10191, there are spreadsheets for Versions 4.0, 5.0 and 6.0.

It is recommended that you read the notes carefully in the user manual before importing a schedule from a non Primavera format and even consider importing into a blank database to clearly understand how the data is imported.

The loading of **Microsoft Project 2007** disables the Microsoft Project mpp import function in Primavera Versions 5.0 and 6.1. This was corrected in Version 6.2.

4.6 Copy an Existing Project

A Project or Projects may be copied in the **Projects Window** by:

- Highlighting the project(s) you wish to copy and select **Edit, Copy** or **Ctrl+C**,

- Highlighting the EPS Node that you wish to associate the new project with and select **Edit, Paste** or **Ctrl+V**,

- The **Copy Project Options** form will then be displayed, enabling you to choose which Project data items you wish to copy with the project; select OK ,

- The **Copy WBS Options** form will be displayed, allowing you to choose which WBS data items you wish to copy with the project;

- After making a selection, click OK ,

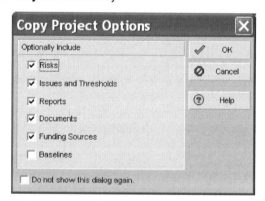

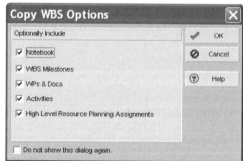

- The **Copy Activity Options** form will be displayed, allowing you to choose the Activity data items you wish to copy with the project; select ,

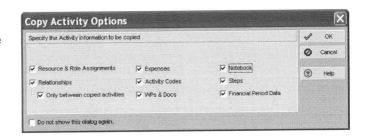

- Open and edit the new project.

A EPS Node may also be selected and copied in the **Projects Window**, and pasted to another location which will copy the projects and add another EPS Node.

> Primavera Version 6.0 added the ability to copy **Baselines** and **High Level Resource Planning Assignments** when copying a project. Earlier versions did not copy project baselines when the project was copied. The Baselines must be manually reassigned after copying the project using the **Assign Baseline** form.

4.7   Project Dates

At this point, a project would not have normally started and you would set the project start date sometime in the future using the **Planned Start** field in the **Projects** Window, **Details** form, **Dates** tab. To open this form:

- Highlight your new project,

- Select **View**, **Show on Bottom**, **Project Details** and click the **Dates** tab:

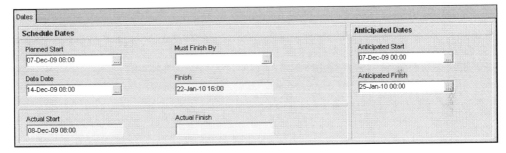

- **Scheduled Dates**
    - The **Planned Start** is the date before which no activity will be scheduled to start.
    - The **Must Finish By** date is an optional date. When this date is entered it is used to calculate the **Late Finish** of activities, thus all **Total Float** will be calculated to this date. This topic is covered in the **Adding Relationships** chapter.
    - The **Finish date** is a calculated date and is the date of the completion of all activities.
    - The **Data Date** is used when updating a project. This topic is covered in the **Tracking Progress** chapter.
    - The **Actual Start** date is inherited from the first stated activity.
    - The **Actual Finish** date is inherited from the last completed activity when all activities are complete.

- **Anticipated Dates**
  - ➢ The **Anticipated Start** and **Anticipated Finish** dates may be assigned before a WBS structure and Activities have been created. The start and finish dates columns and bars at the EPS level adopt these dates when there are no activities. After Activities have been created, they may remain as a historical record only and are not displayed or inherited anywhere else.
  - ➢ **Anticipated Dates** may be assigned to **WBS Nodes**.

4.8 Saving Additional Project and EPS Information - Notebook Topics

Often additional information about a Project or EPS Node is required to be saved with the project such as location, client and type of project. This data may be saved in the **Projects Window**, **Details** form, **Notebook** tab.

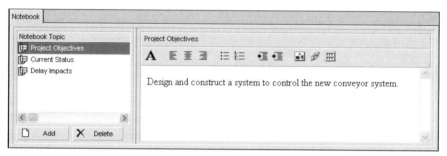

To add a **Note** to a Project:

- Click [Add] to open the **Assign Notebook Topic** form.
- Select a **Topic** from the list by clicking on the **Notebook Topic** you wish to select and click on the ⬛ button to add the topic to the Notebook.
- Close the form by clicking on the ⬛ button.
- You may now add notes to the selected **Project Notebook Topic**.
- Notes may be added to **EPS** Nodes, **Activities** and **WBS Nodes** in the same way as Projects.
- Primavera version 6.0 introduced the search facility when assigning Notes.

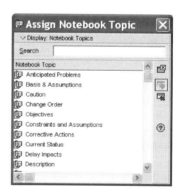

To create a new **Notebook Topic**:

- Select **Admin**, **Admin Categories…** to open the **Admin Categories** form and select the **Notebook Topics** tab.
- The check boxes make the Categories available to EPS Nodes and/or Projects.

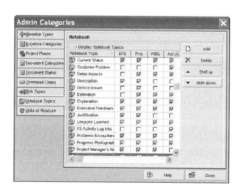

4.9   Workshop 2 - Creating Your Project

Background
You are an employee of OzBuild Pty Ltd and are responsible for planning the Bid preparation required to ensure that a response to an RFQ (Request For Quote) from Wilson International is submitted on time. While short-listed, you have been advised that the RFQ will be available on 05 December 2011 at 8:00hrs (8:00am) and you will be required to submit 3 bound copies of the proposal before 26 January 2012 at 16:00hrs (4:00pm).

NOTE: The Database Administrator or Instructor should create an EPS Node for each student to work in when multiple users are working in a single database, each student should also be assigned a unique Project ID to use and they should start this workshop at paragraph 5.

1.   Close any open project.

Assignment – Students working in a stand alone database start here:

2.   From the **Projects Window** create a new EPS Node by selecting **Enterprise, Enterprise Project Structure...,** [Add], move the node to the top of the list of Nodes using the arrows and add the following information:

- EPS ID – OZ
- EPS Name – OzBuild Projects
- Responsible Manager – Select an appropriate one from your database OBS.

3.   Create a second level EPS Node:

- EPS ID – BIDS
- EPS Name – Bid Projects
- Responsible Manager – Select an appropriate one from your database OBS
- See the picture to the below,
- Close the **Enterprise Project Structure (EPS)** form.

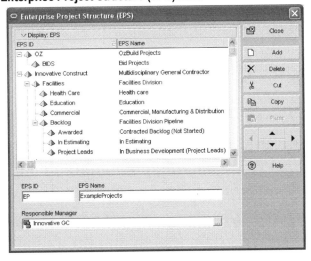

Continued...

Assignment – Students working in a shared database with multiple users start here:

4. Create a new project with the following information by selecting **File**, **New...** to open the **Create a New Project** wizard:

   - EPS - BIDS – Bid Projects (or the nominated node when working in a shared database)

   - Project ID – OZB. **NOTE:** This Project ID may not be accepted if you are working in a shared database when there is another project with this Project ID. You may need to use another Project ID in this situation.

   - Project Name – Bid for Facility Extension

   - Planned Start Date – 05 December 2011 at 08:00

   - Must Finish By – Leave Blank

   - Responsible Manager – Accept the default

   - Rate Type – Price/Unit

   - Project Architect – Do not run

   - Click [⊞ Finish] to create the project.

5. The project should now be open, check the text in the top left side of the screen, the project name should be displayed after "Primavera:".

6. Ensure the project is selected by clicking on it.

7. Add the following project information in the **Project Details** in the **Bottom Pane**:

   - Set the **Status** in the **General** tab to **What-if**, the project needs to be open to change the **Status**.

   - **Dates** tab
     - ➤ Set the Data Date to 05 Dec 11 08:00
     - ➤ Anticipated Start 05 Dec 11 08:00
     - ➤ Anticipated Finish 25 Jan 12 16:00

     You should now see a bar in the Bar Chart above spanning these dates although there are no activities in the schedule. If no bar is displayed double click in the Gantt chart area level with the project.

   - Add a Notebook Topic using a suitable topic such as Vendor Issues stating, "RFQ will not be available prior to 05 December 2011."

8. Your project should look like this:

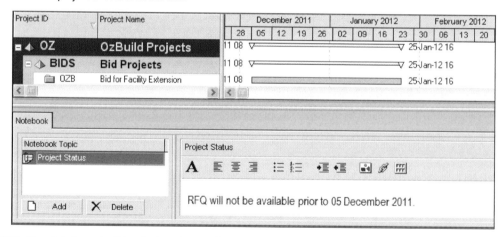

NOTE: The date format will be displayed according to the **User Preferences** settings set by selecting **Edit**, **User Preferences...** and selecting the **Dates** tab.

5   DEFINING CALENDARS

The release of Primavera P6 Version 7 included some changes to the calendar functions are these are covered in this chapter.

The finish date (and time) of an activity is calculated from the start date (and time) plus the duration over the calendar associated with the activity. Therefore, a five-day duration activity that starts at the start of the workday on a Wednesday, and is associated with a five-day workweek calendar (with Saturday and Sunday as non-work days) will finish at the end of the workday on the following Tuesday.

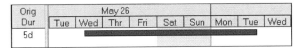

Primavera has three categories for calendars:

- **Global** – These calendars are available to all Projects and Resources.
- **Project** – These calendars are only available to the projects they are created in. These may only be created for a project when that project is open.
- **Resource** – A Resource calendar may be assigned to one or more Resources, which in turn may be assigned to an activity in any project. A Resource will be scheduled according to a Resource Calendar when the **Activity Type** is set to **Resource Dependent**, otherwise the activity is scheduled according to the Activity calendar.

   When an activity is made **Resource Dependent**, unlike some other software, it still acknowledges the Activity Calendar for calculating the start of the resource work. Other software ignore the Activity Calendar and ONLY acknowledge the resource calendars when an activity is made resource driven. You may wish to place resource driven activities on a 24 hour 7 day/week calendar to prevent a delay to start of resource driven activities.

You may create a new, or edit, an existing Calendar to reflect your project requirements, such as adding holidays or additional workdays or adjusting work times. For example, some activities may have a 5-day per week calendar and some may have a 7-day per week calendar.

This chapter covers the following topics:

Topic	Menu Command
• Assigning the **Default Activity / Project Calendar**.	This calendar is assigned to new activities. From the **Projects** Window, click the **Defaults** tab in the **Details** form.
• Creating, copying, editing or deleting calendars	**Enterprise, Calendars…**, select the **Global, Project**, or **Resource** button then click [☐ Add] (to create a new calendar by copying an existing calendar) or [▨ Modify…], or [✕ Delete].
• Renaming an existing calendar	**Enterprise, Calendars…**, select **Global, Project**, or **Resource**, click the description and then modify it.
• Database **Default Calendar**	Select **Enterprise, Calendars** and select the database **Default Calendar** from the **Default** column.

5.1 Accessing Global and Project Calendars

Calendars may be accessed from the **Calendars** form for copying, editing and deleting by selecting **Enterprise**, **Calendars…** from Windows such as **Home**, **Projects** and **Activities**. The following rules dictate when you are able to access the calendars:

- **Global** and **Resource Calendars** may be accessed with or without any projects open.
- A **Project Calendar** may only be copied, edited, and deleted when the project has been opened.
- To list, create and edit more than one existing **Project Calendar** at the same time all the projects in question must be open. To open more than one project:
  - ➤ **Ctrl-click** the projects and select **File**, **Open**, or
  - ➤ Highlight an **EPS Node** and select **File**, **Open**, or
  - ➤ Open a **Portfolio** of projects.

5.2 Assigning the Project Default Project Calendar

A **Default Project Calendar** is assigned to each project from the **Global** or **Project** calendar list:

- All new activities are assigned the project **Default Project Calendar** when they are created. Unlike Microsoft Project changing the **Default Project Calendar** will **NOT** affect the calendar assigned to any tasks.
- The **Default Project Calendar** may be selected for calculating leads and lags in the **Schedule Options** form.

To assign the **Default Activity Calendar** to a project:

- Open the **Projects Window** and highlight the project,
- Click on the **Defaults** tab in the **Details** form; you will see the current **Default Project Calendar** in the **Calendar** box.

To change the project **Default Project Calendar**:

- Click the ⬚ button to the right of the heading **Calendar** to open the **Select Default Project Calendar** form

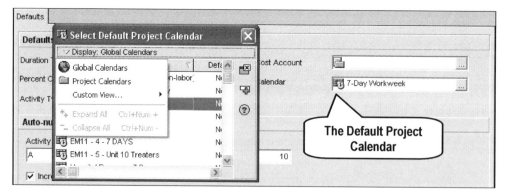

- Select either the **Global Calendars** or **Project Calendars** menu item from the drop down box under the ⬚ Display: Project Calendars heading, and
- Select the calendar to be the **Default Project Calendar**, then
- Click the ⬚ button or **Double-Click** on the calendar to assign the new calendar.

5.3   Creating a New Calendar

A project must be active to create a **Project Calendar** for the project and this function copies a Global calendar. To create a new calendar:

- Select **Enterprise**, **Calendars…**,
- Select the **Global**, **Project**, or **Resource** button, depending on the type of calendar required,
- Then click either the [D   Add] button to create a new calendar, or
- Select an existing Global calendar to copy, you may not copy a Project or Resource calendar,
- Assign a name, it is best to keep these short as then they are then easily displayed in a column.

5.4   Moving a Project Calendar to Global

A **Project Calendar** may moved to become a **Global Calendar**:

- Open the project that the calendar currently resides in,
- Select **Enterprise**, **Calendars…**,
- Select the **Project** button and highlight the calendar to be copied, and
- Click the [⊙ To Global] button.
- The calendar will no longer be a Project calendar so this function is not a copy function.

5.5   Copy a Calendar from One Project to Another

To copy a calendar from one project to another:

- Copy the **Project Calendar** as a **Global Calendar**, and
- Create a new **Project Calendar** in both projects by copying the new **Global Calendar**.

5.6   Renaming a Calendar

To rename a calendar:

- Select **Enterprise**, **Calendars…**,
- Double click the calendar description to edit in the same way as renaming a directory in Explorer.

5.7   Deleting a Calendar

To delete a calendar:

- Select **Enterprise**, **Calendars…**,
- Select the calendar and click the [X Delete] button.

5.8   Resource Calendars

A **Resource** or a **Global** calendar may be assigned to one or more Resources. This is different to the philosophy of Microsoft Project, P3 and SureTrak, where each resource has its own calendar based on a project calendar and many resources are not able to share one calendar.

  A Resource will be scheduled according to the assigned **Resource Calendar** when the **Activity Type** is set to **Resource Dependent**; otherwise the activity is scheduled according to the **Activity Calendar**.

Resource availability is displayed in **Resource Usage Profiles** and is based on the Resource Calendar even when it is assigned to a **Task Dependent** activity.

5.9 Editing the Calendar Working Days of an Existing Calendar

Prior to editing a calendar, particularly if it is a global calendar, click the [🖳 Used By...] button to open the **Calendar Used By** form to determine which other Projects and Resources also use the calendar.

To edit a calendar:

- Select **Enterprise**, **Calendars…**,
- Select the **Global**, **Project**, or **Resource** button,
- Then click [🖳 Modify...] to open the **Calendar** form and modify an existing calendar:

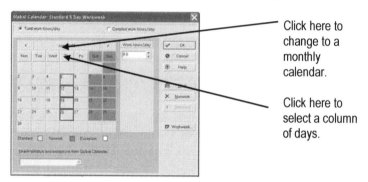

Click here to change to a monthly calendar.

Click here to select a column of days.

- Click in the month name to change the calendar view to monthly. This makes it quicker to navigate around the calendar and works in the other calendar view:

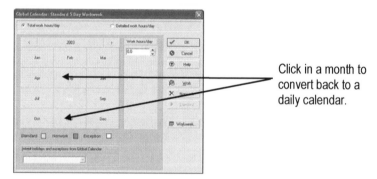

Click in a month to convert back to a daily calendar.

- To make **Nonwork Days** into **Work Days**, highlight the day(s) you want to edit by:
  - ➢ Click on an individual day, or
  - ➢ Ctrl-click to select multiple days, or
  - ➢ Click on a column or columns of days by clicking the day of the week box, which is located below the month and year. Ctrl-click will allow multiple columns to be selected.
  - ➢ Then click the [🗂 Work] button to make these days working.
- To make **Work Days** into **Nonwork Days**, highlight the day(s) you want to edit as described in the paragraph above and then click the [✕ Nonwork] button to make these days nonworking days.
- To return individual days to the default setting, select the day and click the [▷ Standard] button.

5.10 Adjusting Working Hours

The working hours of a standard week are termed **Calendar Weekly Hours**. The working hours of selected individual days may now be edited.

5.10.1 Editing Calendar Weekly Hours

There are two methods of editing the hours of every weekday of a calendar:

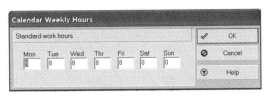

- From the **Calendar** form:
  - ➤ Select **Total work hours**/day and then
  - ➤ Click [Workweek...] to open the **Calendar Weekly Hours** form.

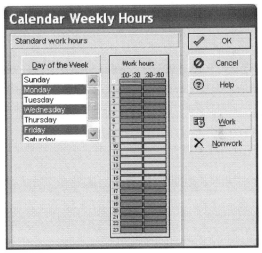

- Or from the **Calendar** form:
  - ➤ Select **Detailed work hours**/day and then
  - ➤ Click [Workweek...] to open the second Calendar Weekly Hours form.
  - ➤ Individual days of the week may be selected using Ctrl-clicking and then the work hours for multiple days edited all at the same time.

- Adjust the hours for each day in this form and click [OK] to accept the changes.

5.10.2 Editing Selected Days Working Hours

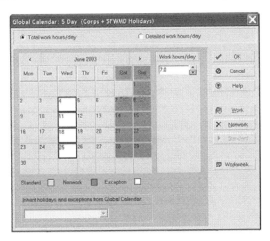

To edit the working hours of individual days:

- Select the days you wish to edit by Shift-clicking, Ctrl-clicking individual days or selecting one or more columns,
- Adjust the hours in the box below the title **Work hours/day**.
- The edited days will now adopt the color of the **Exception** days.

5.10.3 Editing Detailed Work Hours/Day

To edit the **Detailed working hours/day** of individual days:

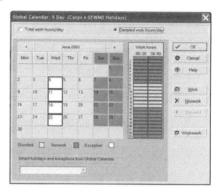

- Select the days to edit by Shift-clicking, Ctrl-clicking individual days, or selecting one or more columns,

- Click the **Detailed work hours/day** button,

- Adjust the hours to the nearest half hour by double-clicking on the table below the title **Work hours** to change them from working to nonworking.

- The edited days will now adopt the color of the **Exception** days.

When any calendar is changed or edited, the end date of all activities assigned with the calendar will be recalculated based on the new calendar. This may make a considerable difference to your project schedule dates.

When calendars have different start and end times some activities will span one day more than the duration of the activity, because for example the last hour of the task will roll into the next day.

5.11   Inherit Holidays and Exceptions from a Global Calendar

When creating a new Project or Resource calendar, a Global Calendar may be selected from the dropdown box and this function will copy the calendar holidays from the selected Global Calendar into the displayed calendar.

The Global and the new Project or Resource calendars will remain linked (in the same way as a Global Calendar in SureTrak and P3) and a change to a Global calendar holiday will be reflected in a calendar with Inherited Holidays.

It is suggested that this option is never used and each calendar is created as stand alone without inheriting holidays from another calendar and therefore will not change if another calendar has holidays changed.

5.12   Start Day of the Week

The start day of the week is best set as a Monday and then the date shown in the Gantt Chart timescale is a work day. Select **Admin**, **Admin Preferences** form, **General** tab, **Starting Day of Week** section:

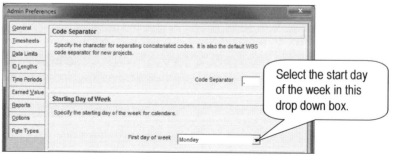

5.13 Summary Durations - Primavera 6.2 and Earlier

5.13.1 Calculation of Activity Summary Duration in Days

Primavera effectively calculates in hours and the Activity Durations in days or weeks are calculated by the factors set up in the **Admin**, **Admin Preferences...**, **Time Periods** tab.

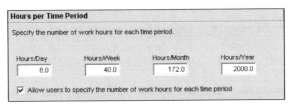

When **Allow users to specify the number of work hours for each time period** is checked then users may set their own time periods in the **Edit**, **User Preferences...**, **Time Units** tab.

These options need to be understood because they affect how durations in days and weeks are displayed. Primavera calculates in hours, but Activity Durations may be summarized and displayed in days or weeks or months.

These options calculate correctly when all database calendars are have the same number of work hours per day and days per week. When tasks are scheduled with calendars that do not conform to the **Edit**, **User Preferences...**, **Time Units** tab settings (e.g. when settings are set for 8 hours per day but there are tasks scheduled on a 24 hour/day calendar), the Activity durations in days or weeks will be incorrect. These results often create confusion for new users and people reviewing the schedule.

The following illustration shows how two activities with the same duration on different calendars are displayed:

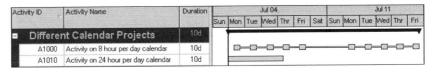

Therefore if you are a contractor and have some projects on a 10 hour a day, some on a 24 hour per day, and some projects on an 8 hour per day, then you need to be careful on how these defaults are set, otherwise your Activity Durations in Days may become very misleading. There are some options that may be considered to resolve this issue.

1. Create a database per project and set the defaults to match the dominant calendar in the project.
2. Create a User that represents each project, allow the user only access to the project that the User represents and set the Users Hours per Time Period to suit the predominant calendar of project.
3. Consider only displaying the durations in hours.
4. Use a Global Change to populate a User Defined field with the elapsed duration in days.

Other scheduling software such as SureTrak and Microsoft Project also exhibit this Activity duration in days conversion problem but P3 and Asta Powerproject do not.

5.13.2 Database Default Calendar, WBS and Project Durations

The durations of all bands such as Project, WBS, and Resources are calculated from the Database **Default Calendar** and the **Hours/Day** setting in the **Edit, User Preferences..., Time Units** tab (or the **Admin, Admin Preferences, Time Periods** field when you have not been granted access to edit this field). These may not be relevant to you project if your **Time Units** field does not match the number of hours in the **Default Calendar**. To set the **Default Calendar** select **Enterprise, Calendars** and select the database from the **Default** column.

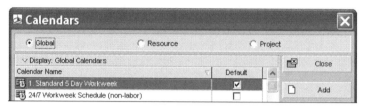

Therefore, if the database **Default Calendar** is changed, or if you change your **Units/Hour**, then every WBS and Project duration in days in the whole database days will change. Also, other users with different **Units/Hour** or database **Default Calendar** will see different WBS and Project durations.

The following picture show the duration of the workshop used in this publication set at firstly 5 days per week, 8 hours per day and a duration of 35 days with an Hours/Day setting of 8 hours.

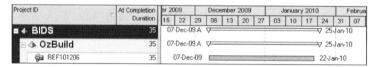

Now with the **Default Calendar** changed to a 7 day/week 24 hour per day the duration of 139 days is clearly misleading.

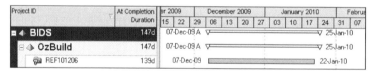

The duration of the Project Summary WBS Nodes are also clearly misleading, the Research Node is not 31 days long.

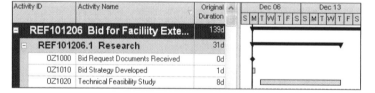

There are some issues that need to be carefully considered when planning and controlling multiple projects with different calendars in one database when correct durations in days are important.

The author also found that the durations in days of projects in the Projects Window also changed depending on if the project was open or closed.

5.14   Summary Durations - Primavera P6 Version 7

5.14.1   Calendars Hours per Time Period

In earlier version of P6 the calculation of the durations in hours for all calendars was set either by the Administrator in **Admin**, **Admin Preferences…**, **Time Periods** tab or by the User in the **Edit**, **User Preferences…**, **Time Units** tab.

Primavera Version 7 has removed these two options above and has created of a new calendar function titled **Hours per Time Period**:

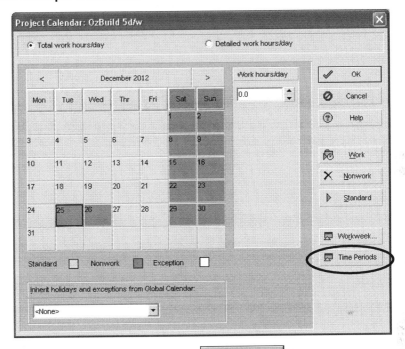

When creating or editing a calendar there is a new 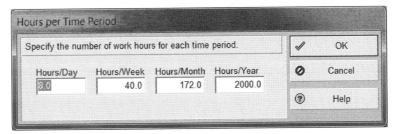 button in the **Enterprise**, **Calendars**, **Modify** form that allows the definition of the number of hours per day for each calendar, which in turn will enable the activity durations in days to be calculated and displayed correctly as long as the number of hours per day is the same for each work day in the calendar.

5.14.2 Calendars for Calculating WBS and Other Summary Durations

In Version 7 the summary durations, including the project duration in the Projects Window are calculated in a similar way as SureTrak:

- When all the activities in a band share the same calendar then the summary duration is calculated on the calendar of the activities in the band and
- When they are different the summary duration is calculated on the Project Default calendar.

The picture below has the Project Default calendar set as the 8hr/d & 5d/w and the picture shows that when the calendars are different then the Project Default calendar is used to calculate the summary duration for WBS Nodes, Projects etc:

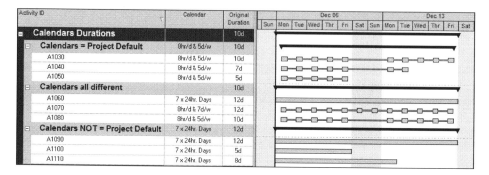

5.14.3 Database Default Calendar

The **Database Default Calendar** is set in the **Enterprise, Calendars** form and is used to display the Non Working times in all Views and all projects in a database.

 It is not possible for users to display different non-work periods for different projects or views, as in many other packages without affecting all other projects in a database. This may become an issue with projects that have different work periods and may be solved by creating another database with a different **Database Default Calendar**.

5.15 Tips for Mixed Calendar Schedules

When a project has mixed calendars, say a 8 and 10 hour per day, then at change of calendar from a predecessor on an 8 hour per day calendar to successor on a 10 hour calendar, the successor activity may have one hour of work on the on the same day as the predecessor and span two days. This situation leads to interesting Float calculations and confusion to no schedulers.

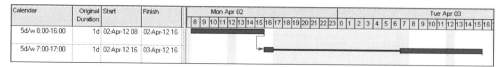

Primavera P6 does not have a "Start on a New Day", function found in other products such as Asta Powerproject, but which in itself brings on a new set of calculation issues. Techniques that may be considered to ensure one day activities span one day and two day activities span two days, etc are:

- Apply an appropriate lag to the relationship, or
- When the Start and Finish Times are not an important scheduling consideration then assign all the calendars the same Start and Finish time but adjust the duration of the lunch break so the days have the desired number of hours. For example a 10 hour day calendar could start at 07:00 and finish at 17:00 without any lunch break and an 8 hour calendar could start at 07:00 and finish at 17:00 and be assigned a 2 lunch break.

5.16   Workshop 3 - Maintaining the Calendars

Background

The normal working week at OzBuild Pty Ltd is Monday through Friday, 8 hours per day excluding public holidays. The installation staff works Monday through Saturday, 8 hours per day.

The company observes the following holidays:

	2010	2011	2012	2013
New Year's Day	1 January	3 January*	2 January*	1 January
Easter	2 – 5 April	22 – 25 April	6 – 9 April	29 March- 1 April
Christmas Day	27* December	26 December *	25 December	25 December
Boxing Day	28* December	27 December*	26 December	26 December

* These holidays occur on a weekend and the dates in the table above have been moved to the next weekday.

NOTE: Boxing Day is a holiday the day after Christmas celebrated in many countries.

Assignment
Although we could use a standard calendar we will create two new calendars for this project.
1.   Ensure your new OzBuild Bid project is open.
2.   Select **Enterprise**, **Calendars...** to open the **Calendars** form.
3.   Click on the **Project** radio button.
4.   Create a new Project Calendar titled "OzBuild 5 d/w" by copying the most appropriate calendar such as the "Standard 5 Day per Week".
5.   Click on the ⊞ Modify... button to open the **Calendars** form.
6.   Select the **Detailed work hours/day** radio button.
7.   Click on the ⊞ Workweek... button to open the **Calendar Weekly Hours** form.
8.   Make the work hours from 8:00 to 16:00 without a lunch break from Monday to Friday and close the form.
9.   Select **<None>** for **Inherit holidays and exceptions from Global Calendar**.
10. If you are using Primavera P6 Version 7 then click on the 🖵 Time Periods button and check the Hours per Time Period and then close the form:

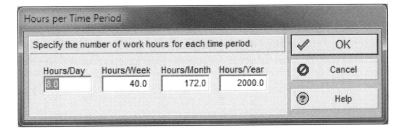

Continued.....

11. Add the holidays above in 2011 and 2012 only.
12. Make any existing calendar holidays not listed above into work-days.

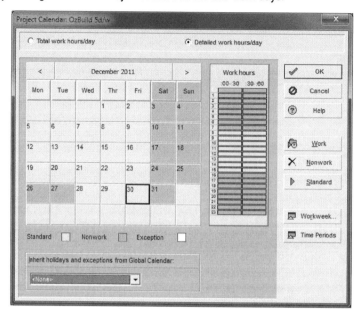

13. Create a new calendar titled "OzBuild 6 d/w" for the 6-day week by copying the same Global calendar.
14. Make the work hours from 8:00 to 16:00 from Monday to Saturday and close the form.
15. Select **<None>** for **Inherit holidays and exceptions from Global Calendar**.

16. If you are using Primavera P6 Version 7 then click on the ▨ Time Periods button and check the Hours per Time Period:

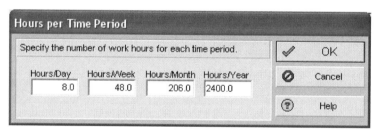

17. Add the holidays above in 2011 and 2012 only.
18. Make any existing calendar holidays not listed above into work days.

6   CREATING A PRIMAVERA PROJECT WBS

This chapter outlines how to create a WBS structure to enable activities to be assigned to a WBS Node so a schedule may be created.

The **Project WBS** function is designed to record a hierarchical WBS that has been developed on a traditional basis as outlined in many project management documents. A well structured WBS should:

- Include all the project deliverables and
- Be set at the appropriate level for summarizing project activities and reporting project progress.

The **Project WBS** function is used to group and summarize activities under a hierarchical structure in the same way as the WBS function in P3 and SureTrak, and the Custom Outline Codes in Microsoft Project. It is also similar to Outlining in all versions of Microsoft Project, however, in Primavera the Activities are assigned to a hierarchical WBS Node and are not demoted under a Parent task as with Outlining with Microsoft Project. The WBS structure is used to organize and summarize your project activities, including costs and resources during the planning, scheduling, and updating of Projects.

The project should be granulated (broken down) into manageable areas by using a project breakdown structure based on attributes of the project such as the Phases or Stages, Systems and Subsystems, Processes, Disciplines or Trades, and Areas or Locations of work. These headings are normally the basis of the project breakdown structure and are used to create the Primavera WBS structure, and the WBS should present the primary view of your project.

Defining the project breakdown structure may be a major task for project managers. The establishment of a Primavera Methodology in Methodology Manager, more commonly called project templates, makes this operation simpler because a standard breakdown is predefined and does not have to be created for each new project. Methodology Manager is a software package supplied with the Primavera planning software.

Primavera also has an **Activity Code** function similar to the **Activity Code** function in Primavera P3 and SureTrak software, Codes in Asta Powerproject and the Custom Outline Codes in Microsoft Project. This feature enables the grouping of activities under headings other than the "WBS Structure." Unlike in Primavera P3 and SureTrak software, **Activity Codes** are not the primary method of organizing activities Primavera. They are covered in the **Activity Codes and Grouping Activities** chapter.

Topic	Menu Command
• Creating and Deleting a WBS Node	The menu commands **Add**, **Delete**, **Copy**, **Cut** and **Paste** all work to create, delete, move and copy WBS Nodes.
• WBS Categories	WBS Categories are created using the **Admin**, **Admin Categories...**, **Project Phase** tab and are assigned to WBS Nodes by inserting the **Project Phase** column in the WBS Window.

A **WBS Node** is a term used by Primavera that is often called a **WBS Code** and is a single point in the WBS structure that activities are assigned to. A Primavera WBS Node may record more information than P3, SureTrak or Microsoft Project including the following data:

- **Anticipated Dates**, which are used to create a bar in the WBS Window when there are no activities under the WBS Node, but do not summarize in the Projects Window.

- **Notes**, which are recorded under **Notebook Topics**,

- **Budget**, **Spending Plan** and **Budget Change Log**,

- **WBS Milestones** which may be used for assigning progress at WBS Node,

- Links to documents,

- The rules for calculating **Earned Value** for each WBS Node, and

- Displaying **Planning Resources** that may be assigned to WBS Nodes using **Primavera Web** (earlier versions were called myPrimavera), the web interface.

The start and finish dates of a WBS Node are adopted from the earliest start date and latest finish date of the detailed activities under that WBS Node and use the Anticipated Dates to create a bar when there are no activities assigned to a WBS Node.

The duration of a WBS Node is calculated from the start and finish dates, the database **Default Calendar** and the **User Options**.

6.1 Opening and Navigating the WBS Window

To view, edit, or create a **WBS** structure:

- The project must be opened.

- The **WBS Window** is displayed by selecting **Project**, **WBS** or by clicking on the [icon] **WBS** icon in the **Directory** bar.

- The following picture is of the Lincoln Hospital project showing the WBS Nodes on the left side of the screen and the WBS bars on the right side of the screen.

- The buttons in the **WBS** toolbar enable different views of the WBS. Click on each button to see its purpose.

- The **Print** and **Print Preview** buttons were added in Version 6.0, circled in the following picture.

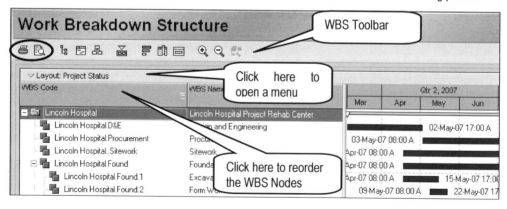

6.2   Creating and Deleting a WBS Node

Right-click to display the menu or select the **Edit** menu command. The commands **Add**, **Delete**, **Copy**, **Cut** and **Paste** all work to create, delete, move, and copy WBS Nodes.

- **Add** will add a new WBS Node under the level currently highlighted.
- **Delete** will delete the WBS Node. When a WBS Node has been assigned activities you will be given the option to either delete the activities or reassign the activities by selecting the **Merge Element(s)** option in the **Merge or Delete WBS Element(s)** form.

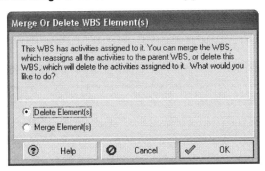

- **Copy** copies a WBS Node and the associated activities.
- **Cut** prepares to move a WBS Node and the associated activities to another location.
- **Paste** pastes a **Cut** or **Copied** WBS Node. After selecting **Paste**, the **Copy WBS Options** form is presented which enables the selection of the data to be pasted with the WBS Node.

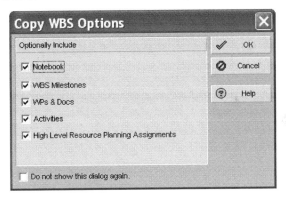

NOTE: The **High Level Resource Planning Assignments** option was added in Primavera Version 6.0 web access software called Primavera Web (earlier versions were called myPrimavera).

6.3   WBS Node Separator

The Default WBS Node Separator is assigned in **Admin**, **Admin Preferences**, **General** tab.

Each individual project WBS Node separator is defined in the **Settings** tab of the **Project Details** form in the **Projects Window** and overrides the default set in the **Admin Preferences** form, **General** tab.

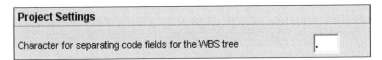

6.4   Work Breakdown Structure Lower Pane Details

The lower pane has nine tabs. **Planning Resources** was added in Primavera Version 6.0.

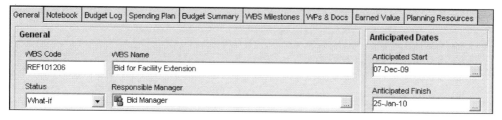

- **General**, in this tab you may assign:
  - ➢ The **WBS Code** has to be unique for each project.
  - ➢ **WBS Name** is the description for the WBS Node.
  - ➢ The **Responsible Manager** is an interesting function as it enable access to data to be controlled at the WBS Node level. When a User has access to change data in one WBS Node only then they are able to see the whole project but only change data in the one node.
  - ➢ **Anticipated Dates** as with the Project Anticipated Dates will display a bar when the WBS Node has no activities, but does not summarize in the Projects Window.
  - ➢ The **Status**, there are four WBS Status types, **Planned**, **Active**, **Inactive**, and **What-if**. The status of a WBS Node controls viewing and access to the Nodes and Activities assigned to the nodes by Primavera Timesheet users. These may be used in filtering and reporting.
- **Notebook** is used in the same way as the activity Notebook and is used to record notes about the WBS Node.
- **Budget Summary**, **Budget Log**, and **Spending Plan** are used together as a top-down method of assigning budgets and are independent of the costs assigned at the activity level.
- **WBS Milestones** are created at the **WBS Node** level and provide a summary method of assigning a **Performance Percent Complete** to activities assigned to that node. For this function to operate there must be at least one activity assigned to a **WBS Node**.
- **Earned Value** is where the rules for calculating the Estimate to Complete, ETC and other Earned Value parameters are set.
- **WPs & Docs** enables the assignment of documents to a WBS Node and operates in the same way as the activities **WPs & Docs** tab.
- Displaying **Planning Resources** that may be assigned to WBS Nodes using **Primavera Web** (earlier versions were called myPrimavera), the web interface.

6.5   WBS Categories

WBS Nodes may be assigned categories, which enables WBS Nodes within an EPS to be grouped and sorted in a different way. WBS Categories are to WBS Nodes in a similar way as Activity Codes are to Activities.

- WBS Categories are created using the **Admin**, **Admin Categories…**, **Project Phase** tab.
- WBS Categories are assigned to and removed from WBS Nodes by inserting the **Project Phase** column into the WBS Window.

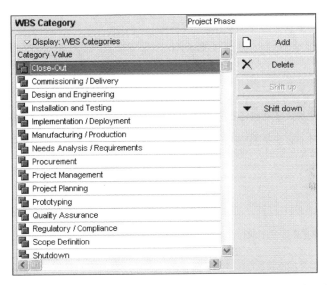

One use of a WBS Category could be, for example, to tag the WBS Nodes with the phase such as Design, Procure and Install and then the Activities may be Grouped by WBS Category and then WBS or some other Activity Code.

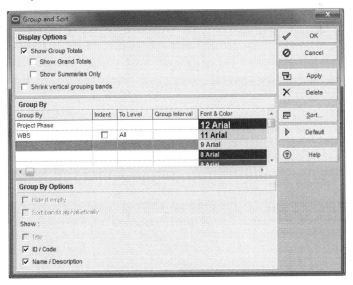

This topic is covered in more details in **Grouping, Sort and Layouts** chapter.

6.6 Why a Primavera WBS is Important

People converting from P3 and SureTrak will be used to using Activity Codes and Activity ID Codes. Primavera does not have Activity ID codes.

You may be tempted to ignore the WBS and use Activity Codes instead. This paragraph will explain the main purposes of the WBS function:

- **User Access** may be assigned at this level, so two schedulers may open the same project and one only change activities in WBS Nodes assigned to each user.
- **Earned Value** calculations and **Project Performance** may be performed at this level.
- Progress at the WBS level may be measured with the use of **WBS Milestones**.
- **Anticipated Dates** may be assigned at the WBS level to provide a bar when no activities have been added to a WBS Node.
- The **Tracking Window** operates down to WBS Node level.
- There are a number standard **Reports** that function at WBS Node level.

6.7   Workshop 4 - Creating the Work Breakdown Structure

Background

A review of the scope identifies three deliverables:

- Technical Specification
- Delivery Plan
- Bid Document

Assignment

1. Click on the ▣ button to open the **WBS** Window.
2. Click in the WBS field header until the sort indicator is displayed as three horizontal bars, as displayed in the picture below, the WBS will be displayed hierarchically now:

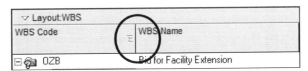

3. Select the Project WBS Node and right-click and select **Add** to add the WBS Node and continue to add three WBS Nodes for the three Phases above.
4. If the WBS Nodes are not indented click the **WBS Code** heading as described in para 2, until they are indented.
5. Use the arrows on the command bar to put them in the correct order and indent.
6. Your answer should be displayed like the following picture:

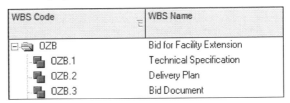

7. Return to the Activities View by clicking on the ▣ or the [Activities] icon on the Director toolbar, you screen may look like this:

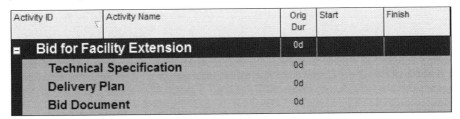

Continued....

8. If your view looks different, select **View**, **Layout**, **Open**…, select the **Classic WBS Layout** and click the ![Open] button.

9. Depending on the Layout that your software has loaded your data may be displayed in different columns and with different bar formatting. Layouts are covered in the **Group, Sort and Layouts** chapter. Should your layout not enable you to review your data entry try selecting a different layout using the command **View**, **Layouts**, **Open...** and select another layout from the list such as the Classic or Default WBS Layout.

10. If it is still not displayed correctly select **View**, **Group and Sort...**, and under the **Group By** box select **WBS** as per the form below:

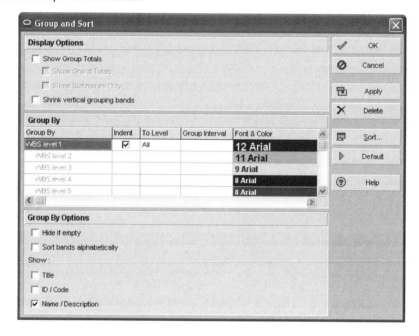

7   ADDING ACTIVITIES AND ORGANIZING UNDER THE WBS

Activities should be well-defined, measurable pieces of work with a measurable outcome. Activity descriptions containing only nouns such as "Bid Document" have confusing meanings. Does this mean read, write, review, submit or all of these? Adequate activity descriptions always have a verb-noun structure to them. A more appropriate activity description would be "Write Bid Document" or "Review and Submit Bid Document." The limit for activity names is 120 characters, but try to keep activity descriptions meaningful yet short and concise so they are easier to print.

When activities are created, they may be organized under other coding structures such as Activity Codes or User Defined Fields.

This chapter will cover the following topics:

Topic	Menu Command
• Setting **Auto-numbering Defaults** and other defaults for new Activities	Select the **Default** tab from the **Bottom** pane in the **Project Window**.
• **Adding New Activities**	Select a line in the schedule and strike the **Ins (Insert Key)** or right-click and select the **Add** menu item.
• **Activity Details** form	May be displayed in the bottom pane by selecting **View**, **Show on Bottom**, **Activity Details**.
• **Copying** activities in **Primavera**	Select the activities and copy and paste to the required location.
• **% Complete Type**	Use the **% Complete Type** drop down box in the **General** tab of the **Activity Details** form.
• **Milestones**	Use the **Activity Type** drop down box in the **General** tab of the **Activity Details** form.
• Assigning **WBS Nodes** to activities	• Create an activity in an existing WBS band, • Drag one or more activities into the desired band, • Display the WBS column and click the WBS cell to display the **Select WBS** form, or • Open the **General** tab in the lower window.

7.1 New Activity Defaults

After creating a new project and before adding activities it is important to set the defaults such as the Activity ID Numbers and Calendars. By setting them correctly before adding activities you will save a significant amount of time because you will not have to change a number of attributes against all activities at a later date. These defaults are set in the **Defaults** tab of the **Project Details** form:

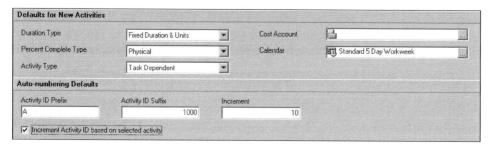

7.1.1 Duration Type

None of the **Duration Type** options affects how the schedule calculates until one or more resource is assigned to an Activity. The following options are available:

- **Fixed Units**
- **Fixed Duration and Units/Time**
- **Fixed Units/Time**
- **Fixed Duration & Units**

If you do not plan to add resources to Activities, then you do not need to assign a **Duration Type** and it may be left as the default.

This topic will be covered in detail in the **Assigning Roles and Resources Expenses** chapter.

7.1.2 Percent Complete Type

The **Percent Complete** type should be understood if it is intended to be used to update (status or progress) the schedule. In Primavera this option may be set for each activity individually and the default for new activities is set in the **Percent Complete Type** drop down box. Primavera has many Activity Percent Complete fields that may be displayed in columns and we will discuss four of them now:

- **Activity % Complete**, which may be linked to one only of the three following % Complete fields and is always linked to the % Complete displayed in the bars:
- **Physical % Complete**, which is independent of activity resources and durations,
- **Duration %Complete**, which is lined to activities durations, and
- **Units % Complete**, which is linked to resources Units.

There are three percent complete options; each new activity is assigned the project default **Percent Complete Type** and then this may be edited for each activity as required.

Therefore if the option of **Physical % Complete** is selected for an activity then the **Activity % Complete** and the **Physical % Complete** are linked and a change to one will change the other.

Default % Complete

The **Default % Complete Type** for each new activity in each project is assigned in the **Defaults** tab of the **Details** form in the **Project Window**:

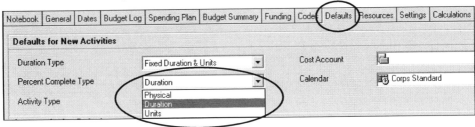

- A new activity Percent Complete Type is set to the Default Percent Complete when created and may be changed at any time.

Percent Complete Types

- **Physical % Complete** – This field enables the user to enter the percent complete of an activity and this value is independent of the activity durations. This is similar to the way P3 and SureTrak calculates the % Complete when the **Link Remaining Duration and Percent Complete** option is NOT selected.

- **Duration % Complete** – This field is calculated from the proportion of the **Original Duration** and the **Remaining Duration** and they are linked. A change to one value will change the other. When the **Remaining Duration** is set to greater than the **Original Duration** this percent complete is always zero. This is similar to the way P3 and SureTrak calculates the % Complete when the **Link Remaining Duration and Percent Complete** option is selected

- **Units % Complete** – This is where the percent complete is calculated from the resources Actual and Remaining Units, a change to one value will change the other and when more than one resources is assigned then all the Actual Units for all resources will be changed proportionally. This will be covered further in the **Updating Resources** chapter. This is similar to the Microsoft Project % Work Complete.

Activity % Complete

The field this is linked with is determined by the **% Complete Type** assigned to an activity in the **General** tab of the **Details** form in the **Activities Window** or from a column:

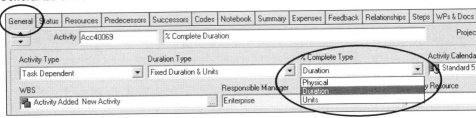

Therefore the **Activity % Complete** is linked to the value from one of the other three % Completes, thus only the **Activity % Complete** needs to be displayed irrespective of the **% Complete Type**. See the following picture:

Percent Complete Type	Original Duration	Remaining Duration	Activity % Complete	Duration % Complete	Physical % Complete	Units % Complete	Actual Labor Units	At Completion Labor Units	Oct 24	Oct 31	No
% Co...	10d	6d		40%		33.33%	5	15			
Duration	10d	6d	40%	40%	5%	0%	0	0			
Physical	10d	6d	12%	40%	12%	0%	0	0			
Units	10d	5d	33.33%	50%	5%	33.33%	5	15			

7.1.3   Activity Types and Milestones

An Activity may be assigned one the following default Activity Types using the drop down box in the Project Defaults tab:

- **Finish Milestone**
- **Level of Effort**
- **Resource Dependent**
- **Start Milestone**
- **Task Dependent**
- **WBS Summary**

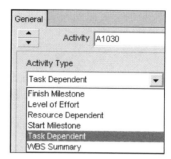

TASK TYPE	DESCRIPTION
• **Task Dependent**	These Activity Types have a duration and will only calculate the duration using the assigned calendar even when one or more resources are assigned to an activity.
• **Resource Dependent**	These Activity Types have a duration and will calculate the duration only using the calendar assigned to the activity when NO resources are assigned to the activity. These activities acknowledge Resource Calendars when resources are assigned. This is similar to an Independent Activity Type in P3 and SureTrak. They acknowledge the Activity calendar to calculate the Early Start date.
• **Level of Effort**	This Activity type is covered in the **Assigning Roles, Resources and Expenses** chapter, and are similar to P3 and SureTrak Hammock activities. It spans from the start or finish of one or more predecessor activities to the start or finish of one or more activities successor activities which are linked by relationships.
• **Start Milestone**	A Start Milestone has a start date and no finish date and is scheduled at the start of a timeperiod and may not be assigned Resources.
• **Finish Milestone**	A Finish Milestone has a finish date, no start date and is scheduled at the end of a timeperiod and may not be assigned Resources. Changing a milestone from Start to Finish would not affect a schedule when all the tasks are on one calendar but would move the milestone from the start of a day to the finish of the previous day.
• **WBS Summary**	This Activity type is covered in the **Assigning Roles, Resources and Expenses** chapter, and calculates in the same way as P3 and SureTrak WBS activities. It spans all activities with the same WBS code.

A Milestone has zero duration and is used to mark the start or finish of a major event. Primavera differentiates between **Start** and **Finish Milestones** in the same way as P3 and SureTrak, where a Start Milestone has a start date and no finish date and a Finish Milestone has a finish date and no start date. This is unlike Microsoft Project, which only has one type of Milestone. Later versions of Microsoft Project allow Milestones with durations.

7.1.4   Cost Account

This drop down box is used to select the default Cost Account for all new Resources and Expenses and is blank by default. Cost Accounts are covered in detail in the **Other Methods of Organizing Activities** chapter.

7.1.5   Calendar

This topic was covered in detail in the **Calendars** chapter. This drop down box is used to select the default calendar for an activity. A **Default Project Calendar** is assigned to each project from the **Global** or **Project** calendar list.

All new activities are assigned the project **Default Project Calendar** when they are created however individual calendars may be assigned for each activity.

7.1.6   Auto-numbering Defaults

The **Auto-numbering Defaults** decide how new activities are numbered. The first activity added to a new project will be based on the defaults set in this form.

- The **Increment Activity ID based on selected activity** check box controls which of the **Auto-numbering Defaults** rules are acknowledged after the first activity is added:
  - ➢ When checked, new activities will inherit the number of the highlighted activity plus the **Increment** number, and
  - ➢ When unchecked, new activities will use the **Activity ID Prefix,** plus the **Activity ID Suffix** plus the Increment from the last activity.

 There are no Activity ID Codes such as found in P3 and SureTrak.

7.2   Adding New Activities

It is often quicker to create a schedule in a spread sheet and import the data into the scheduling software. Primavera offers a spreadsheet import function found under **File**, **Import…** which is very user friendly. This is covered in detail in **Utilities** chapter.

 Some data associated with an imported activity must exist before the activity is imported from Excel otherwise it will not be imported. This includes items such as Roles, Resources and Activity Codes. These data items may be imported using the Primavera SDK (which is loaded from the installation CD and instructions are available on the Administration Guide) and an Excel spreadsheet available from the Oracles Primavera Knowledgebase.

To add an Activity to a project in the **Activities Window** you must first open the project, select the appropriate WBS Node and then:

- Select **Edit**, **Add**, or
- Press the **Insert** key on the keyboard.

7.3   Default Activity Duration

The default activity duration for newly created activities is specified in the **Admin, Admin Preferences…**, **General** tab **Activity Duration cell**.

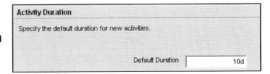

7.4   Copying Activities in Primavera P6 Version 7

Activities may be copied from another project when both projects are open at the same time or copied from within the same project using the normal Windows commands, **Copy** and **Paste**, by using the menu commands **Edit, Copy** and **Edit, Paste** or **Ctrl+C** and **Ctrl+V**.

One or more activities may be selected to be copied by:

- **Ctrl**-clicking, or
- Holding the **shift** key and clicking on the first and last activity in a range, or
- Dragging a range with the mouse.

With this operation be sure to select the whole activity or activities, not just a cell.

P6 Version 7 has a new function that allows the renumbering of pasted activities, the options are self explanatory:

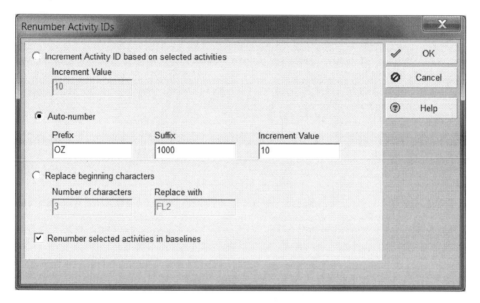

Should you attempt to renumber to Activity IDs that exist then a further form is presented to allow manual renumbering:

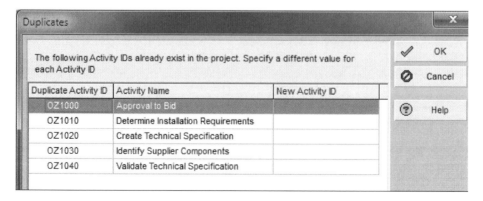

7.5   Copying Activities in Primavera P6.2 and Earlier

Activities may also be copied from another project when both projects are open at the same time or copied from within the same project using the normal Windows commands, **Copy** and **Paste**, by using the menu commands **Edit, Copy** and **Edit, Paste** or **Ctrl+C** and **Ctrl+V**.

One or more activities may be selected to be copied by:

- **Ctrl**-clicking, or
- Holding the **shift** key and clicking on the first and last activity in a range.

With this operation be sure to select the whole activity or activities, not just a cell.

When pasting, you are presented with the **Copy Activity Option** form where you may select which data is to be copied and pasted:

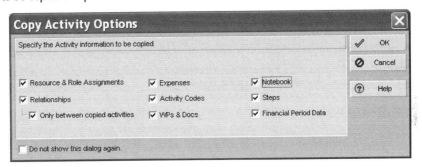

To copy an activity from one project to another, both projects must be open.

7.6   Renumbering Activity IDs in P6 Version 7

There is a new function in P6 Version allowing the renumbering of activities, to use this function:
- Select the activities that are to be renumbered,
- Select from the menu **Edit, Renumber Activity IDs** or right click in the columns area and select **Renumber Activity IDs**,
- This opens the **Renumber Activity IDs** form allowing renumbering of the activity IDs.

7.7   Copying Activities from other Programs

Activity data may NOT be copied from, or updated from other programs (such as Excel), by cutting and pasting.

7.8   Elapsed Durations

An activity may NOT be assigned an **Elapsed** duration as in Microsoft project and the activity should be scheduled on a 24hrs/day and 7 days per week calendar.

7.9   Finding the Bars in the Gantt Chart

At times you will find there are no bars displayed in the Gantt Chart because the Timescale has scrolled too far into the past or future. Double-click in the Gantt Chart in line with an activity and the Timescale will scroll to display the activity bar. There are no rolling dates as in P3 or SureTrak associated with the Gantt Chart.

7.10 Activity Information – Bottom Layout

The Bottom Layout has a number of tabs where information about the highlighted activity may be viewed and edited. (These are not in any specific order as the tabs may be reordered on the screen.)

• **General**	This form displays the: • **Activity ID** and **Activity Description** • **Project** and **Responsible Manager**, these may not be edited here. It also displays activity attributes including some which were set as defaults in the **Project Window**: • **Activity Type, Duration Type, % Complete Type, Activity Calendar, WBS**, and **Primary Resource**.
• **Status**	This is where the following data is displayed/edited: • The **Durations**, • The **Status**, where Actual Dates and % Complete may be entered, • Where **Constraints** are entered and • By selecting from the drop down box the **Labor** and **Nonlabor Units** or **Costs** and **Material Costs** may be displayed. **NOTE:** It is possible to assign resource Units in the **Status** tab without a resource being assigned to the activity and the rate will be taken from the **Project Properties Calculations** tab.
• **Summary**	This form displays summary information about the activity. It has three buttons that select which data will be displayed: • **Units**, or **Costs**, or **Dates**
• **Resources**	**Resources** and **Roles** may be assigned to activities and assignment information displayed.
• **Expenses**	**Expenses** may be added and edited here. These are intended for one off costs that do not require a resource to be created. **NOTE:** These are often used for material costs on construction and maintenance projects to prevent clogging up the **Resource Window**.
• **Notebook**	Notes about activities may be made here by adding a **Notebook Topic** and then adding notes about the topic.
• **Steps**	This function enables an activity to be broken down into increments titled **Steps** that may be marked up as complete as work on the Activity progresses.
• **Feedback**	This is where comments made in the timesheet module may be viewed.
• **WP's & Docs**	This is where files that have been listed in the **Work Products and Documents Window** may be associated with activities and then opened from this form.
• **Codes**	Project Codes may be created and activities associated with these codes with this form. These codes are similar to P3 and SureTrak Activity Codes and activities may be organized in a similar way.
• **Relationships** **Predecessors** **Successors**	This is where the activity's predecessors and successors are added, edited and deleted. This is covered in the **Adding the Dependencies** chapter.

7.11 Assigning Calendars to Activities

Activities often require a different calendar from the default **Project Calendar** that is assigned in the **Project Information** form. Primavera enables each activity to be assigned a unique calendar. An **Activity Calendar** may be assigned by the **General** tab of the **Bottom Layout** or by displaying the **Calendar** column.

7.11.1 Assigning a Calendar Using General Tab of the Bottom Layout Form

- Select one activity that you want to assign to a different calendar. Multiple activity selection may not be used, Open the **General** tab of the **Bottom Layout**,
- Click on the ⬛ button in the **Activity Calendar** box to open the **Select Activity Calendar** form,
- Select either **Global** or **Project** from the drop down list in the top left menu and
- Select an Activity calendar by clicking in the ⬛ button.

7.11.2 Assigning a Calendar Using a Column

You may also display the **Calendar** column and edit the activity calendar from this column. The process of displaying a column is covered in the **Formatting the Display** chapter.

Edit, **Fill Down** may be used to assign a new calendar to multiple selected activities.

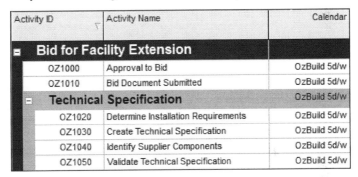

Activity ID	Activity Name	Calendar
Bid for Facility Extension		
OZ1000	Approval to Bid	OzBuild 5d/w
OZ1010	Bid Document Submitted	OzBuild 5d/w
Technical Specification		OzBuild 5d/w
OZ1020	Determine Installation Requirements	OzBuild 5d/w
OZ1030	Create Technical Specification	OzBuild 5d/w
OZ1040	Identify Supplier Components	OzBuild 5d/w
OZ1050	Validate Technical Specification	OzBuild 5d/w

7.12 Undo

Primavera Version 5.0 introduced a multiple **Undo** function that operates on Resources, Resource Assignments, and Activities windows, but no **Redo** function.

There are many functions that will erase the Undo memory such as scheduling, summarizing, importing, opening a project, opening Code forms, opening User and Admin Preferences and closing the application.

7.13 Assigning Activities to a WBS Node

Activities are assigned to a WBS Node from the Activities Window. They may be assigned using the following methods:

- A new activity will inherit the WBS Node that is highlighted when an activity is created.

- A new activity will inherit the WBS Node of a selected existing activity when the project is organized by WBS Nodes and an activity is created.

- Select the activity and click the WBS box in the **General** tab in the lower window. This will open the **Select WBS** form where you may assign the WBS Node. The $\boxed{+}$ and the $\boxed{-}$ are used to expand or rollup the WBS structure.

  Click on the $\boxed{\oplus}$ button to assign the node.

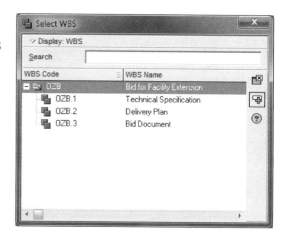

- Select one or more activities and move the mouse to the left of the activity description and the mouse will change into the shape displayed in the following picture. You may then drag the activities to another WBS Node.

  Be sure the Mouse pointer changes to this shape before dragging.

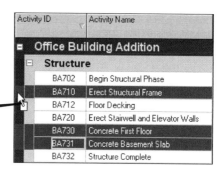

- Insert the WBS column by clicking on the $\boxed{\boxplus}$ button and selecting WBS from the Columns form under General. Clicking in the WBS column of an activity will open the Select WBS form.

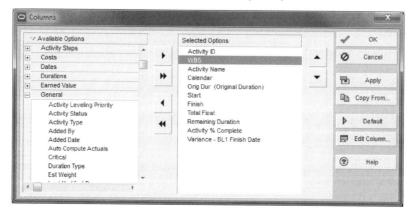

7.14   Reordering or Sorting Activities

You may not drag activities up or down the schedule in the same way as other products.

There are two principal methods of ordering activities after they have been added:

- Using the **Sort** function. To open the **Sort** form:

  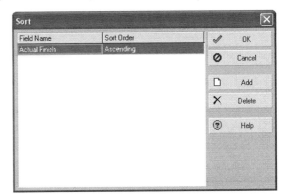

  > Select **View**, **Group and Sort...** and click the ⟦ Sort... ⟧ button, or

  > Click on the ⟦⟧ **icon** and click the ⟦ Sort... ⟧ button to open the **Sort** form,

 It is unfortunate that with Primavera, as soon as you use the option below for sorting activities then the sorting fields entered into the **Sort** form above are overwritten by the column that has been used to sort the activities.

- Highlighting a column title and clicking with the mouse. The activities within a band will be reordered within that band in the order indicated with an arrow in the right side of the column header. The order will be either Ascending or Descending:

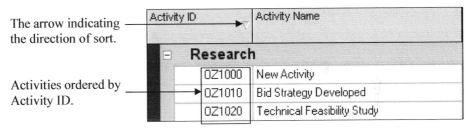

The arrow indicating the direction of sort.

Activities ordered by Activity ID.

This function changes all the settings made in the **Sort** form on a permanent basis.

 The Activities ID's are not renumbered when they have been reordered as they are with Microsoft Project.

7.15 Summarizing Activities Using WBS

The WBS bands may be summarized in the same way as in other project planning and scheduling software. The following picture shows the activities displayed under the WBS Nodes:

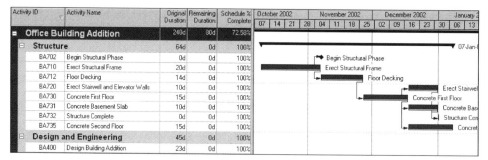

The following picture shows the activities summarized under the WBS Nodes:

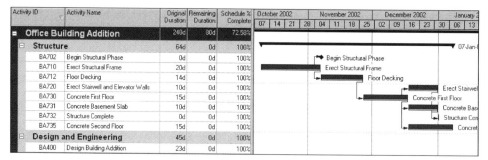

WBS Nodes may be summarized or expanded by:

- Double-click any WBS band description. The band will either roll up when expanded or expand when rolled up.

- Select **View**, **Expand All** or **View**, **Collapse All** from the menu.

- Right-click and select **Expand All** or **Collapse All** from the menu.

- Click on the [+] or the [-] to the right of the WBS Node description to expand or collapse the WBS Node.

WBS Nodes may be reordered by clicking the arrow buttons in the Command Toolbar to the right side of the WBS Window.

 The durations in days of the WBS Nodes in Primavera Version 6.2 and earlier is covered the **Calendar** chapter. These are calculated from the Database **Default Calendar** and the **Hours/Day** setting in the **Edit**, **User Preferences...**, **Time Units** tab (or the **Admin**, **Admin Preferences**, **Time Periods** field if you have not been granted access to edit this field). These durations may not be relevant to your project if your **Time Units** field does not match the number of hours in the **Default Calendar**.

7.16 Spell Check

To spell check a project, open the **Spell Check** form by:

- Select **Edit**, **Spell Check**, or

- Hit the F7 key:

This form is simple to use.

7.17   Workshop 5 - Adding Activities

Background
We need to setup the defaults and add the activities to the schedule.

Assignment
1. Go to the **Projects Window**, highlight the OzBuild project and select the **Defaults** tab in the **Activity Details** pane. If required, adjust the following parameters.

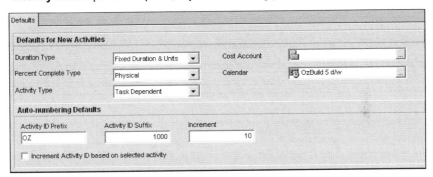

2. Open the **Activities Window** and add the following activities under the appropriate WBS.
3. Click on the Activity ID column header if the activities become out of order.

Activity ID	Activity Name	Orig Dur	Calendar	Activity Type
	Technical Specification			
OZ1000	Approval to Bid	0d	OzBuild 5d/w	Start Milestone
OZ1010	Determine Installation Requirements	4d	OzBuild 5d/w	Task Dependent
OZ1020	Create Technical Specification	5d	OzBuild 5d/w	Task Dependent
OZ1030	Identify Supplier Components	2d	OzBuild 5d/w	Task Dependent
OZ1040	Validate Technical Specification	2d	OzBuild 5d/w	Task Dependent
	Delivery Plan			
OZ1050	Document Delivery Methodology	4d	OzBuild 5d/w	Task Dependent
OZ1060	Obtain Quotes from Suppliers	8d	OzBuild 5d/w	Task Dependent
OZ1070	Calculate the Bid Estimate	3d	**OzBuild 6d/w**	Task Dependent
OZ1080	Create the Project Schedule	3d	**OzBuild 6d/w**	Task Dependent
OZ1090	Review the Delivery Plan	1d	OzBuild 5d/w	Task Dependent
	Bid Document			
OZ1100	Create Draft of Bid Document	6d	OzBuild 5d/w	Task Dependent
OZ1110	Review Bid Document	4d	OzBuild 5d/w	Task Dependent
OZ1120	Finalise and Submit Bid Document	2d	OzBuild 5d/w	Task Dependent
OZ1130	Bid Document Submitted	0d	OzBuild 5d/w	Finish Milestone

Continued.....

4. Assign the **Activity Type** and **6 day per week calendar** where required in the **General** tab of the **Activity Details** form.
5. Reschedule the project by pressing F9 and check that the Data Date is set at the 5 December 2011 at 08:00.
6. Your answer should look like the following picture, but you may have different columns displayed and there may be text on the bars, ensure the sort order is by Activity ID:

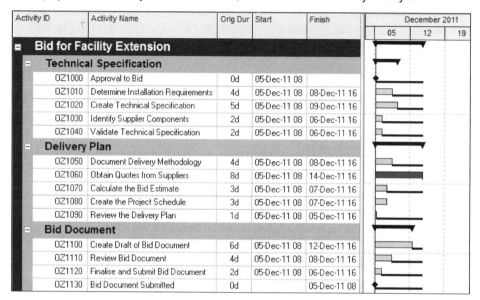

NOTE:
1. Depending on the Layout that your software has loaded your data may be displayed with different columns and bar formatting. Should your layout not enable you to review your data entry try selecting a different layout using the command **View**, **Layouts**, **Open...** and select another layout from the list such as the Classic or Default WBS Layout which may be similar to the picture above. If this does not solve your problem then refer to the Layouts and Formatting sections of this book.
2. The durations against the WBS Nodes have been hidden as these may calculate differently depending on the version of the software that you are using and the Default Global Calendar.
3. If your timescale week start date is different to the one above, for example the first day in the timescale is 4 Dec where as the first day above is 5 Dec then you may change this if you have the access rights. Select **Admin**, **Admin Preferences** form, **General** tab, **Starting Day of Week** section:

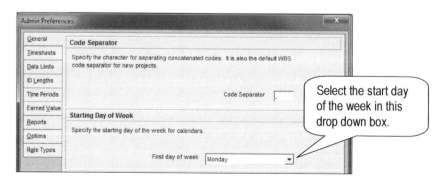

8 FORMATTING THE DISPLAY

This chapter shows you how to set up the on-screen presentation so that the schedule will be easier to read and more consistent. This chapter covers the following display customizing topics:

Topic	Menu Command
• Formatting Columns	Open the **Column** form: • Select **View**, **Columns...**, or • Click on the ⬚ button.
• Formatting Activity Bars	Open the **Bar** form: • Select **View**, **Bars...**, or • Click on the ⬚ button.
• Format Gridlines	**Bar Chart Gridlines** are formatted in the **View**, **Bar Chart Options...** form, **Sightlines** tab.
• Format Data Date	The **Data Date** is formatted in the **Bar Chart Options...** form, **Data Date** tab.
• Formatting Row Height	Open the **Table, Font and Row** form by: • Selecting **View, Table Font and Row....**
• Formatting Colors	There are limited options for formatting colors: • **Text** colors are formatted in the **Color** form accessed from the **Table, Font and Row** form which is opened by selecting **View, Table Font and Row...**, AaBbYyZz button. • **Bar Colors** are covered in the **Formatting the Bars** paragraph of this chapter. • **Band** colors are selected as part of the formatting of the layout by selecting **View, Group and Sort...** or clicking on the ⬚ button.
• Formatting Fonts	There are limited options for formatting fonts: • **Text** fonts are formatted in the **Font** form accessed from the **Table, Font and Row** form which is opened by selecting **View, Table Font and Row...**, AaBbYyZz button. • **Notebook** entries may be edited when entered.
• Format Timescale	• Click on the ⬚ button, or • Select **View, Timescale...**, or • Right-click in the Bar Chart area and select **Timescale...**.

The formatting is applied to the current **Layout** and is automatically saved as part of the Layout when another Layout is selected. Views are covered in the **Group, Sort and Layouts** chapter.

8.1   Formatting the Project Window

The formatting of the Project Window is very similar to the formatting of the Activity Window and will not be covered separately. Formatting, Filters and Layouts all work in the same way, except one is dealing with projects and not activities.

8.2   Understanding Forms

Unlike many software packages Primavera has sorting and filtering functions in most forms and the principals are the same in most forms. This section will demonstrate some of the functions but you must be prepared to experiment with each form to see how they operate.

- Clicking in the **Resource ID** column of the Resources Window take the formatting from hierarchical to alphabetical to reverse alphabetical. This function works in other forms with a hierarchical structure.

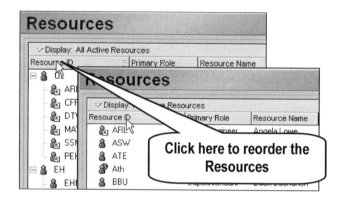

- The **Assign Successors** form has a **Filter** and **Group and Sort By** option which affect which data and how it is Grouped.

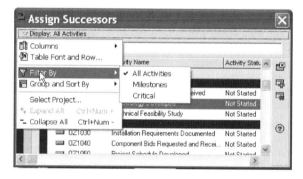

- The **Assign Resource** form has a **Filter** and **Group and Sort By** option which affect what data is available.

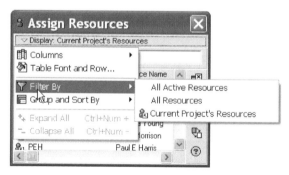

8.3 Formatting Columns

8.3.1 Selecting the Columns to be Displayed

The columns are formatted through the **Columns** form which may be opened by:

- Select **View**, **Columns...**, or
- Click on the ⊞ button, or
- Right-click to open a menu and select **Columns...**:

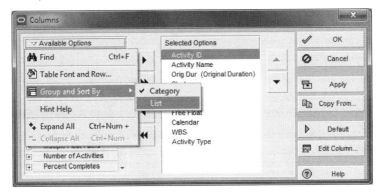

The **Column** form may be resized by dragging the edges.

- The available columns are displayed in the right window and may be listed under **Categories** or as a single **List**.
- To select how the column titles are displayed, click the **Available Options** drop down box and then select **Group and Sort By** to choose either **List** or **Categories**, as per the picture above.
- The columns to be displayed are listed in the right **Selected Options** window and are copied from the **Available Options** to and from **Selected Options** using the ⊡ and ⊡ buttons.
- The ▷ Default button sets the columns back to the default column display.

8.3.2 Column Header Alignment

- Select **View**, **Columns...**, or
- Click on the ⊞ button, then
- Select the ☒ Edit Column... , (☒ Edit Title... in Version 5.0) and earlier, option which opens the **Edit Column** form and enables a user definable column title to be created in the **New Title:** cell and the **Column Title Alignment** to be set to Left, Center or Right.

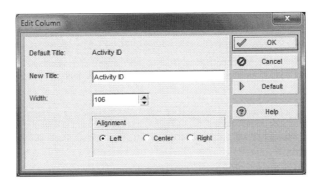

8.3.3 Adjusting the Width of Columns

You may adjust the width of the column in two ways:

- By dragging the column title separator; move the mouse pointer to the nearest vertical line of the column. A ↔ icon will then appear and enable the column to be adjusted by Right-clicking and dragging.

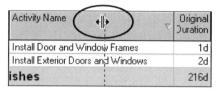

- From the **Column** form select the ⊞ Edit Column... , (⊞ Edit Title... in Version 5.0) and earlier, to open the **Edit Column Title** form and enter the width of the column in pixels.

8.3.4 Setting the Order of the Columns from Left to Right on the Screen

The order of the columns on the screen, from left to right, is the same as the order in the **Columns** form **Selected Options** window from top to bottom. The order of the columns may be altered:

- Highlight the column in the **Columns** form **Selected Options** window and use the ▲ and ▼ buttons, or
- Right-click the column title in a Window and drag the column.

8.4   Formatting the Bars

The bars in the Gantt Chart may be formatted to suit your requirements for display. Primavera does not have the option to format individual bars but is able to assign a filter to a bar style so that a style is applied to activities that meet a filter definition.

8.4.1   Formatting Activity Bars

To format all the bars you must open the **Bar** form:

- Select **View**, **Bars...**, or
- Click on the ▦ button, or
- Right-click in the bars area and select **Bars...** from the menu.

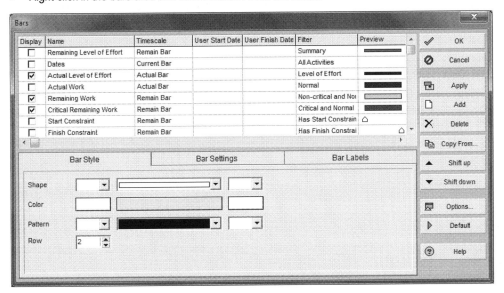

The following notes are the main points for using this function. Detailed information is available in the help facility by searching for "Bar styles dialog box."

- Each bar listed in the table may be displayed on the bar chart by checking the box in the **Display** column.
- New bars may be added by clicking on the [□ Add] button and deleted by clicking on the [X Delete] button.
- The bar at the top of the list is placed on the screen and then the one below drawn over the top of it, so it would be simple to hide one bar with a second. The [▲ Shift up] and [▼ Shift down] buttons are used to move the bars up or down the list and therefore determine which bar is drawn on top of the next.
- The **Name** is the title assigned to the bar and may be displayed in the printout legend.
- The **Timescale** option is similar to the **Show For ... Tasks** option in the Microsoft Project **Bar Styles** form or the **Data Item** in the SureTrak **Format Bars** form, and enables the nomination of a predefined bar which is selected from the drop down box.
- Version 4.1 introduced **User Defined Dates** that may be used for formatting **User Defined Bars Styles**, see the first line on the bars form above.

- Double clicking on a cell in the **Filter column** opens the **Filters** form where you are able to select the filter/s which will determine which activities are displayed with the assigned bar format. Filters will be covered in detail in the **Filters** chapter.

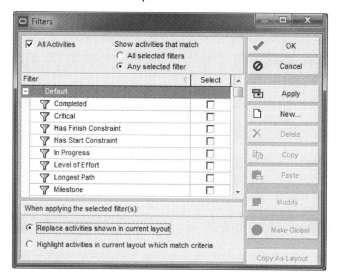

- **Negative Float** is displayed in a similar way as in Microsoft Project and requires another bar in addition to the **Positive Float** bar and both the **Timescale** and **Filter** selected as Negative Float.
- The **Float** bar shows **Total Float**; there is no **Free Float** bar available, as in P3.
- The **% Complete** bar is linked to the **Activity % Complete**.

8.4.2   Formatting Bars Issues

There are a number of issues with the Primavera standard bar formatting that need to be understood so the user may display the activity bars logically:

- It is recommended that you use the Primavera default bar display options displaying the **Actual Work** (this bar is displayed from the **Start** date to the **Data Date**), **Remaining Work** and **Critical Remaining Work** bars (these bars are displayed from the **Data Date** to the **Finish** date with the appropriate filter) because the **Early** bar will not display actual progress as in other software packages. Please read the **Understanding Dates** section in the **Tracking Progress** chapter to understand how the dates are calculated that are used to draw each bar.
- When a Baseline Bar is displayed then the Planned Dates are displayed as the Baseline Bar so ensure you have a Baseline set before displaying a Baseline Bar.
- The relationships are displayed on the Baseline Bar when the Baseline Bar is listed in the Bars form above other bars. To prevent this the Baseline Bars should be moved below all other bars in the Baseline form.
- Displaying a Baseline Bar does not display the Baseline Milestones and the Baseline Milestones have to be displayed separately.
- The Total Float Bar is called the Float Bar in the Bars form.
- The default total **Float Bar** displays a float bar on completed activities, but the Total Float field will not display a value. To prevent this happening you should edit the total **Float Bar Filter** in the **Bars** form so it is only displayed for and Not Started and In Progress activities:

Display	Name	Timescale	User Start Date	User Finish Date	Filter	Preview
☑	Float Bar	Float Bar			Not Started or In Progress	▬▬▬

8.4.3 Bar Style Tab

The appearance of each bar is edited in the lower half of the form. The bar's start, middle, and end points may have their color, shape, pattern, etc., formatted.

The bars may be placed on one of three rows numbered from 1 to 3, from top to bottom one bar above the other. If multiple bars are placed on the same row, the bar at the top of the list will be drawn first and the ones lower down the list will be drawn over the top.

8.4.4 Bar Settings Tab

Grouping Band Settings
This sets the style for summary bars only, which may be displayed when the WBS Node is both summarized and not summarized.

- This would not normally be used when a Summary Bar has been defined as the result would be two summary bars.
- **Show bar when collapsed** option displays the detailed bars on a single line when the WBS Node has been summarized; see the two pictures following:

  ➢ Before summarizing:

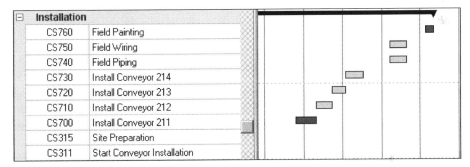

  ➢ After summarizing:

This is similar to the Microsoft Project **Always roll up Gantt bars** option in the **Layout** form.

Show bar for grouping bands
This shows a summarized bar all the time and converts the filter automatically to "Summary" bars only.

 When formatting the **Bar Style** for Milestones it is important to take note of the checked boxes and Filter format. If the box **Show bar for grouping bands** is checked, Milestones will appear at the ends of Summary Bars and not in line with the actual activities they belong too. The filter in this case will read **Summary** and not **Milestone**.

Bar Necking Settings

Bar Necking displays a thinner bar during times of inactivity such as weekends and holidays and applies only to Current Bar setting column in the **Bars** form.

Un-necked bars

Necked bars

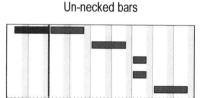
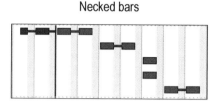

- **Calendar nonwork time** necks the bar based on the activity's calendar.

- **Activity nonwork intervals** necks the bar when Out of Sequence Progress options of Actual Dates or Retained Logic causes a break in the work. See the **Advanced Scheduling Options** paragraph.

 There is no Resource Bar available and Primavera will not neck on the resource calendar so when an activity is Resource Dependent and the resource is on a different calendar to the activity then the bar may neck when the resource is working or not necked when the resource is not working.

8.4.5 Bar Labels Tab

This tab enables the placement of text with a bar, above, below, to the left and to the right. The following pictures show how the start and finish dates are formatted and displayed on the bar chart:

- Select the bar that you wish to add the label to.

- Click on the [Add] and the [X Delete] buttons at the bottom of the **Bars** form to add and delete a **Label** item.

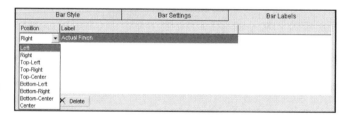

- Select the **Position** and **Label** from the drop down boxes in the **Bar Labels** tab.

- The dates on the bar chart are adopted from the **User Preferences** and may not be formatted separately.

 It is often useful to create a bar that only displays the text. This bar may be displayed or not displayed as required, which is much simpler than reformatting a bar to show text.

- Each **Notebook Topic** may be displayed on a bar one at a time by selecting the topic in the **Bar Labels** tab. After the box containing the label is displayed on the screen it may be adjusted in size by dragging.

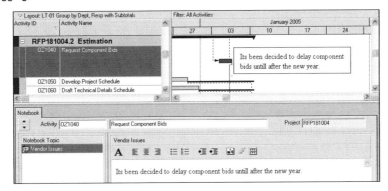

8.4.6   Bar Chart Options Form

The **Bar Chart Options** form is displayed by clicking on the [⬛ Options...] button from the **Bars** form or by selecting **View**, **Bar Chart Options...**:

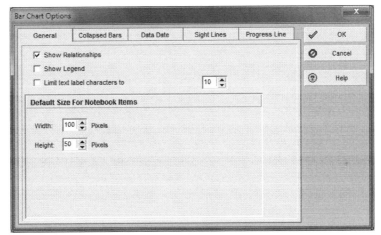

- The **General** tab has a variety of options for formatting the bar chart which are mainly self explanatory.
  - ➢ **Show Relationships** has the same result as clicking on the ⬛ icon and displays the relationships.
  - ➢ **Show Legend** Displays a legend on the bar chart in the Activities view, see the following picture:

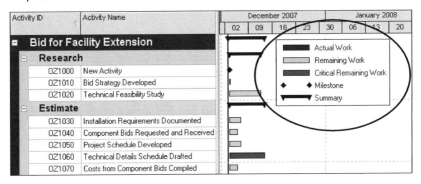

> ➤ The default size of the box displaying a **Notebook** topic may be set in the **Bar Chart Options** form, **General** tab, which is displayed by clicking on the [Options] button from the **Bars** form.

- The **Collapsed Bar** tab is to format the bars when a WBS band has been collapsed and displays a summarized bar.

- The **Data Date** tab is for formatting the Data Date, its style, color and size.

- Primavera Version 5.0 introduced the **Sight Lines** tab which enables the specification of both Major and Minor vertical and horizontal Sight Lines, which brings this functionality up to match P3, SureTrak and Microsoft Project.

- Primavera P6 Version 7 introduced the **Progress Line** Display on the Gantt Chart which is covered in detail in the next paragraph.

8.5 Row Height

Row heights may be adjusted to display text that would otherwise be truncated by a narrow column.

- The height of all rows may be formatted by selecting **View, Table Font and Row...** to open the **Table, Font and Row** form. The options in this form are self-explanatory.

- The **Show Icons** option will display a different icon in front of the Activity and WBS.

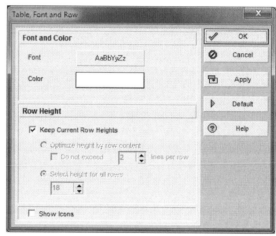

> ➤ In the **Projects Window** a 🖳 indicates a **What-if** project, 📁 a **Planned** project and 🖥 an **Active** or **Inactive** project.

> ➤ In the **Activity Window** 🖫 indicates a WBS Node, a blue ▬ a complete activity, a blue and green ▬ an in-progress activity and a green ▬ an un-started activity.

> ➤ In the **Resources Window** 🧍 indicates a Resource, 🗂 a resource assigned to an open project, 🗂 and 🗂 an unassigned and assigned **Nonlabor Resource** and 🔖 and 🔖 a unassigned and assigned **Material Resource**,

- The height of a single row may be manually adjusted in a similar way to adjusting row heights in Excel, click the row; the pointer will change to a double-headed arrow ⬍; then drag the row with the mouse. These manually adjusted rows are not saved with a Layout.

8.6 Progress Line Display on the Gantt Chart

A progress line displays how far ahead or behind activities are in relation to the Baseline. Either the Project Baseline or the Primary User Baseline may be used and there are four options:

- Difference between the Baseline Start Date and Activity Start Date,
- Difference between the Baseline Finish Date and Activity Finish Date,
- Connecting the progress points based on the Activity % Complete,
- Connecting the progress points based on the Activity Remaining Duration.

There are several main components of displaying a Progress Line in P7:

- Firstly the progress line is formatted using the **View**, **Bar Chart Options** form, **Progress Line** tab, which may also be opened by right clicking in the Gant Chart area:

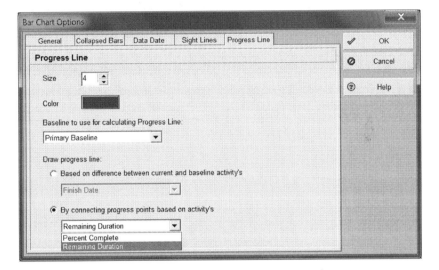

- Selecting **View**, **Progress Line** to hide or display the **Progress Line**.
- If you use either of the options of Percent Complete or Remaining Duration then you must display the appropriate Baseline Bar that has been selected as the **Baseline to use for calculating Progress Line:**.
- The picture below shows the option highlighted above of **Percent Complete**:

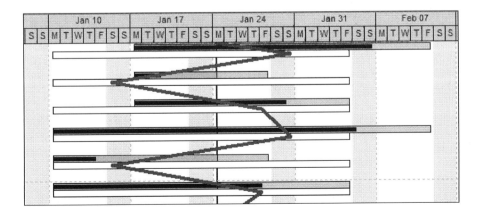

8.7   Format Fonts and Font Colors

The format font options are:

- The **Activity Data** fonts are formatted in the **Table, Font and Row** form (displayed in the paragraph above) by selecting **View, Table Font and Row**....

  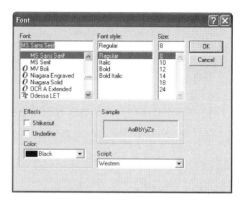

  - ➢ Clicking on the [AaBbYyZz], the **Font** button, will open the font form where normal Windows functions are available.
  - ➢ Clicking on the **Color** button will enable the selection of a color for the background of both the **Bar Chart** and the **Columns** area.

- The **Notebook Topics** may be formatted using the formatting features above where the Notebook items are entered in the lower pane.

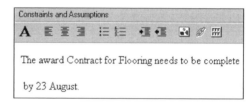

- Some forms may have the fonts for displaying data edited when there is a menu on the top left side with the **Table Font and Row...** menu item.

  The award Contract for Flooring needs to be complete by 23 August.

- The text in a **Text Box** that has been inserted onto the Bar Chart may be formatted when the box is created.

8.8   Format Colors

These are the main options for formatting colors:

- **Band** colors in layouts are formatted in the **Group and Sort** form by clicking on the [⊞] button or selecting **View, Group and Sort**....

- **Text** colors were covered in the **Format Font and Colors** paragraph.

- **Bar Colors** were covered in the **Formatting the Bars** paragraph.

- **Timescale** and **Column Headers** see the **Format Timescale Command** paragraph.

- **Sight Lines (Gridline)** colors may not be formatted.

- The **Progress Line** color is selected in the **Bar Chart Options** for **Sight Line** tab.

- The **Data Date** is formatted in the **Bar Options** form, **Data Date** tab.

- The **Relationship Lines**, also known as **Dependencies**, **Logic**, or **Links**, may not be formatted and are displayed with the following characteristics:

  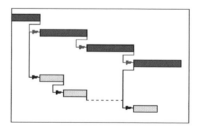

  - ➢ Solid Red for Critical,
  - ➢ Solid Black for Driving, and
  - ➢ Dotted Black for Non-driving.

8.9   Format Timescale

8.9.1   Moving and Rescaling the Timescale

To display hidden parts of the schedule the timescale may be grabbed and moved by placing the cursor in the top half of the Timescale, the cursor will turn into a 🖑, right-click and drag left or right.

The timescale may be rescaled, therefore increasing or decreasing the length of the bars and displaying more or less of the schedule by placing the cursor in the bottom half of the Timescale, the cursor will turn into a 🔍, right-click, and drag left to make the bars shorter and right to make the bars longer.

When there are no bars in view when you are viewing a time ahead or behind the activity dates you may double-click in the **Gantt Chart** area to bring them back into view.

8.9.2   Format Timescale Command

The **Timescale** form provides a number of options for the display of the timescale, which is located above the Bar Chart. To open the **Timescale** form:

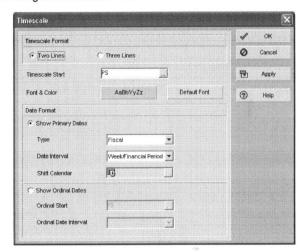

- Click on the 🖾 button, or

- Select **View**, **Timescale…**, or

- Right-click in the Bar Chart area and select **Timescale…**

The options available in the **Timescale** form are:

- **Timescale Format** in Primavera Version 6.0 now has the options of:
  - ➢ Two Lines, or
  - ➢ Three lines

- **Font and Color**
  - ➢ The ⬚ AaBbYyZz button opens the **Edit Font and Color** form which enables the timescale and column headers font and color to be changed.
  - ➢ By clicking on the ⬚ Default Font button all changes will be reversed.

- **Date Interval** sets the timescale and has the options in the picture to the right:

  > The **Week/Day 1** displays the Days like this:

Sep 27							Oct 04					
M	T	W	T	F	S	S	M	T	W	T	F	S

  > The **Week/Day 2** displays the Days like this:

Sep 27						
Mon	Tue	Wed	Thr	Fri	Sat	Sun

  Year/Quarter
  Year/Month
  Quarter/Month
  Month/Week
  Week/Day 1
  Week/Day 2
  Day/Shift
  Day/Hour

  > The **Date Interval** may also be adjusted by clicking on the ⊕ or the ⊖ which moves the timescale setting up and down the list shown above.

- **Shift Calendar** breaks the day into time intervals to suit the shift intervals when the **Day/Shift** option has been selected.

- **Date Format**

  > **Calendar** displays a normal calendar.
  > **Fiscal Year** displays the fiscal year in the year line. The Fiscal Year Start Month is set in the **Settings** tab of the **Project Details** form in the **Projects Window**.
  > **Week of the Year** displays the week of the year starting from "1" for the first week in January and is often termed **Manufacturing Week**.
  > **Ordinal Dates** displays the timescale to be counted by the unit selected in the **Date Interval**. This is useful for displaying a schedule when the start of the project is unknown. Ordinal dates display the time scale by counting in the selected units starting from a user definable start date. This option works in a similar way to the P3 function where the Ordinal start date may be selected. When 3 lines are displayed the ordinal dates and calendar dates may be displayed

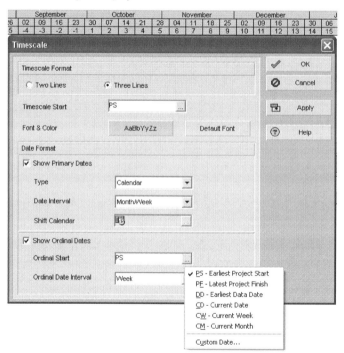

Fiscal Year: When the scale was set to Month/Week on the author's system the Fiscal Year did not display in accordance with date formatting settings. When the scale was set to Week and Days, the Date were displayed in US format (MM/DD/YYYY) which is not correct for countries that use the DD/MM/YYYY format.

8.9.3 Non Work Period Shading in Timescale

The non work period shading behind the bars is set by the database **Default Calendar** and is selected by selecting **Enterprise, Calendars** and checking a calendar in the **Default Column**. The **At Completion Duration** of 30d is calculated from the user database **Default Calendar**.

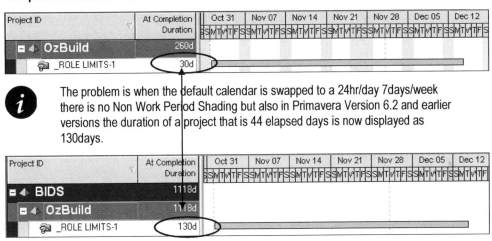

 The problem is when the default calendar is swapped to a 24hr/day 7days/week there is no Non Work Period Shading but also in Primavera Version 6.2 and earlier versions the duration of a project that is 44 elapsed days is now displayed as 130days.

8.10 Inserting Attachments - Text Boxes and Curtain

8.10.1 Adding a Text Box

A text box may be inserted in a bar chart area:

- Select the Activity which the new Text Box is to be associated with, either
- Right-click in the Bar Chart to open the menu, select **Attachments**, **Text** or
- Select **View, Attachments, Text** and
- The **Text Attachment** form will be displayed,

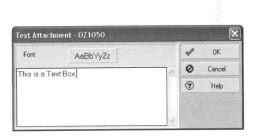

- Type in the text and format the font by clicking on the  button.
- A **Text Box** may be repositioned by clicking on the text and using the curser to drag the corners and sides.

8.10.2 Adding a Curtain

Primavera Version 5.0 introduced a function allowing the placing of multiple curtains on the Gantt Chart which may be all hidden or displayed. A **Curtain**, used to highlight periods of time over part of the bar chart, may be displayed in a similar way to P3 and SureTrak. Select **View**, **Attachments** to display the **Curtain** menu or right-click a bar and select **Attachments, Curtain**:

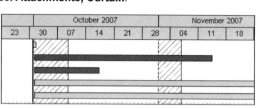

- **Add Curtain** opens the **Curtain Attachment** form used to create a curtain:

- **Show All** shows all the curtains,

- **Hide All** hides all the curtains and

- Clicking on a curtain in the Gantt Chart also opens the **Curtain Attachment** form where individual curtains may be deleted or hidden.

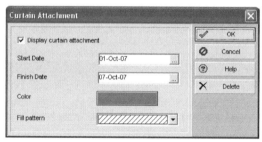

- Using the **Start Date** and **Finish Date** boxes, or

- Grabbing the left or right edge of the Curtain in the Bar Chart (the cursor will change to a) and dragging the start or finish date, or

- Grabbing the Curtain in the centre (the cursor will change to a) and dragging the whole Curtain.

8.11 Workshop 6 - Formatting the Bar Chart

Background
Management has received your draft report and requests that some changes be made to the presentation.

Assignment
Format your schedule as follows:
1. Depending on the default settings your Gantt Chart view may differ from that shown, e.g., there may be no summary bars.
2. Apply the **Classic WBS Layout**.
3. Add a **Calendar** and **Activity Type** columns, from the **General** section of the **Columns** form, to the right of the Activity Name.
4. Adjust the column widths by dragging the column headers divider lines.
5. Press the **F9** key and click the ⏵ Schedule button which will schedule the project and calculate the float.
6. Edit the **Float Bar** Filter (Total Float bar) so the only show float for Not Started or In Progress activities. Ensure you select the **Any selected filter** in the **Filters** form.

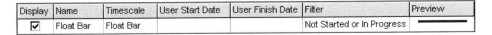

Display	Name	Timescale	User Start Date	User Finish Date	Filter	Preview
☑	Float Bar	Float Bar			Not Started or In Progress	——

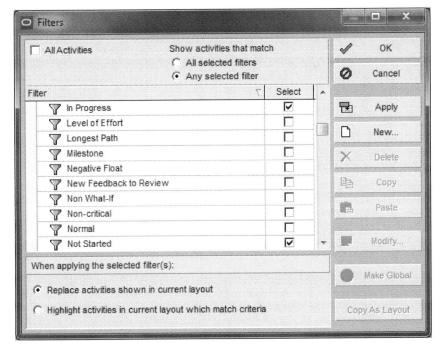

7. Now hide and display the **Float Bar** (Total Float bar) and **Neg Float Bar** (Negative Total Float bar), view the results and then leave the bars displayed.

Continued…

8. Remove all text from all bars in the bars form and delete the Current Bar Label bar if it exists.

9. Create a bar titled 'Activity Name' which does not display a bar and shows the Activity Name to the right of a bars and display it.

10. Change the Row Height to 30 points by selecting **View, Table Font and Row...**.

11. Now check the **Optimize height by row content box**, not exceeding 1 line per row.

12. Now change the setting to 18 point height for all rows.

13. Format Timescale to Year and Month, then Week and Day (two options), then Month and Week by using the 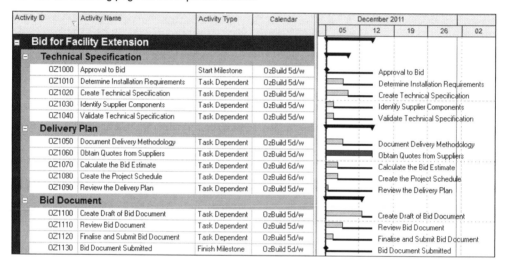 buttons

14. Format the Vertical lines with a solid Major line every month and a Minor line every week by selecting **View**, **Bar Chart Options...** and select the **Sight Lines** tab.

15. Expand and contract the timescale and adjust it so that all the descriptions and bars are visible.

16. See the following page for the expected results:

Activity ID	Activity Name	Activity Type	Calendar	December 2011				
				05	12	19	26	02
Bid for Facility Extension								
Technical Specification								
OZ1000	Approval to Bid	Start Milestone	OzBuild 5d/w	Approval to Bid				
OZ1010	Determine Installation Requirements	Task Dependent	OzBuild 5d/w	Determine Installation Requirements				
OZ1020	Create Technical Specification	Task Dependent	OzBuild 5d/w	Create Technical Specification				
OZ1030	Identify Supplier Components	Task Dependent	OzBuild 5d/w	Identify Supplier Components				
OZ1040	Validate Technical Specification	Task Dependent	OzBuild 5d/w	Validate Technical Specification				
Delivery Plan								
OZ1050	Document Delivery Methodology	Task Dependent	OzBuild 5d/w	Document Delivery Methodology				
OZ1060	Obtain Quotes from Suppliers	Task Dependent	OzBuild 5d/w	Obtain Quotes from Suppliers				
OZ1070	Calculate the Bid Estimate	Task Dependent	OzBuild 6d/w	Calculate the Bid Estimate				
OZ1080	Create the Project Schedule	Task Dependent	OzBuild 6d/w	Create the Project Schedule				
OZ1090	Review the Delivery Plan	Task Dependent	OzBuild 5d/w	Review the Delivery Plan				
Bid Document								
OZ1100	Create Draft of Bid Document	Task Dependent	OzBuild 5d/w	Create Draft of Bid Document				
OZ1110	Review Bid Document	Task Dependent	OzBuild 5d/w	Review Bid Document				
OZ1120	Finalise and Submit Bid Document	Task Dependent	OzBuild 5d/w	Finalise and Submit Bid Document				
OZ1130	Bid Document Submitted	Finish Milestone	OzBuild 5d/w	Bid Document Submitted				

9 ADDING RELATIONSHIPS

The next phase of a schedule is to add logic to the activities. There are two types of logic:

- **Relationships** (**Dependencies** or **Logic** or **Links** between activities), and
- Imposed **Constraints** to activity start or finish dates. These are covered in the **Constraints** chapter.

The Primavera Help file and other text use the terms **Relationships** and **Logic** for **Relationships** but does not use the terms **Dependencies**.

We will look at the following techniques in this chapter:

Topic	Notes for creating a SF Relationship
• Graphically in the Bar Chart.	Drag the ⌐ mouse pointer from one activity to another to create a dependency.
• By opening the **Activity Details** form.	Predecessor and Successors may be added and deleted from the **Relationships**, **Predecessor** or **Successor** tabs.
• By editing or deleting a dependency using the **Edit Relationship** form.	Double-click an activity link in the **Bar Chart** or **PERT** view.
• Opening the **Assign Predecessor** form or the **Assign Successor** form from the menu.	• Select **Edit**, **Assign**, **Predecessors...**, or • Select **Edit**, **Assign**, **Successors....**
• By displaying the **Predecessor** and/or **Successor** columns.	Double clicking in the Predecessor or Successor cells will open the **Assign Predecessor** form and the **Assign Successor** form.
• Chain Linking or Automatically Linking activities with a start to finish relationship.	Select the activities in the order they are to be linked, right-click and select **Link Activities**.

Relationships

There are two types of dependencies that are discussed in scheduling:

- **Hard Logic**, also referred to as **Mandatory** or **Primary Logic**, are dependencies that may not be avoided: for example, a footing excavation has to be prepared before concrete may be poured into it.
- **Soft Logic**, also referred to as **Sequencing Logic**, **Discretionary Logic** or **Preferred Logic** or **Secondary Logic** may often be changed at a later date to reflect planning changes: for example, determining in which order the footing holes may be dug.

There is no simple method of documenting which is hard logic and which is soft logic as notes may not be attached to relationships. A schedule with a large amount of soft logic has the potential of becoming very difficult to maintain when the plan is changed. As a project progresses, soft logic converts to hard logic due to commitments and commencing activities.

Constraints

Constraints are applied to Activities when relationships do not provide the required result and are often as a result of **External Dependencies**. Typical applications of a constraint are to constrain an activity to a date for:

- The availability of a site to commence work.
- The supply of information by a client.
- The required finish date of a project.

Constraints are often entered to represent contract dates and may be directly related to contract items using Notebook Topics.

Constraints are covered in detail in the **Constraints** chapter.

9.1 Understanding Relationships

There are four types of dependencies available in Primavera Version 5.0:

- Finish-to-Start (**FS**) (also known as conventional)
- Start-to-Start (**SS**)
- Start-to-Finish (**SF)**
- Finish-to-Finish (**FF**)

Two other terms you must understand are:

- **Predecessor**, an activity that controls the start or finish of another immediate subsequent activity.
- **Successor**, an activity where the start or finish depends on the start or finish of another immediately preceding activity.

The following pictures show how the dependencies appear graphically in the **Bar Chart** and **Activity Network** (also known as PERT, Network Diagram and Relationship Diagram views).

The **FS** (or conventional) dependency looks like this:

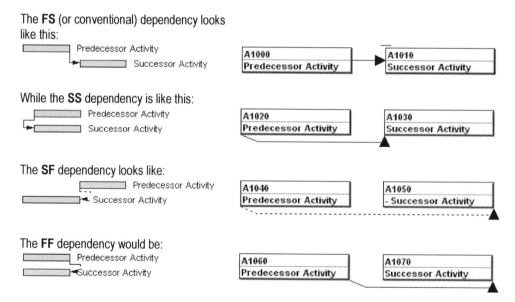

While the **SS** dependency is like this:

The **SF** dependency looks like:

The **FF** dependency would be:

9.2 Understanding Lags and Leads

A **Lag** is a duration that is applied to a dependency to make the successor start or finish earlier or later.

- A successor activity will start later when a positive **Lag** is assigned. Therefore, an activity requiring a 3-day delay between the finish of one activity and start of another will require a positive lag of 3 days.

- Conversely, a lag may be negative when a new activity may be started before the predecessor activity is finished. This is called a **Lead** or **Negative Lag**

- **Leads** and **Lags** may be applied to any relationship type, including Summary Activity relationships.

An example of a **FS** with positive lag

An example of a **FS** with negative lag:

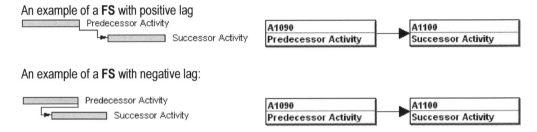

Here are some important points to understand about Lags:

- The lag duration is calculated on the lag as per Microsoft Project and other Primavera products and a lag is not assigned to one or both of the Predecessor and Successor activities as in Asta Powerproject.

- Lags may be assigned one of four calendars from the **Calendar for Scheduling Relationship lag** drop down box in the **General Schedule Options** form. This form is opened by selecting **Tools**, **Schedule...** and clicking on the [▷ Advanced...] tab. The four Lag Calendar options are:
  - ➢ Predecessor Activity Calendar,
  - ➢ Successor Activity Calendar,
  - ➢ 24 Hour Calendar, and
  - ➢ Project Default Calendar.

NOTE: Lags are by only calculated by Primavera P3 and SureTrak software using the predecessor's calendar. Microsoft Project 2002 to 2007 uses the Successor Calendar or may have an Elapsed Duration Lag. Microsoft Project 2000 uses the Project Calendar.

 You must be careful when using a lag to allow for delays such as curing concrete when the Lag Calendar is not a seven-day calendar. Because this type of activity lapses non-work days, the activity could finish before Primavera calculated finish date.

You must be extremely careful when opening multiple projects when the Lag Calendar option is different for each project. This is because all the projects options are changed permanently to be the same as the **Default Project** and therefore some of your projects may not calculate the same way as they did before opening the projects together. Please read the **MULTIPLE PROJECT SCHEDULING** for more details on this topic.

9.3 Formatting the Relationships

Relationships lines may not be formatted like in SureTrak, but unlike Microsoft Project they do not adopt the color of the predecessor activity which is often misleading.

- The relationships may be displayed or hidden by clicking on the ⬛ button on the **Activity Toolbar** or by checking and un-checking the **Show Relationships** box in the **Bar Chart Options** form, **General** tab.
- When displayed the color of the relationship represents:
  - ➤ Red is a Critical and therefore a Driving relationship,
  - ➤ Solid Black a Non Critical Driving relationship, and therefore has Free Float,
  - ➤ Dotted Black a Non Critical Non Driving relationship, and has Free Float, and
  - ➤ Blue is a selected relationship and may be deleted.
- A relationship is displayed on the **Baseline** bar when the Baseline bar is above the Actual and Remaining bars in the **Bars** form. To place the relationships onto the Early bar which is more logical them move the Baseline bars in the **Bars** form to below the Actual and Remaining bars in the **Bars** form.

Relationships on the Baseline Bar

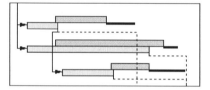

Relationships on the Current Bar

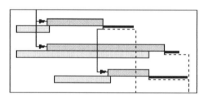

9.4 Adding and Removing Relationships

9.4.1 Graphically Adding a Relationship

To add relationships you can click the end of the predecessor activity bar, which will change the mouse arrow to a ⌐. Then simply hold down the left mouse, drag to the start of the successor activity and release the mouse button.

To create other relationships such as **Start to Start**, drag from the beginning of the predecessor to the beginning of the successor bar.

To confirm or edit the link or add lag after a link has been added, the **Edit Relationship** form may be opened:

- Select the relationship line on the Gantt Chart; it will turn to blue and an arrow, ↑ , will appear, then
- Double-click to open the **Edit Relationship** form:

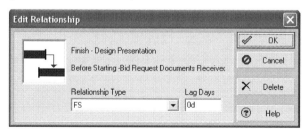

9.4.2 Graphically Deleting a Relationship

Select a relationship and when it turns blue strike the delete key to delete it. Another relationship may turn blue and if you wish to delete this relationship then you may strike the delete key again.

9.4.3 Adding and Deleting Relationships with the Activity Details Form

The **Activity Details** form in the lower pane may be used for adding and deleting relationships.

Opening the Form

- Select either the **Predecessor, Successor** or the **Relationship**s tab (they all operate in a similar way). The **Successor** tab is displayed in the following picture:

Editing the Form

- The **Predecessor** and **Successor** tabs may both be formatted and the columns you require may be displayed:
  - ➤ Right-click in the **Predecessor** or **Successor** tabs and
  - ➤ Select [Customize Successor Columns...] to open the **Predecessor** or **Successor Columns** form.
  - ➤ The following picture displays the fields that are available:

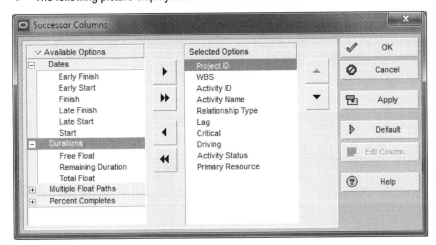

  - ➤ The data fields you require are added, deleted and reordered using the arrows. The title may also be edited using the **Edit Column Titles** form by clicking on the [Edit Title...] button.

Adding a Relationship

- To **Add** a predecessor or successor:

  ➢ Click on the [⬚ Assign] button, or

  ➢ Double-click in the Predecessor or Successor column of an activity to open the **Assign Predecessor** or **Successor** form,

  ➢ Format the form as required by clicking on [▽ Display: All Activities] button,

  ➢ Then select the relationship from the list:

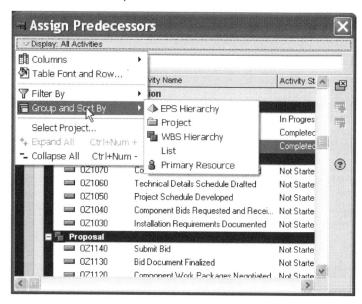

  ➢ You may use the **Search** function and type in the first characters of either the Activity ID or the Description to narrow down your search.

  ➢ Double-click the Activity or click the [⬚] icon to assign the predecessor or successor.

- Enter the Relationship Type from the **Relationship Type** drop-down list and the lag, if required, from the **Lag** drop-down list.

- To enter another relationship click the next activity line. The **Assign Predecessor** or **Successor** form will remain open.

- **Delete** a relationship by selecting a relationship and clicking on the [⬚ Remove] button.

- It is possible to follow the network path by jumping to an activity highlighted in the **Predecessor** or **Successor** form by clicking on the [⬚ GoTo] button.

- Move up and down the list of activities by clicking on the [▲▼] buttons in the top left side of the **Predecessor** or **Successor** tabs. This button exists in every lower pane tab.

9.4.4 Chain Linking

Activities may also be linked by selecting two or more activities in the order you wish them to be linked, right-click and select **Link Activities:**

- This option will only create Start to Finish relationships.

- This option does not enable the user to Chain Unlink.

9.5 Using the Command Toolbar Buttons to Assign Relationships

The **Assign Predecessors** button, , may be used to open the **Assign Predecessors** form and the **Assign Successors** button, , may be used to open the **Assign Successors** form.

9.6 Dissolving Activities

When an activity is deleted then a chain of logical activities may be broken. The **Edit**, **Dissolve** command and the right-click **Dissolve** command will delete an activity but join the predecessors and successors with a Finish to Start relationship.

9.7 Circular Relationships

A **Circular Relationship** is created when a loop is created in the logic. The relationship will be blue and when you reschedule you will be presented with the **Circular Relationships** form, which identifies the loop.

> To remove a circular relationship either select the first activity in the list and remove the offending predecessor which is the last Activity in the list or go to the last activity in the list and remove the offending successor which is the first activity in the list.

9.8 Scheduling the Project

After you have your activities and the logic in place, Primavera calculates the activities' dates/times. More specifically, Primavera **Schedules** the project to calculate the **Early Dates**, **Late Dates**, **Free Float** and the **Total Float**. This will enable you to review the **Critical Path** of the project. (Microsoft Project uses the term **Slack** instead of the term **Float**.) To schedule a project:

- Select **Tools**, **Schedule…,** or
- Strike the **F9** button to open the **Schedule** form:

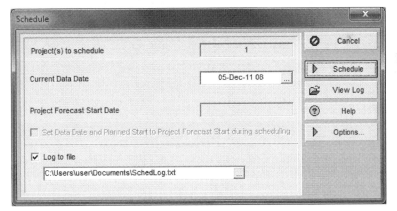

- Check the **Current Data Date**, which before a schedule is progressed should be the start date of the project.
- Click on the ▷ Schedule button.

Sometimes it is preferable to have the software recalculate the schedule each time an edit is made to an activity which affects any activity dates. To turn on automatic calculation, select **Tools, Schedule...,** ▷ Advanced.. button. Select **Schedule automatically when a change affects dates**.

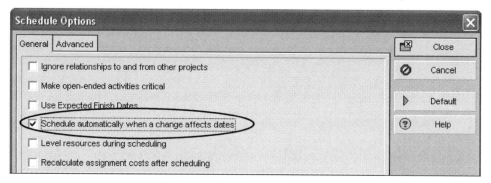

The default calculation setting for Microsoft Project and SureTrak is Automatic Calculation and Manual for P3 and Primavera Versions 3.5 to 6.0.

9.9   Critical Activities Definition

Critical Activities Definition criteria is defined in the **Settings** tab of the **Project Details** in the **Projects Window.**

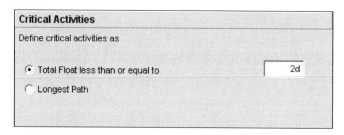

Defining critical activities affects how the activities are displayed.

- **Total Float less than or equal to** enables float to be set at any value. It is useful to set this at 2 days when multiple calendars are used, say a 5 day/week and a 7 day/week. This is because when there is a relationship from a 7 day/week predecessor to a 5 day/week successor over a weekend then float will be generated on the first activity although this is the driving relationship, the activity will have two days float:

Activity Name	Calendar	Total Float	Dec 27							J
			e Wed	Thr	Fri	Sat	Sun	Mon	Tue	We
Predecessor	7-Day Workweek	2								
Successor	Standard 5 Day Workweek	0								
New Activity	Standard 5 Day Workweek									

- **Longest Path** compensates for multiple calendars and selects the longest path through the schedule normally displaying a single chain of activities.

9.10   Workshop 7 - Adding the Relationships

Background
You have determined the logical sequence of activities, so you may now create the relationships.

Assignment

1.   Display the **Predecessor** column from the **Lists** section of the **Columns** form, to the right of the Activity Name.

2.   Input the logic below using several of the methods detailed in this chapter:

Activity ID	Activity Name	Predecessors
Bid for Facility Extension		
Technical Specification		
OZ1000	Approval to Bid	
OZ1010	Determine Installation Requirements	OZ1000
OZ1020	Create Technical Specification	OZ1010
OZ1030	Identify Supplier Components	OZ1020
OZ1040	Validate Technical Specification	OZ1030
Delivery Plan		
OZ1050	Document Delivery Methodology	OZ1040
OZ1060	Obtain Quotes from Suppliers	OZ1030
OZ1070	Calculate the Bid Estimate	OZ1050, OZ1060
OZ1080	Create the Project Schedule	OZ1070
OZ1090	Review the Delivery Plan	OZ1080
Bid Document		
OZ1100	Create Draft of Bid Document	OZ1050
OZ1110	Review Bid Document	OZ1090, OZ1100
OZ1120	Finalise and Submit Bid Document	OZ1110
OZ1130	Bid Document Submitted	OZ1120

3.   Hide and display the Logic Links using the ⌐ button, leave them displayed.

4.   Open the **Bars** form and display the Milestones, Actual Work, Remaining Work, Critical Remaining Work, Summary, Total Float and Neg Float bars.

5.   Reschedule the project and review your results against the diagram on the next page.

Continued.....

Answer to Workshop 7

6. Format the columns as per the following picture:

Activity ID	Activity Name	Predecessors	Successors	Orig Dur	Start	Finish	Total Float
Bid for Facility Extension							
Technical Specification							
OZ1000	Approval to Bid		OZ1010	0d	05-Dec-11 08		0d
OZ1010	Determine Installation F	OZ1000	OZ1020	4d	05-Dec-11 08	08-Dec-11 16	0d
OZ1020	Create Technical Spec	OZ1010	OZ1030	5d	09-Dec-11 08	15-Dec-11 16	0d
OZ1030	Identify Supplier Comp	OZ1020	OZ1040, OZ1060	2d	16-Dec-11 08	19-Dec-11 16	0d
OZ1040	Validate Technical Spe	OZ1030	OZ1050	2d	20-Dec-11 08	21-Dec-11 16	2d
Delivery Plan							
OZ1050	Document Delivery Me	OZ1040	OZ1100, OZ1070	4d	22-Dec-11 08	29-Dec-11 16	2d
OZ1060	Obtain Quotes from Su	OZ1030	OZ1070	8d	20-Dec-11 08	03-Jan-12 16	0d
OZ1070	Calculate the Bid Estim	OZ1050, OZ1060	OZ1080	3d	04-Jan-12 08	06-Jan-12 16	0d
OZ1080	Create the Project Sch	OZ1070	OZ1090	3d	07-Jan-12 08	10-Jan-12 16	0d
OZ1090	Review the Delivery Pl	OZ1080	OZ1110	1d	11-Jan-12 08	11-Jan-12 16	0d
Bid Document							
OZ1100	Create Draft of Bid Doc	OZ1050	OZ1110	6d	30-Dec-11 08	09-Jan-12 16	2d
OZ1110	Review Bid Document	OZ1090, OZ1100	OZ1120	4d	12-Jan-12 08	17-Jan-12 16	0d
OZ1120	Finalise and Submit Bid	OZ1110	OZ1130	2d	18-Jan-12 08	19-Jan-12 16	0d
OZ1130	Bid Document Submitte	OZ1120		0d		19-Jan-12 16	0d

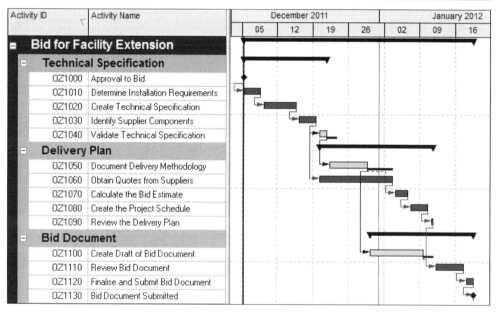

10 ACTIVITY NETWORK VIEW

The **Activity Network**, also known as the **PERT View**, displays activities as boxes connected by the relationship lines. See the following picture:

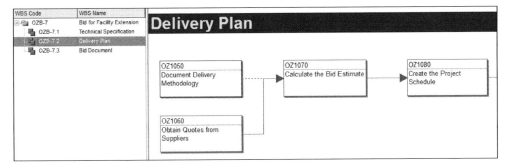

This chapter will not cover this subject in detail but will introduce the main features.

Many features available in the **Gantt Chart View** are also available in the **Activity Network** View, including:

Topic	Menu Command
• Viewing a Project Using the **Activity Network View**	• Select **View**, **Layout**, **Open...**, and select an Activity Network layout, or • Click on the **Layout Options** bar, just below the **Activities** toolbar on the left side of the screen, and select **Layout**, **Open...**, or • Select **View**, **Show on Top**, **Activity Network**, or • Click on the ⬚ button on the **Activities** toolbar.
• Adding and Deleting Activities in the **Activity Network** View	• Use the **Add** and **Delete** keys, or • Use the menu commands **Edit**, **Add** and **Delete**.
• Adding, Editing and Deleting Relationships	• Graphically drag from one activity to another, or • Use the **Predecessor** and **Successor** tabs in the **Activity Details** form.
• Formatting the Activity Boxes	• Select **View**, **Activity Network**, **Activity Network Options...**, or • Right-click in the **Activity Network** area and select **Activity Network Options...**.

10.1 Viewing a Project Using the Activity Network View

To view your project in the Networking View either:

- Open the **Open Layout** form by:
  - ➢ Select **View**, **Layout**, **Open...**, or
  - ➢ Click on the **Layout Options** bar, just below the **Activities** toolbar on the left side of the screen and select **Layout**, **Open...**.
  - ➢ Then select an Activity Network Layout, for example the **PERT Predecessor/Successor**, from the drop down list.

- Or click the [icon] icon on the **Activity** toolbar.

10.2 Adding, Deleting and Dissolving Activities in the Activity Network View

A **New Activity** may be created without a relationship by:

- Using the **Insert** key, or
- Selecting **Edit**, **Add**.

Activities may be deleted by:

- Using the **Delete** key, or
- Selecting **Edit**, **Delete**.

Activities may be **Dissolved**, which deletes the activity but maintains the logic with its predecessors and successors connected with FS relationships. Select **Edit**, **Dissolve**.

10.3 Adding, Editing and Deleting Relationships

Relationships may be added, deleted or edited using the following methods:

10.3.1 Graphically Adding a Relationship.

- To create a FS relationship, move the mouse to the right side of the predecessor activity box (the pointer will change to a ↳) and drag to the left side of the successor activity. Selecting the left or right side of the predecessor and successor activity bar will determine the type of relationship that is created.
- To edit the relationship, select the relationship (it will change to blue), double-click to open the **Edit Relationship** form and edit the relationship.

10.3.2 Using the Activity Details Form

Open the **Relationships** tab in the **Activity Details** form:

- When the **Activity Details** form is not displayed, select **View**, **Show on Bottom**, **Activity Details**.
- Then add, edit and delete activities in the same way as with the Bar Chart.

10.4 Formatting the Activity Boxes

Activity Boxes may be formatted from the **Activity Network Options** form, which is displayed when an Activity Network view is displayed. The formatting affects both the **Trace Logic** and **Activity Network Window** formatting for the layout that is being formatted:

- Select **View**, **Activity Network**, **Activity Network Options...**, or
- Right-click in the PERT area and select **Activity Network Options...**:

  ➢ A selection of box templates are available from the drop down box under the Activity Box Template title. These templates display different data in the box.

  ➢ Click on [Font & Colors...] to format the text font and colors,

  ➢ Click on [Box Template...] to edit the template or add and remove data items from the activity boxes.

NOTE: This option also formats the **Trace Logic** boxes with the same format.

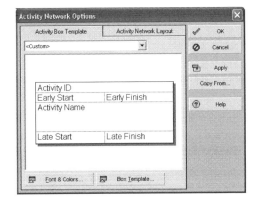

- Click on the **Activity Network Layout** tab to display further options which are self-explanatory:

  ➢ **Show progress** will place a diagonal line through an in-progress activity and a cross through a completed activity.

  ➢ The **spacing factors** are a percentage of the box sizes.

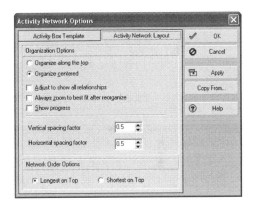

10.5 Reorganizing the Activity Network

Activities in the **Activity Network** view may be repositioned by dragging. There are two functions available when right-clicking in the **Activity Network** view:

- **Reorganize** will reposition activities that have not been manually positioned and
- **Reorganize All** will reposition all activities including those that have been manually positioned.

10.6 Saving and Opening Activity network Positions

When activities are manually dragged into new positions on the screen for presentation purposes, it is possible to save and reload these positions at a later date:

- **View**, **Activity Network**, **Save Network Positions...** will create a *.anp file and
- **View**, **Activity Network**, **Open Network Positions...** will enable a *.anp file to be located and loaded which will reposition the activities as they were saved.

10.7 Early Date, Late Date and Float Calculations

To help understand the calculation of late and early dates, float and critical path, we will now manually work through an example. The boxes below represent activities.

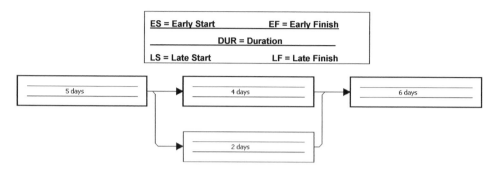

- The forward pass calculates the early dates: EF = ES + DUR – 1

Start the calculation from the first activity and work forward in time.

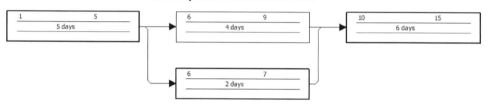

- The backward pass calculates the late dates: LS = LF – DUR + 1

Start the calculation at the last activity and work backwards in time.

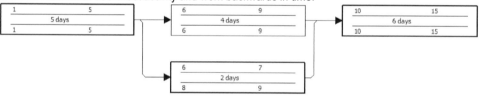

Total Float is the difference between either the **Late Finish** and the **Early Finish** or the difference between the **Late Start** and the **Early Start** of an activity. The lower 2 days' activity has float of 14 – 12 = 2 days. None of the other activities have float.

The **Critical Path** is the path where any delay causes a delay in the project and runs through the top row of activities. **Free Float** is the difference between the Predecessor Early Finish and the Successor Early Start.

 An activity may not be on the Critical Path and may have more than one predecessor. A **Driving Relationship** is the predecessor that determines the Activity Early Start.

10.8 Workshop 8 - Scheduling Calculations and Activity Network View

Background

We want to practice calculating early and late dates with a simple manual exercise.

Assignment

1. Apply the Activity Network View of your OzBuild schedule by clicking on the icon.
2. Click on each node of the WBS and notice how only activities assigned to each node are displayed.

3. Click on the three Zoom icons and notice their effect of the schedule.

4. Calculate the Early Dates, Late Dates and Total Float for the following activities, assuming a Monday-to-Friday working week and the first activity starting on 01 Oct 12.

4. See over the page for the answer:

Answer to Workshop 8

Forward Pass   EF = ES + DUR –1

Backward Pass   LS = LF – DUR +1

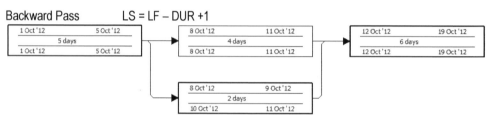

Float Calculation   TF = LS - ES

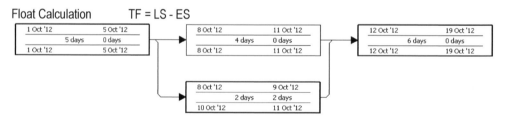

The Early Bar is the upper bar, the Late Bar the lower bar and the end of the Total Float bar which is the thin bar ends at the Late Finish date.

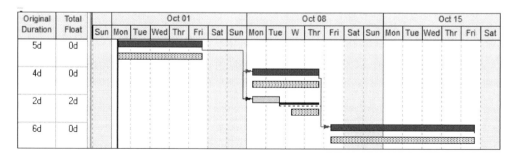

11 CONSTRAINTS

Constraints are used to impose logic on activities that may not be realistically scheduled with logic links. This chapter will deal with the following constraints in detail:

- **Start On or After**
- **Finish On or Before**

These are the minimum number of constraints that are required to effectively schedule a project.

Start On or After (also known as an "Early Start" or "Start No Earlier Than" constraint as it only affects the Early dates calculation) is used when the start date of an activity is known and does not have a predecessor. Primavera will not calculate the activity early start date prior to this date.

Finish On or Before (also known as "Late Finish" or "Finish No Later Than" constraint as it only affects the Late dates calculation) is used when the latest finish date is stipulated. Primavera will not calculate the activity's late finish date after this date.

The following table summarizes the methods used to assign Constraints to Activities or how to add notes to activities:

Topic	Notes for Creating a Constraint
• Setting a **Primary** and **Secondary** constraint with the **Activity Details** form.	Open the **Status** tab on the **Activity Details** form.
• Setting Constraints using columns.	The following columns may be displayed and the constraints assigned or edited: • Primary Constraint • Primary Constraint Date • Secondary Constraint • Secondary Constraint Date • Expected Finish Date
• Adding Notes, these could be about constraints or other activity information.	The **Activity Details** form has a **Notebook** tab, which enables Notes to be assigned to **Notebook Topics**.

Primavera will permit two constraints against a given activity. P3 and SureTrak also allow two constraints but Microsoft Project only permits one except when a Deadline constraint is applied.

A full list of **constraints** available in Primavera are:

- **<None>**   This is the default for a new activity. An activity by default is scheduled to occur **As Soon As Possible** and does not have a Constraint.

- **Start On**   Also known as **Must Start On** and sets a date on which the activity will start. Therefore, the activity has no float. The early start and the late start dates are set to be the same as the Constraint Date.

- **Start On or Before**   Also known as **Start No Later Than** or **Late Start**, this constraint sets the late date after which the activity will not start.

- **Start On or After**   Also known as **Start No Earlier Than** or **Early Start**, this constraint sets the early date before which the activity will not start.

- **Finish On**   Also known as **Must Finish On**, this constraint sets a date on which the activity will finish and therefore has no float. The early finish and the late finish dates are set to be the same as the Constraint Date.

- **Finish On or Before**   Also known as **Finish No Later Than** or **Late Finish**, this sets the late date after which the activity will not finish.

- **Finish On or After**   Also known as **Finish No Earlier Than** or **Early Finish**, this sets the early date before which the activity will not finish.

- **As Late As Possible**   Also known as **Zero Free Float**. An activity will be scheduled to occur as late as possible and does not have any particular Constraint Date. The Early and Late dates have the same date.

- **Mandatory Start**   This relationship prevents float being calculated through this activity and effectively breaks a schedule into two parts.

- **Mandatory Finish**   This relationship prevents float being calculated through this activity and effectively breaks a schedule into two parts.

- **Expected Finish**   An **Expected Finish** sets the Early Start to equal the Expected Finish constraint date and calculates the Remaining Duration from the Early Start date for an un-started activity, or Data Date if the activity is in-progress, and the assigned Expected Finish date.

Earlier Than constraints operate on the **Early Dates**, and **Later Than** constraints operate on **Late Dates**. The following picture demonstrates how constraints calculate Total Float of activities (without predecessors or successors) against the first activity of 10 days' duration:

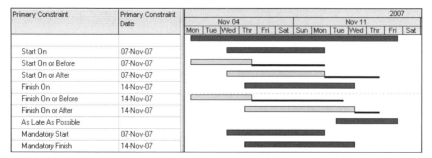

     An activity assigned with an **As Late as Possible** constraint in Primavera P6, Primavera Contractor, Primavera P3 and SureTrak software will schedule the activity so it absorbs only **Free Float** and will not delay the start of successor activities. In Microsoft Project, an activity assigned with an **As Late as Possible** constraint will be delayed to absorb the Total Float and delay all its successor activities, not just the activity with the constraint.

11.1 Assigning Constraints

11.1.1 Number of Constraints per Activity

Two constraints are permitted against each activity. They are titled Primary and Secondary Constraint. After the Primary has been set, a Secondary may be set when the combination is logical and therefore a reduced list of constraints is available from the Secondary Constraint list after the Primary has been set.

11.1.2 Setting a Primary Constraint Using the Activity Details Form

To assign a constraint using the **Activity Details** form:

- Select the activity requiring a constraint,
- Open the **Status** tab on the **Activity Details** form,
- Select the **Primary Constraint** type from the **Date** drop down list under **Primary**:

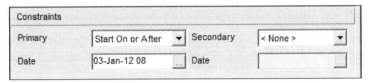

11.1.3 Setting a Secondary Constraint Using the Activity Details Form

To assign a constraint using the **Activity Details** form:

- Select the activity requiring a constraint,
- Open the **Status** tab on the **Activity Details** form,
- Select the **Secondary Constraint** type from the **Date** drop down list under **Secondary**:

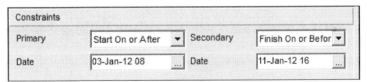

The picture above shows that after a **Primary Start On or After** constraint is set there are only two Secondary Constraints available. After a constraint is set the date will have an asterisk "*" next to it.

> ➢ Start Constraints will have the "*" next to the Start Date, and
> ➢ Finish Constraints will have the "*" next to the Late Start Date.
> ➢ Unlike P3 and SureTrak one does not have to display the Late Dates to see a Late Constraint "*".

11.1.4 Expected Finish Constraint

This constraint is set in the dates **Status** area above the **Constraints** area and will only work if the **Tools, Schedule…**, ▷ Options… **Use Expected Finish dates** check box is checked.

The author found when setting constraints that sometimes the constraint time was not at the start or finish of the activity calendar but set at 00:00. Therefore when setting constraints you may consider displaying the time by selecting **Edit, User Preferences…, Dates** tab to ensure the constraint time is compatible with the activity calendar.

11.1.5 Setting Constraints Using Columns

The following constraint columns may be displayed and the Constraints edited or assigned using these columns:

- Primary Constraint
- Primary Constraint Date
- Secondary Constraint
- Secondary Constraint Date
- Expected Finish

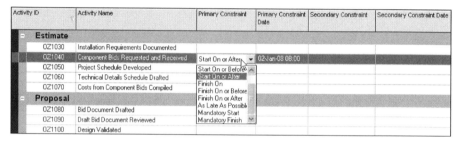

11.1.6 Typing in a Start Date

A **Start On or After** constraint may be assigned from the **Activity Status** tab or the **Start Date** column by typing a date into the **Start** field:

- A **Start On or After** constraint is assigned by overtyping the Start date, and the **Confirmation** form will confirm this action.

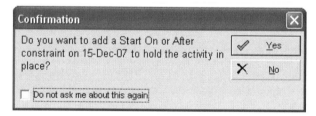

 A date typed into the finish date will not assign a Finish Date constraint but will adjust the duration of the activity.

In Microsoft Project, a date typed into either the Start or Finish field will set a constraint; Primavera does not operate in this way.

11.1.7 Expected Finish Date

This constraint is set in **Status** section of the **Activity Details**, **Details** tab, not as one would expect under constraints:

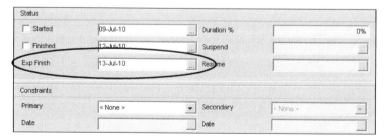

11.2 Project Must Finish By Date

An absolute finish date may be imposed on the project using the **Project Window**, **Dates** tab:

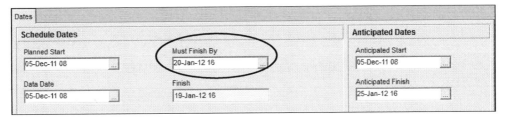

Imposing a **Must Finish By** date makes Primavera calculate the late dates from the **Must Finish By** date rather than the calculated early finish date. This will introduce positive float to activities when the calculated **Early finish** date is prior to the **Must Finish By** date:

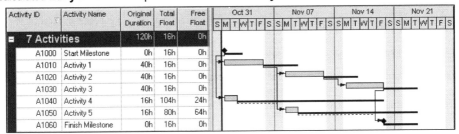

This will also create negative float when the activity's calculated early finish date is after to the must finish by date, but it is not obvious where the negative float is being driven from as there are no constraints assigned to activities:

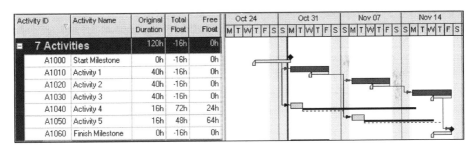

When opening multiple projects some further issues need to be considered when a **Project Must Finish By** date is set and these are covered in the **Multiple Project Scheduling** chapter.

To remove a **Project Must Finish By** date, highlight the date, press the Delete key and then the Enter key or Tab out of the cell to ensure the date is removed.

This function is similar to the P3 and SureTrak function but very different to the way Microsoft Project "Project Information, Finish Date" operates. After a Finish Date is set in Microsoft Project all new Tasks are set with an As Late As Possible constraint and the Start Date is calculated. Primavera does not set As Late As Possible constraints after a **Must Finish by** date is set and the Project Start Date is still editable.

It is not obvious where the float is being generated after a **Must finish by** date is imposed on a project. This is often confusing to people new to scheduling and it is recommended that you do not use a **Must finish by** date. Instead tie all activities to a **Finish milestone** which has a **Late finish** constraint.

11.3   Activity Notebook

It is often important to note why constraints have been set. Primavera has functions that enables you to note information associated with an activity, including the reasons associated for establishing a constraint.

The **Activity Details** form has a **Notebook** tab, which enables Notes to be assigned to **Notebook Topics** and has some word processing-type formatting functions.

11.3.1   Creating Notebook Topics

Notebook Topics are created by selecting **Admin**, **Admin Categories...** and then selecting the **Notebook Topics** tab. After a topic has been created this topic may be made available to the following data fields by checking the appropriate box:

- EPS
- Project
- WBS, and
- Activities

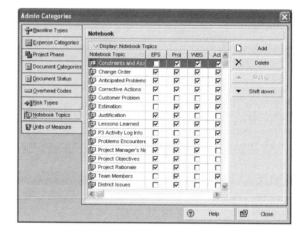

11.3.2   Adding Notes

To add a note to an activity:

- Select the **Notebook** tab in the **Activity Details** form,
- Add a **Topic**, and
- Type in the note.

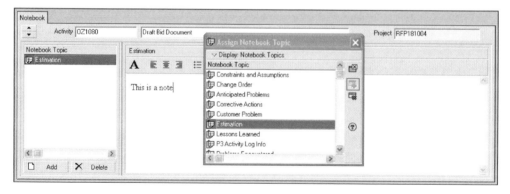

11.4   Workshop 9 - Constraints

Background
Management has provided further input to your schedule as the client has said that they require the submission on 26 Jan 2012.

Assignment

1. Observe the calculated finish date and the critical path of the project before applying any constraints.

2. Columns - Display the **Activity ID**, **Activity Name**, **Original Duration**, **Start**, **Finish**, **Total Float** and **Free Float** columns,

3. Bars - Display the **Float Bar (Total Float Bar)** and **Neg Float Bar (Negative Float Bar)**.

4. The client has said that they require the submission on 26 Jan 2012. Apply a **Finish On or Before** constraint and assign a constraint date of 26 Jan 2012 16:00 to the **Bid Document Submitted** activity from the **Status** tab.

    NOTE: The author has in the past found that constraint times have not always matched the activity calendar start times (e.g. 08:00) and finish times (e.g. 16:00) and have been set to 00:00. If you find the floats do not calculate correctly then open the **User Preferences** form and display the time and review if the times are correct and if not edit them to suit your calendar.

5. Schedule and there should be no change in the Total Float as a **Finish On or Before** constraint will not develop Positive Float.

6. Remove the **Finish On or Before** constraint from the **Bid Document Submitted** activity.

7. Now move to the **Project Window**, **Dates** tab and assign a **Project Must Finish By** constraint of 26 Jan 2012 16:00, return to the **Activity Window** and reschedule. All activities now have their float calculated to this date and have positive float.

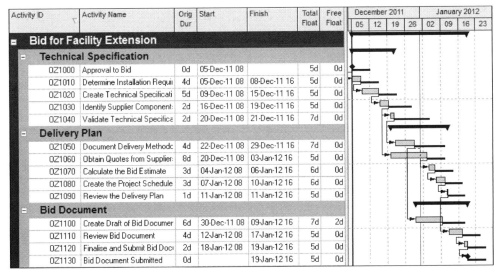

Activity ID	Activity Name	Orig Dur	Start	Finish	Total Float	Free Float	December 2011	January 2012
Bid for Facility Extension								
Technical Specification								
0Z1000	Approval to Bid	0d	05-Dec-11 08		5d	0d		
0Z1010	Determine Installation Requi	4d	05-Dec-11 08	08-Dec-11 16	5d	0d		
0Z1020	Create Technical Specificati	5d	09-Dec-11 08	15-Dec-11 16	5d	0d		
0Z1030	Identify Supplier Component:	2d	16-Dec-11 08	19-Dec-11 16	5d	0d		
0Z1040	Validate Technical Specifica	2d	20-Dec-11 08	21-Dec-11 16	7d	0d		
Delivery Plan								
0Z1050	Document Delivery Methodc	4d	22-Dec-11 08	29-Dec-11 16	7d	0d		
0Z1060	Obtain Quotes from Supplier:	8d	20-Dec-11 08	03-Jan-12 16	5d	0d		
0Z1070	Calculate the Bid Estimate	3d	04-Jan-12 08	06-Jan-12 16	6d	0d		
0Z1080	Create the Project Schedule	3d	07-Jan-12 08	10-Jan-12 16	6d	0d		
0Z1090	Review the Delivery Plan	1d	11-Jan-12 08	11-Jan-12 16	5d	0d		
Bid Document								
0Z1100	Create Draft of Bid Documer	6d	30-Dec-11 08	09-Jan-12 16	7d	2d		
0Z1110	Review Bid Document	4d	12-Jan-12 08	17-Jan-12 16	5d	0d		
0Z1120	Finalise and Submit Bid Doci	2d	18-Jan-12 08	19-Jan-12 16	5d	0d		
0Z1130	Bid Document Submitted	0d		19-Jan-12 16	5d	0d		

Continued.....

8. Remove **Project Must Finish By** constraint of 26 Jan 2012 16:00 (by highlighting the date and pressing the delete key and tab out of the cell to ensure the date has been deleted) and then schedule. The Critical Path should return.

9. Apply a **Finish On or Before** constraint and assign a constraint date of 26 Jan 2012 16:00 to the **Submit Bid** activity and schedule.

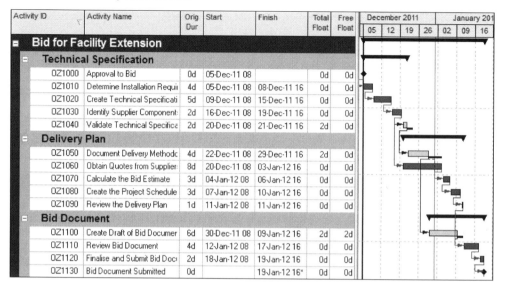

10. Due to the proximity to Christmas, management has requested that you delay the **Obtain Quotes from Suppliers** until first thing in the New Year (03 Jan 2012). Consensus is that a better response and sharper prices will be obtained after the Christmas rush.

   ➤ To achieve this, set a **Start On or After** constraint date of 03 Jan 2012 08:00 on the **Obtain Quotes from Suppliers** activity.

   ➤ Now reschedule. Observe the impact on the critical path and end dates.

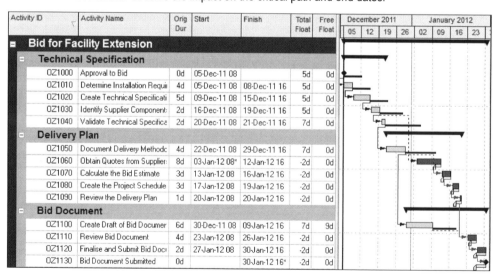

You will notice that the Finish Constraint on the **Bid Document Submitted** activity has created some negative float, which is displayed in the **Total float** column and the **Negative Float** bar.

Continued.....

11. Add a Notebook Topic against the **Obtain Quotes from Supplier** activity indicating why there is a constraint of 3 Jan 2010.

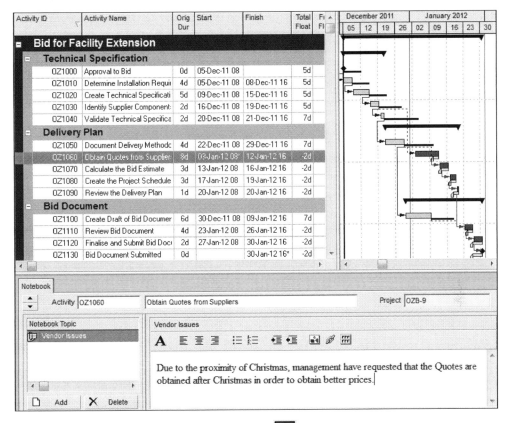

12. Open the **Group and Sort** form by clicking on the ⬚ button and group by **Total Float** and close the form.

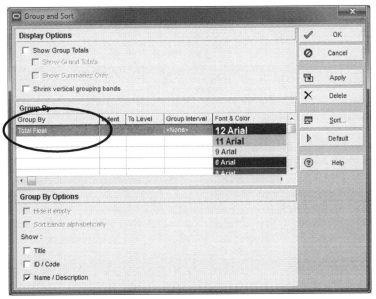

Continued.....

13. Sort on duration (by clicking in the **Original Duration** column) to bring the longest activity to the top. It is normally the longest task that may be shortened.

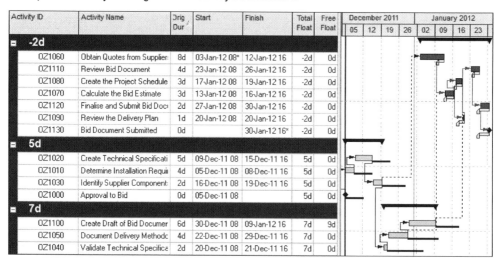

14. After review, it is agreed that two days may be deducted from **Review Bid Document** activity. Change the duration of this activity to 2 days and reschedule.

15. Now organize by WBS and sort by Activity ID:

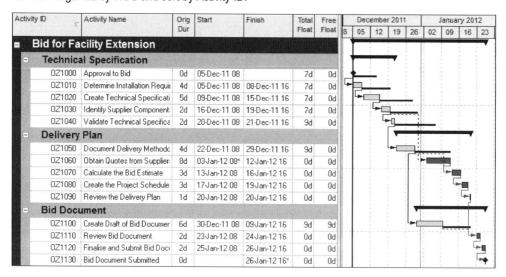

16. Notice that activities with constraints have an "*" by their dates.

12 GROUP, SORT AND LAYOUTS

Group and Sort enables data such as activities in the **Activity Window**, WBS Nodes in the **WBS Window**, projects in the **Project Window** and many other data items to be sorted and organized under other parameters such as **Dates** and **Resources** or user-defined **Activity** and **Project Codes**. This function is similar to **Organize** in P3 and SureTrak and **Grouping** in Microsoft Project and Asta Powerproject.

Layouts is a function in which the formatting of parameters such as the **Group and Sort**, **Columns** and **Bars** is saved and reapplied later. This function is similar to **Layouts** in P3 and SureTrak or **Views** in Asta Power Project and Microsoft Project. A **Layout** may be edited, saved or reapplied at a later date and may have a **Filter** associated with it. Layouts contain the formatting for all options of both the top and bottom pane.

Although Group and Sort is available in many forms, Layouts are only available in a few places including the following Windows:

- Projects
- WBS
- Activities
- Resources
- Tracking

This chapter will concentrate on how Group and Sort and Layouts are applied in the Activity Window but the same principals apply to the other Windows. This chapter covers the following topics:

Topic	Notes on the Function
• Reformat the Grouping and Sorting of activities by opening the **Group and Sort** form:	• Click on the ⊞ button, or • Select **View, Group and Sort….**
• Group and Sort Projects at Enterprise Level	Projects may be Grouped and Sorted at Enterprise level in a similar method to activities in a project.
• Create or edit a Layout	Select either: • From the menu **View, Layout, Save As…**, or • From the **Layout** bar **Layout, Save As….**

The **Layout** bar location is indicated in the following picture:

12.1   Group and Sort Activities

The **Group and Sort** function has been used in this publication to group activities under WBS bands.

To Group and Sort activities open the **Group and Sort** form by:

- Clicking the 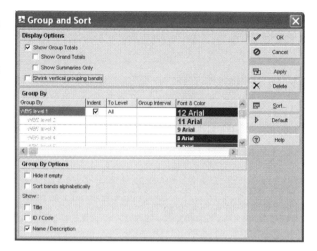 button, or
- Selecting **View, Group and Sort**....

12.1.1   Display Options

Show Group Totals

Show Group Totals is a new function in Primavera Version 6.0 which when unchecked hides the summary data in the bands, which prevents the truncating of Band titles.

Summary Data Displayed

Activity ID	Original Duration	Start	Finish	Total Float
■ Bid for Fac	139d	08-Dec-09 A	22-Jan-10	0d
⊟ Research	31d	08-Dec-09 A	21-Dec-09	6d
OZ1000	0d	08-Dec-09 A		
OZ1010	1d	08-Dec-09 A	08-Dec-09 A	
OZ1020	8d	09-Dec-09 A	21-Dec-09	2d
⊟ Estimate	52d	22-Dec-09	08-Jan-10	3d
OZ1070	2d	07-Jan-10	08-Jan-10	0d

Summary Data Hidden

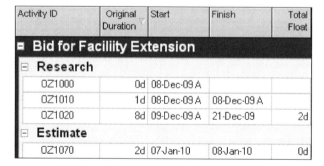

Activity ID	Original Duration	Start	Finish	Total Float
■ Bid for Faciliity Extension				
⊟ Research				
OZ1000	0d	08-Dec-09 A		
OZ1010	1d	08-Dec-09 A	08-Dec-09 A	
OZ1020	8d	09-Dec-09 A	21-Dec-09	2d
⊟ Estimate				
OZ1070	2d	07-Jan-10	08-Jan-10	0d

 The Summary Data Hidden option may be the best option to use in P6.2 and earlier versions when you have a database with multiple calendars that have different hours per day and the WBS Summary Durations are not displaying the correct value. They may now be hidden when incorrect.

Show Grand Totals

Show Grand Totals is the same as inserting a Project band in P3, or SureTrak with Organize, or displaying a **Project summary task** in Microsoft Project.

This displays a Summary band for the project and adds up all the costs and hours for a project, displays the earliest and latest dates and a summary duration for the whole project. This feature is very useful when the project is not organized by WBS and therefore has no project total line, or when multiple projects have been opened to calculate all the projects' values.

Activity ID	Activity Name	Original Duration	Actual Labor Cost	Remaining Labor Cost	Start	Finish
■ **Total**		**37**	**$3,220**	**$45,920**	**03-Dec-07 A**	**22-Jan-08**
0Z1000	Bid Request Document Received	0	$0	$0	03-Dec-07 A	
0Z1010	Bid Strategy Developed	1	$1,300	$0	03-Dec-07 A	03-Dec-07 A
0Z1150	New Activity	1	$0	$0	03-Dec-07 A	03-Dec-07 A
0Z1020	Technical Feasibility Study	8	$1,920	$4,800	04-Dec-07 A	17-Dec-07
0Z1030	Installation Requirements Documented	4	$0	$5,120	18-Dec-07	21-Dec-07
0Z1060	Technical Details Schedule Drafted	9	$0	$9,360	18-Dec-07	02-Jan-08
0Z1050	Project Schedule Developed	4	$0	$2,880	22-Dec-07	28-Dec-07
0Z1040	Component Bids Requested and Received	3	$0	$3,840	02-Jan-08*	04-Jan-08
0Z1070	Costs from Component Bids Compiled	2	$0	$1,280	07-Jan-08	08-Jan-08
0Z1080	Bid Document Drafted	3	$0	$6,720	09-Jan-08	11-Jan-08

Show Summaries Only

Show Summaries Only hides all the activities and displays only the WBS or Codes that have been used to summarize the activities:

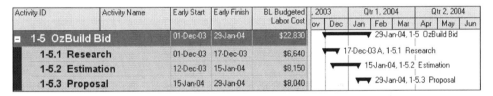

Shrink Vertical Grouping Bands

Shrink vertical grouping bands is new to Primavera Version 6.0 and narrows the Vertical Bands on the left of the screen. This is useful in projects with a number of levels in the WBS as this provides more usable screen space and paper width for printing.

Option Unchecked   Option Checked

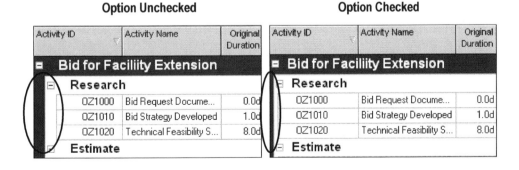

12.1.2   Group By

The Group By box has several options:

- **Group By and Indent**

When a hierarchical code such as a **WBS** and the **Indent** is selected, the subsequent bands are completed by the software and there are no other banding options available. The WBS is then displayed hierarchically:

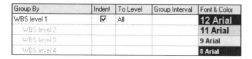 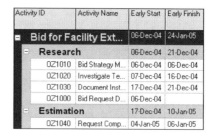

When a hierarchical code such as a **WBS** is selected and the **Indent** is **NOT** selected on a line then the subsequent bands are **NOT** completed by the software and other bands may be selected. The WBS is not displayed hierarchically:

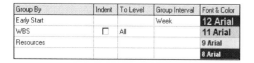 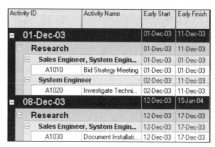

- **To Level**

The **To Level** option decides how many levels of the hierarchical code structure such as the WBS will be displayed. All activities are displayed under the lowest level of WBS, as chosen from the **To Level** drop down box.

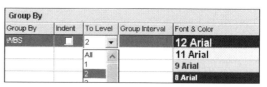

This option enables other banding below the select level which is not permitted with the **All** option.

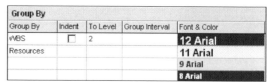

- **Group Interval**

This option is available with some fields such as **Total Float**, where the interval may be typed in, and **Date** fields, where a drop down box enables the selection of the time interval used to group activities:

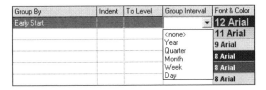 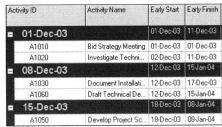

- **Font and Color**

  Double-click these boxes to open the **Edit Font and Color** form to change the font and color of each band.

12.1.3 Group By Options

- **Sort Banding Alphabetically**

  When a hierarchical code is selected, the bands are sorted by the **Code Value**. If this box is checked, the bands will be sorted alphabetically by the **Code Description**.

- **Hide if empty**

  Check this box is used to hide bands that:

  ➢ Have not been assigned an activity, or

  ➢ When activities have been filtered out and only the bands remains.

 This function is useful when you have filtered on a couple of activities and the screen is filled with blank bands. This will remove all the blank bands.

- **Show Title**, **Show ID / Code** and **Show Name / Description**

  These options format the display of the band title. It is not possible to uncheck all the options as there then would not be a title in the band. The options change depending on the data displayed in the band:

With all options checked

Activity ID	Original Duration	Start	Finish	Total Float
Project: REF101206 Bid for Faciliity Extension				
WBS: REF101206.1 Research				
0Z1000	0d	07-Dec-09		4d
0Z1010	1d	07-Dec-09	07-Dec-09	4d
0Z1020	8d	08-Dec-09	17-Dec-09	4d
WBS: REF101206.2 Estimate				
0Z1070	2d	07-Jan-10	08-Jan-10	0d

With only Description Checked

Activity ID	Original Duration	Start
Bid for Faciliity Extension		
Research		
0Z1000	0d	07-Dec-09
0Z1010	1d	07-Dec-09
0Z1020	8d	08-Dec-09
Estimate		
0Z1070	2d	07-Jan-10

NOTE. These options are set for each band individually.

12.1.4 Sorting

The 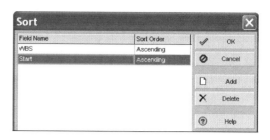 button opens the **Sort** form where the order of the activities in each band may be specified.

NOTE: This order may be easily overridden by clicking on the column titles to reorder activities and therefore the use of this option is problematic as clicking on the column header is very simple and will override options set here.

12.1.5 Reorganize Automatically

Primavera Version 4.1 introduced a function titled Reorganize Automatically, which is similar to the P3 and SureTrak function but applies to all Layouts, not just the selected Layout. Select **Edit, User Preferences...** to open the **User Preferences** form and click the **Application** tab.

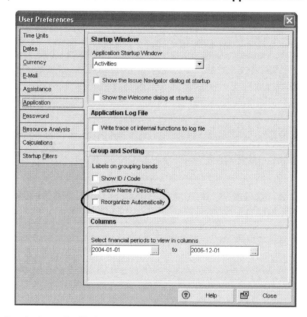

When the **Reorganize Automatically** box is checked, all views will reorganize automatically when data fields are changed that are used in the layout such as Grouping and Sorting.

It is often better to disable **Reorganize Automatically** when data is being edited that is used in the grouping of data in a Layout which will prevent the activities moving to their new position in the Layout until all data has been edited.

To reorganize a view, select **Tools, Reorganize Now** or **Shift+F2**.

The other Group and Sort options in the **Application** tab apply to views that do not have a Group and Sort form such as the predecessor and successor form.

12.1.6 Group and Sort Projects at Enterprise Level

Projects in the **Projects Window** may be Grouped and Sorted in a similar way to the Grouping and Sorting of activities.

When a database is opened, the projects are by default displayed under the Enterprise Project Structure (EPS) in the Projects Window.

The projects may be Grouped and Sorted under a number of different headings by:

- Selecting **Layout: Projects**, **Group and Sort By**, or
- Right-clicking in the columns area and selecting **Group and Sort ...**, or
- Selecting **View**, **Group and Sort By**.

Then selecting the option from the drop down list.

The **Customize...** option will open the projects Group the Sort form which operates in a similar way to the Activities Group and Sort form.

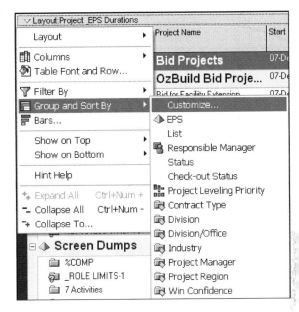

12.2 Understanding Layouts

A standard load of Primavera is supplied with a number of predefined Layouts for some of the Windows which are defined by default as **Global Layouts** and any user on the system may apply these. These layouts may be copied and shared with other users or be available to the current user in a similar way as filters.

Primavera Version 6.0 introduced Project Layouts for the Activity Window. Project Layouts are only available when a project is open and may be exported with a project and therefore minimizes the need for Global Layouts.

In large databases with many users and projects there becomes a need to code layouts so they may easily be found in long lists of filters. Prefixing them with the project number may be considered.

Layouts are not exported with an XER file in Version 5.0 and earlier but may be exported using a PLF file. Therefore to send a person a complete projects schedule you may need to include the layout as a PLF file.

12.2.1 Applying an Existing Layout

Layouts may be applied from the **Open Layout** form by:

- Selecting the **Open** option from the **Layout Options** bar:

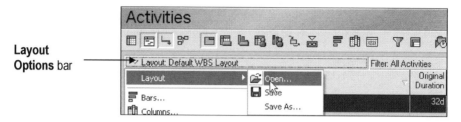

- Or, by selecting **View, Layout, Open….**

When a Layout has been edited by changing any parameter, such as column formatting, a form will be displayed allowing the confirmation of the changes that have been made to the layout.

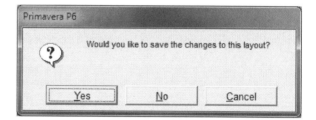

The **Open Layout** form will be displayed and an alternative layout may be selected from the list. The list will has three headings after a project layout has been created, **Global**, **User** and **Project**:

- ➢ Click on the [🖾 Apply] button to apply the layout. This will leave the form open but allow the effect to be viewed, or
- ➢ Click on the [🖙 Open] button to apply the layout and close the form:

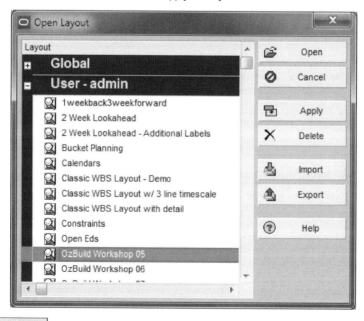

Clicking on [Layout] button to reorder the Layouts.

12.2.2 Creating a New Layout

A new layout may be created by saving an existing layout with a new name and editing it. To create a new Layout:

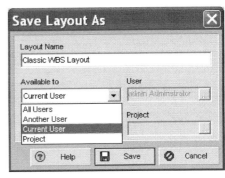

- Apply the layout that closely matches the requirements of the new layout and apply.

- Select either:
  - ➢ From the menu **View**, **Layout**, **Save As...**, or
  - ➢ From the Layout Options bar **Layout**, **Save As...**:

- Type in a new **Layout Name** and select who you wish the layout to be available.
  - ➢ **All Users** will make the Layout Global and therefore available to all users and you will need the appropriate security access to be able to create a Global Layout.
  - ➢ **Another User** will make the layout available to a nominated user.
  - ➢ **Current User** will make a copy for your own use.
  - ➢ **Project** will make the layout available to anyone who has the project open. This option is useful to reduce the number of Global Layouts in a database with a number of projects requiring a number of layouts each.

- Click on the [💾 Save] button.

This layout may now be edited and the edits saved by selecting:
  - ➢ From the menu **View**, **Layout**, **Save**, or
  - ➢ From the Layout bar **Layout**, **Save**.

12.2.3 Layout Types

A layout is comprised of a **Top Pane** and a **Bottom Pane**. Each **Pane** may be assigned a **Layout Type**. The following is a list of the **Layout Types** and the panes they may be applied to the **Activity Window**:

Layout Name	Available in Top Pane	Available in Bottom Pane
• Gantt Chart	Yes	Yes
• Activity Details		Yes
• Activity Table	Yes	Yes
• Activity Network	Yes	
• Trace Logic		Yes
• Activity Usage Profile		Yes
• Resource Usage Spreadsheet		Yes
• Resource Usage Profile		Yes
• Activity Usage Spreadsheet	Yes	Yes

NOTE: The available layouts vary depending on the Window open. This chapter will predominately discuss the Activity Window but experimentation will show the options available in the other Windows.

12.2.4 Changing Activity Layout Types in Panes

The **Activities Toolbar** has icons for the display options in the top and bottom pane:

- [ ] are the top pane buttons, and

- [ ] are the bottom pane buttons.

To change a **Layout Type** in a pane select from the menu:

- **View**, **Show on Top**, or

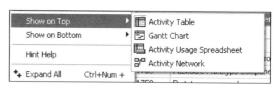

- **View**, **Show on Bottom**.

Then select the Layout Type required from the list.

NOTE: There are more options here than on the **Activity Toolbar**.

12.2.5 Activity Window Layout Panes

Each Layout Type has a number of options and the formatting of these has been discussed in earlier chapters.

Gantt Chart

The Gantt Chart has two sides:

- The left side where the columns are displayed may be formatted with the **Columns**, **Sorting** and **Grouping** functions.

- The right side may be formatted using the **Timescale**, **Bars** and **Gridlines** functions.

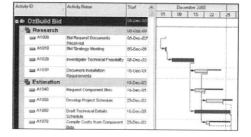

Activity Details

These may be displayed at any time in the Bottom Pane with any of the tabs hidden or displayed.

Activity Table

This layout is the same as the left side of the Gantt Chart and has no Bars and Timescale on the right side.

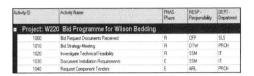

Activity Network

Like the Gantt Chart it has two panes:

- The **left** pane displays the WBS:

  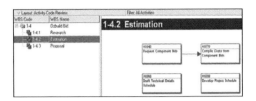

  ➢ This side may not be formatted except by adjusting the width of the columns.

  ➢ The selection of a WBS Node acts like a filter and will only display activities that are associated with the selected WBS Node and lower level member WBS Nodes. This enables the relationships between activities within one WBS Node to be checked.

- The **right** pane displays the activity data in boxes and is organized under headings:

  ➢ The Activity Boxes may be formatted as described in the **Network View** chapter.
  ➢ The activities may be Grouped which is covered in the **Grouping** section of this chapter.

Trace Logic

The Trace Logic options allow the selection of the number of predecessor and successor levels.

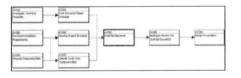

This is achieved by displaying the **Activity Table** in the top view and selecting **View, Show on Bottom, Trace Logic**.

To select the number of levels of predecessors to be displayed you are required to open the **Trace Logic Options** form. The form is then opened by either:

- Right-clicking in the lower pane and selecting **Trace Logic Options....** or
- Selecting View, Bottom Layout Options....

Formatting Trace Logic and Activity Network

Formatting of these boxes in both of these panes is linked to the formatting in the **Activity Network**. The boxes are formatted by right-clicking in the right screen of the **Activity Network** form and selecting **Activity Network Options....**

Resource Analysis Panes

The **Activity Usage Profile**, **Resource Usage Spreadsheet**, **Resource Usage Profile**, **Activity Usage Spreadsheet** views display resource information and will be discussed in the **Resource Optimization** chapters.

12.2.6 WBS and Projects Window Panes

The WBS and Projects Window has three options for the top pane:

- ⊞ shows a table without bars,

- ⊞ shows a table with bars and

- ⊞ displays a chart view of the WBS and the boxes may also be formatted by right-clicking and selecting **Chart Box Template**:

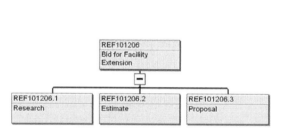

12.3 Copying a Layout To and From Another Database

A layout from any **Window** may be copied to another database by using the Import and Export functions from the **Open Layout** form. The layout is saved in a **Primavera Layout File (*.PLF)** format as a stand-alone file and is then imported into another database.

12.4 Workshop 10 - Organizing Your Data

Background

Having completed the schedule, you may report the information with different Layouts.

Assignment

Display your project in the following formats, noting the different ways you may represent the same data.

1. Hide and display the relationships, use the ⌐ button.
2. Display the **Activity Network**, use the ⊞ button.
3. Zoom in, out and best fit using the ⊕ ⊖ ⊗ buttons.
4. Scroll up and down or click the **WBS** Nodes on the left side of the screen. You will notice that only the Activities associated with the highlighted WBS are displayed.
5. Clt Click and select two WBS Nodes and you will see the relationships between the activities in each WBS Node.
6. Display the **Activity Table** by clicking on the ⊞ button.
7. Hide and display the **Bottom** pane by clicking on the ⊟ button.
8. With the bottom pane displayed click the ⊡ to show the **Trace Logic** form; experiment with the form.
9. Right-click in the **Trace Logic** form, select **Trace Logic Options...** and change the number of Predecessor and Successor Levels displaying 1, 2 and 3 levels and note the change in the layout. Click on the predecessors and successors in each option.
10. Click on the ⊡ button to display the **Activity Details** form.

Continued.....

11. Create a new layout titled **OzBuild Workshop 11 - Without Float**, make it available to only yourself, displaying the columns and formatting the bars as per the following picture; the Total Float and Negative Float bars are not displayed:

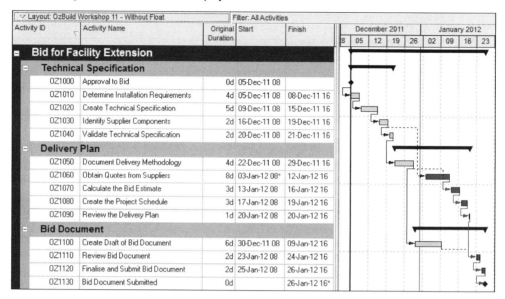

12. Save this layout.
13. Make a copy of it titled **OzBuild Workshop 11 - With Float**, make it available to only yourself, displaying the columns and formatting the bars as per the following picture, this is displaying the **Total Float** and **Negative Float** bars:
14. Save this layout.

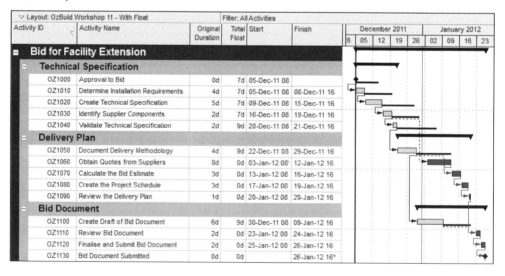

13 FILTERS

This chapter covers the ability of Primavera to control which activities are displayed, both on the screen and in printouts, by using **Filters**.

13.1 Understanding Filters

Primavera has an ability to display activities that meet specific criteria. You may want to see only the incomplete Activities, or the work scheduled for the next couple of months or weeks, or the Activities that are in-progress.

Primavera defaults to displaying all activities. There are a number of pre-defined filters available that you may use or edit. You may also create one or more of your own.

A filter may be applied to display or to highlight only those activities that meet a criteria.

There are four types of filters:

- **Default** filters which are supplied with the system and may not be edited or deleted but may be copied and then edited or modified and are often used in conjunction with the display of bars.
- **Global** filters which are made available to anyone working in the database, and
- **User-Defined** filters which are defined by a user and available only to that user unless it is made into a **Global** filter.
- **Layout** filters which make the filter only available when the current layout is applied. **NOTE:** If the current layout is a **Project** layout then this effectively makes the **Layout** filter a project filter.

The following types of filters are not available:

- Drop down or Auto filters as in Excel and Microsoft Project.
- Interactive filters as available in SureTrak and Microsoft Project. This is when a filter is applied and the user is offered choices from drop down list. The lack of this function may result in an excessive quantity of filters being generated or the user continually editing frequently used filters.

 There are no dedicated project filters (except by creating a Layout filter) available in Primavera, so you might consider placing the project name or number at the start of a filter name so you may identify which filters belong to which projects. When you have a number of **User Filters** or there are a number of **Global Filters**.

Topic	Menu Command
• To apply, edit, create or delete a filter open the **Filters** form.	• Click on the 🖳 button, or • Select **View**, **Filters…**, or • Right-click in the columns area and select **Filters…**.

13.2 Applying a Filter

13.2.1 Filters Form

Filters are applied from the **Filters** form which may be opened by:

- Clicking on the  button, or

- Selecting **View**, **Filters...**, or

- Right-clicking in the columns area and selecting **Filters...**

13.2.2 Applying a Single Filter

A single filter is applied by:

- Checking the **Select** check box beside one filter, and

- Clicking on the `Apply` button to apply the filter and not close the form. If the result is undesirable another option may be selected, or

- Clicking on `OK` to apply the filter and close the form.

- **When applying the selected filter(s):**

  > Only activities that comply to the filter criteria will be displayed when the **Replace activities shown in the current layout button** is checked.

  > These activities will be highlighted in the **Select Activity** color when the **Highlight activities in current layout which match criteria** button is checked.

13.2.3 Applying a Combination Filter

A combination filter has two or more filters selected and has two options under **Show activities that match**:

- **All selected filters** where an activity to be displayed or highlighted has to match the criteria of **ALL** the filters, or

- **Any selected filters** where an activity to be displayed or highlighted has to match the criteria of **ONLY ONE** filter.

In many places in the software there will be an option of either clicking on the `OK` button or the `Apply` button:

- The `Apply` button applies the format however leaves the form open.
- The `OK` button applies the format and closes the form.

13.3 Creating a New Filter

Filters may be created from the **Filters** form by:

- Clicking on the 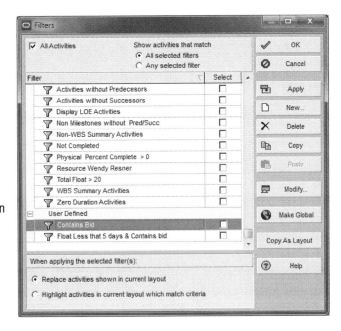 button to open the **Filter** form and creating a new filter, or

- Copying an existing filter using the Copy and Paste buttons and then editing the new filter.

New filters will be created in the **User-Defined** filter area at the bottom of the list.

13.4 Modifying a Filter

There are a large number of options available to create a filter and from the following examples you should be able to experiment and add your own filters. To modify an existing filter, select it from the **Filters** form and click the Modify... button.

13.4.1 One Parameter Filter

The following example is a filter to display incomplete activities:

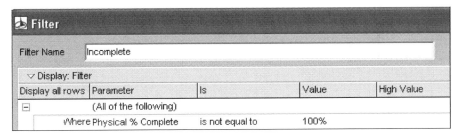

- **Parameter** is used to select any of the available database fields,

- Select one of the options from the **Is** drop down box:

- The parameter selected in the **Is** box determines if it is required to use only the **Value** (which is the same as the **Low Value** in P3 and SureTrak), or **Value** and **High Value**. **Value** and **High Value** are used with only the **is within range of** and **is not within range of** options.

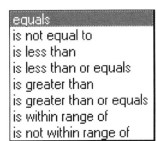

The following example is a filter to display in-progress activities using the **is within range of** and **Value** and **High Value** options:

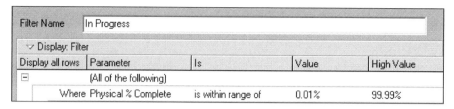

13.4.2   Two Parameter Filter

The following example is a filter to display incomplete activities on the critical path:

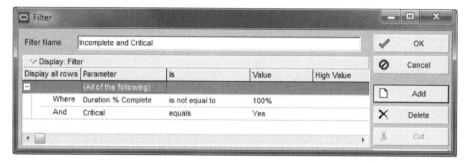

- The drop down box under **Parameter** has two options:
  - ➢ **(All of the following)**. This is used when an activity must meet all of the parameters selected below.
  - ➢ **(Any of the following)**. This is used when an activity must meet any of the parameters selected below.

  In the case of a filter that is to display the **Incomplete Critical Activities** it must be set to **All** and not **Any**, otherwise all of the **Incomplete** and all of the **Critical** activities will be displayed.
- The **Value** options on the second line are now **Yes** or **No**. The options for **Value** change with the data selected in the **Parameter** box.

13.4.3   Multiple Parameter Filter

The following example is a filter to display incomplete activities on the critical path with resources PEH and SEH:

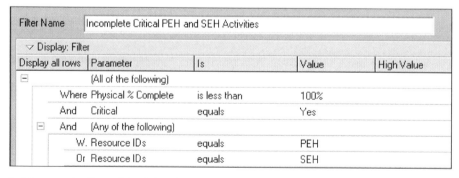

- In this example, **(Any of the following)** was selected from the **Parameters** drop down box which enables a nesting effect of filter parameters.
- This function is similar to the filter levels in P3.

13.4.4 Editing and Organizing Filter Parameters

Lines in a filter are added, copied, pasted and deleted using the appropriate buttons in the **Filters** form.

The arrows allow the filter lines to be moved up and down and indented to the left and outdented to the right in a similar way to indenting and outdenting tasks in Microsoft Project.

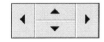

A filter may be optimized to delete the redundant filter lines using the **Optimize** command:

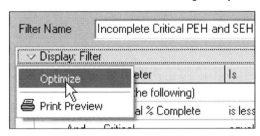

13.5 Workshop 11 - Filters

Background

Management has asked for reports on activities to suit their requirements.

Assignment
Ensure your **OzBuild Bid** project is open.

1. They would like to see all the critical activities.
   ➢ Ensure a column showing the **Total Float** is displayed, and
   ➢ Apply the **Critical** activities filter.
   You will see only activities that are on the critical path and their associated summary activities.

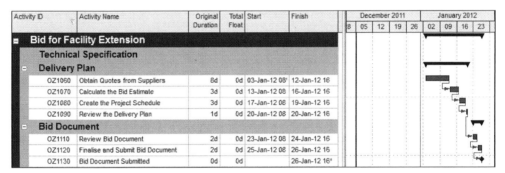

Activity ID	Activity Name	Original Duration	Total Float	Start	Finish
Bid for Facility Extension					
Technical Specification					
Delivery Plan					
OZ1060	Obtain Quotes from Suppliers	8d	0d	03-Jan-12 08	12-Jan-12 16
OZ1070	Calculate the Bid Estimate	3d	0d	13-Jan-12 08	16-Jan-12 16
OZ1080	Create the Project Schedule	3d	0d	17-Jan-12 08	19-Jan-12 16
OZ1090	Review the Delivery Plan	1d	0d	20-Jan-12 08	20-Jan-12 16
Bid Document					
OZ1110	Review Bid Document	2d	0d	23-Jan-12 08	24-Jan-12 16
OZ1120	Finalise and Submit Bid Document	2d	0d	25-Jan-12 08	26-Jan-12 16
OZ1130	Bid Document Submitted	0d	0d		26-Jan-12 16*

2. Open the **Group and Sort** form and check the **Hide if empty** box and notice the **Technical Specification** band is hidden.
3. Management would like to see all the activities with float less than or equal to 8 days:
   ➢ Create a new filter titled: **Float Less Than or Equal to 8 Days**, and
   ➢ Add the condition to display a total float of less than 8 days.

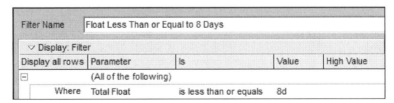

Filter Name	Float Less Than or Equal to 8 Days			
▽ Display: Filter				
Display all rows	Parameter	Is	Value	High Value
⊟	(All of the following)			
Where	Total Float	is less than or equals	8d	

➢ Apply the filter
➢ You should find that activities with 9 days float are hidden:

Continued.....

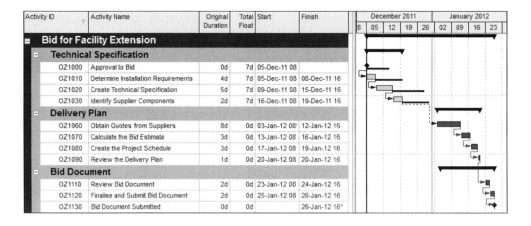

4. They would like to see all the activities that are critical and contain the word "Bid."

    ➤ Copy the **Critical** filter,
    ➤ Edit the filter title to read: **Critical or Contains "Bid,"**
    ➤ Edit the top line to read **(Any of the following),**
    ➤ Add the condition: **Or** Name (Activity Name) contains **Bid,** and

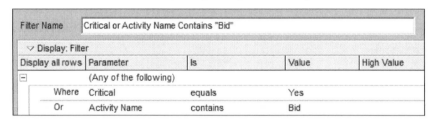

    ➤ Apply the filter.

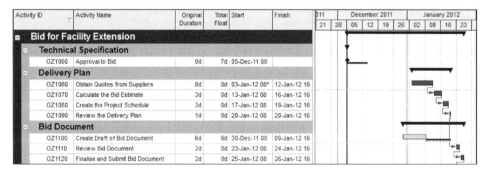

5. Now change the **(Any of the following)** option to **(All of the following)** and see the effect.

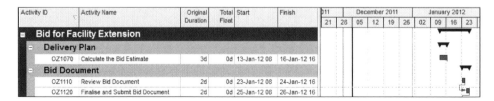

6. Now apply the **All Activities** filter and there should be less activities as you are now displaying activities that meet both conditions.

14 PRINTING AND REPORTS

This is the stage at which the schedule is printed so people may review and comment on it. This chapter will examine some of the options for printing your project schedule.

There are several tools available to output your schedule to a printer:

- The **Printing** function prints the data displayed in the current Layout.
- The **Reporting** function prints reports, which are independent of the current Layout. Primavera supplies a number of predefined reports that may be tailored to suit your own requirements. Reports will not be covered detail in this publication.
- The **Project Web Site Publisher** to publish the schedule to a web site. This function is not covered in this publication but is accessed using the **Tools**, **Publish** command.

 It is recommended that you consider using a product such as Adobe Acrobat to output your schedule in pdf format. You then will be able to e-mail high quality outputs that recipients may print or review on screen without needing a copy of Primavera.

14.1 Printing

When a Layout is split, the lower pane may also be printed at the same time unless it is an **Activity Details** pane. This is similar to P3 and SureTrak, but different from Microsoft Project where only the active View may be printed. Unlike Asta Powerproject multiple resource Histograms may not be printed on one printout.

Print settings are applied to the individual Layouts and the settings are saved with that Layout.

There are three commands used when printing:

- **File**, **Page Setup...**
- **File**, **Print Preview**
- **File**, **Print...** or **Ctrl+P**

Each of these functions will be discussed only for printing the Gantt Chart. Printing all other Layouts is a similar process. Some Layouts will have different options due to the nature of the data being displayed. These other options should be easily mastered after the basics covered in this chapter are understood.

 Each time you report to the client or management, it is recommended that you save a copy of your printout or report. A pdf is an excellent method of saving this data. This enables you to reproduce these reports at any time in the future and keep an electronic copy available for dispute resolution purposes.

It is good practice to keep a copy of the project after each update, especially if litigation is a possibility. A project may be copied either by creating a Baseline, by exporting the project as an XER file or by using the project copy function, then making the **Status** inactive in the **General** tab of the **Projects Window**. It is important to note that although the project may be marked as inactive it may still be opened and modified.

14.2 Print Preview

To preview the printout, use the Primavera **Print Preview** option. Select **File**, **Print Preview** or click the ![] button on the **Activity Toolbar**:

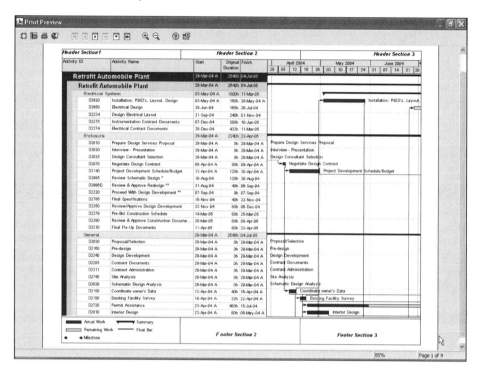

The following paragraphs describe the functions of the icons at the top of the Print Preview screen from left to right:

- The ![] button opens the **Page Setup** form to be covered in the next paragraph.

- The ![] button opens the **Print Setup** form where the printer and paper size etc may be selected.

- The ![] button opens the **Print** form where the printer, the pages to be printed, and the number of copies to be printed may be selected.

- The ![] button opens the **Publish to HTML** form and saves the view in HTML format where both the tables and bar charts are converted.

- The first six icons on the left, ![], allow scrolling when a printout has more than one page.

- The magnifying glass ![] buttons zoom in and out. You may also click in the Preview screen to zoom in.

- The ![] button closes the preview screen.

14.3   Page Setup

To open the **Page Setup...** form:

- Click the ⊞ button on the **Print Preview** toolbar, or
- Select **File**, **Page Setup...** to display the **Page Setup** form:

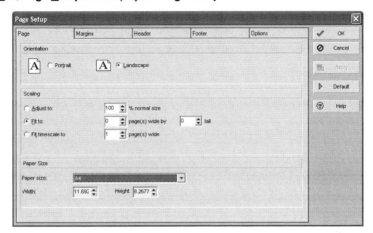

The **Page Setup** form contains the following tabs:

- Page
- Margins
- Header
- Footer
- Options

When changes are made to a header or footer then the buttons on the right side may be used:

- [Apply] – Applies the changes so they are visible without closing the form.
- [Default] – Resets the Page Setup settings to default.
- [OK] – Accepts the changes and closes the form.
- [Cancel] – Cancels the changes and closes the form.

14.3.1   Page Tab

The Primavera options in the **Page** tab are:

- **Orientation** enables the selection of **Portrait** or **Landscape** printing.
- **Scaling** enables you to adjust the number of pages the printout will fit onto:
    - ➢ **Adjust to:** – enables you to choose the scale of the printout that both the bars and column text are scaled to. Primavera will calculate the number of pages across and down for the printout.
    - ➢ **Fit to:** – enables you to choose the number of pages across and down and Primavera should scale the printout to fit.
    - ➢ **Fit timescale to:** – enables the user to select the number of pages the Gantt chart is scaled over but leaves the font of the columns un-scaled. This will often be the best setting with 1 page(s) wide selected. This functions in a similar way as P3 and SureTrak functions.

- Pages are numbered across first and then down, and does not follow the P3 and SureTrak convention of numbers down and letters across or the Microsoft Project convention of numbering pages down and then across.

14.3.2 Margins Tab

With this option, you may choose the margins around the edge of the printout.

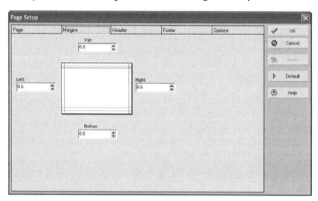

Type in the margin size around the page. It is best to allow a wider margin for an edge that is to be bound or hole punched. 1" or 2.5cm is usually sufficient.

14.3.3 Header and Footer Tabs

Headers appear at the top of the screen above all schedule information and footers are located at the bottom. Both the headers and footers are formatted in the same way. We will discuss the setting-up of footers in this chapter.

Click on the **Footer** tab from the **Page Setup** form. This will display the settings of the default footers and headers. You should modify the output to suit your requirements.

Slide for manually sizing the sections

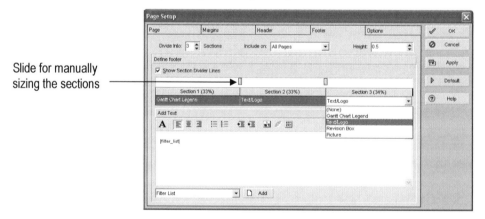

- **Divide Into:** – determines the number of sections the Header/Footer is divided into from 1 to 5 sections.
- **Include on:** – determines on which pages the Header/Footer is to appear: First Page, Last Page, All Pages or No Pages.
- **Height:** – enables the user to select the height of the Header/Footer.

- **Define Footer**
  - ➤ **S̲how Section Divider Lines** – check box, hides or displays the divider lines between the sections.
  - ➤ The sections may be sized by manually moving the divider lines with the mouse and the slide underneath the **S̲how Section Divider Lines**.

- **Section Content**

  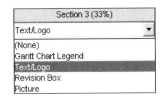

  The Section content may be selected by clicking on the [▼] button under the **Section** title, a subject type to be displayed may be selected.

  - ➤ **(None)** – leaves the section blank.
  - ➤ **Gantt Chart Legend** – displays all the bars checked in the display column of the **Bars** form and only the fonts may be edited by clicking on the little font button at the bottom of the form.
  - ➤ **Text/Logo** – enables many types of data to be displayed including text, a data item selected from the drop down box, the fonts may be formatted by clicking on the formatting buttons [A][E][E][E][E][E][E][E]. A Logo inserted by clicking on the [◨] button, tables added by clicking on the [▦] button, and a Hyperlink added by clicking on the link button [✎] which opens the Hyperlink form.
  - ➤ **Revision Box** has a **Revision Box Title:** – the following information may be entered manually Date, Revision, Checked, Approved.
  - ➤ **Picture** – enables a picture to be placed in the footer, its size can be manually adjusted of to fit the space or automatically adjusted by checking the **Resize picture to fit the selection** box.

14.4 Options Tab

The Options tab has three sections:

- **Timescale Start:** and **Timescale Finish:**

  These options enables the start and finish point of the timescale to be set. Click on the [⋯] button and select a date from the drop down list. A **Custom Date…** may be selected from the menu and a calendar is opened to select the date.

  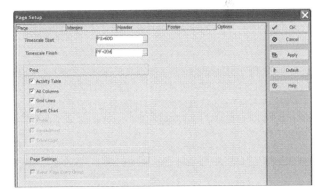

  A lag from the nominated dates may be specified, see the picture above. This function work in a similar way to P3 and SureTrak

- The **Print** options alter depending on the Layout. The checkboxes allow a selection of the data to be printed.

- The **Break Page Every Group** puts a page break at each change of heading in the first group in the **Group and Sort** form.

14.5   Print Form

The **Print** form is be opened by:

- Selecting **File**, **Print…**, or

- Executing the keystrokes **Ctrl+P**, or

- Clicking on the 🖨 print icon in the **Print Preview** screen.

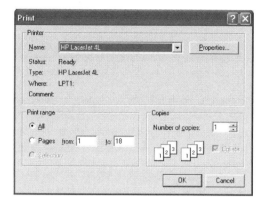

14.6   Print Setup Form

The **Print Setup** form is be opened by:

- Selecting **File**, **Print Setup…**, or

- Clicking on the 🖺 print icon in the **Print Preview** screen.

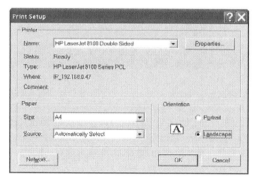

14.7   Reports

Click the 🖽 button on the **Directory Toolbar** or select **Tools**, **Reports**, **Reports** to open the **Reports Window**:

- The reports are grouped under a hierarchical structure that may be modified by opening the **Tools**, **Reports**, **Reports Groups** form.

- Multiple reports may be run by using the **Tools**, **Reports**, **Batch Reports** form or clicking the ⏭ button in the **Reports Window**:

- A single report may be run by right-clicking on a report and selecting **Run**, or clicking the ▷ button in the **Reports Window**:

- Reports may be cut, copied and pasted using the toolbars or right-clicking.

- Some reports are created with the **Report Wizard** and some with the **Report Writer**.

   ➢ Those created with the **Report Wizard** are edited with the **Report Wizard** and have a 📝 by the report name.

   ➢ Those created with the **Report Writer** are edited with the **Report Writer** and have a 📋 by the report name.

- To create a new report or modify an existing report that was created with the **Report Wizard**, run the Report Wizard by clicking the 🪄 button on the **Command** toolbar, or selecting **Tools**, **Report Wizard…** or right-clicking on a report and selecting **Modify**.

- The **Report Editor** may be used to modify any existing report. Refer to the User Manual for full details.

14.8 Workshop 12 - Printing

Background

We want to issue a report for comment by management.

Assignment

Open your **OzBuild Bid** project from the previous workshop to complete the following steps:

1. Apply the OzBuild Workshop 11 - With Float layout.
2. Select **File**, **Print Preview** and click the 🗔 icon to open the **Page Setup** form.
3. In the **Page** tab select the printout to fit on one page by one page in landscape and your paper size; A4 or Letter.
4. In the **Margins** tab set all the settings to 0.5" or 12mm, except for the **Top:** settings which should to be set to 0.75" or 19mm to allow space for binding.
5. In the **Header** tab:
   - ➤ **Divide Into:** 1 **Sections**
   - ➤ Select **Text/Logo** under Section 1, insert the **[project_name]** Project Name from the drop down box at the bottom left side of the form, click the 🗋 Add button and align in center in Arial 12 Bold.
6. In the **Footer** tab:
   - ➤ **Divide Into:** 3 **Sections**
   - ➤ Section 1 – Text/Logo – Date aligned to the left **[date]** in Arial 10.
   - ➤ Section 2 – Text/Logo – Page Number **[page_number]** of Total Pages **[total_pages]** align in center in Arial 10.
   - ➤ Section 3 – Gantt Chart Legend.
   - ➤ Adjust the **Height:** of the footer as necessary to show all the bars in the legend, say 0.75 inch.
7. In the **Options** tab set the **Timescale Start:** from the Project Start minus 5 days and **Timescale Finish:** to the Project Finish plus 5 days, see the Options tab picture on the previous page. Show the Activity Table, All Columns, Grid Line and Gantt Chart.
8. Compare your result with the picture on the next page.

Answer to Workshop 12

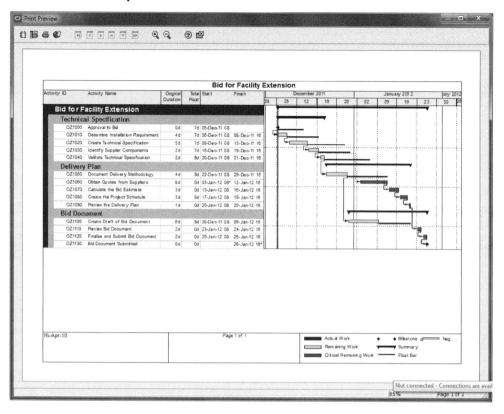

15 TRACKING PROGRESS

Tracking Progress is used after you have completed the plan, or have completed sufficient iterations to reach an acceptable plan, and the project may be progressing. Now the important phase of regular monitoring and control begins. This process is important to help catch problems as early as possible, and thus minimize their impact on the successful completion of the project. The main steps for monitoring progress are:

- Saving a **Baseline** schedule, also known as a **Target**. This schedule holds the dates against which progress is compared. The current project may be copied and used as a baseline or an existing project may be assigned as a baseline.
- Recording or marking-up progress as of a specific date, often titled the **Data Date**, **Status Date**, **Update Date**, **Current Date** and **As-Of-Date**.
- **Updating** or **Progressing** the schedule with **Actual Start** and **Actual Finish** dates where applicable, and adjusting the activity's **Remaining Durations** and **Percent Completes**.
- Scheduling and at the same time moving the **Data Date** to the new **Data Date** and recalculating all the activities dates.
- Comparing and Reporting actual progress against planned progress and revising the plan and schedule, if required.

Comparing the status of an activity against more than one baseline is useful; for example:

- The original plan, which could be Baseline 1, to see the slippage compared to the original plan.
- Last Period, which could be Baseline 2, to see the changes since the last update.

By the time you get to this phase you should have a schedule that compares your original plan with the current plan, showing where the project is ahead or behind. If you are behind, you should be able to use this schedule to plan appropriate remedial measures to bring the project back on target.

This chapter covers the following topics:

Topic	Menu Command
• Saving and Deleting and Setting a **Baseline**	To save a Baseline, select **Project, Maintain Baselines...** to display the **Maintain Baselines** form
• Assigning a Baseline project	The baselines are assigned from the **Project**, **Assign Baselines...** form
• Recording Progress	Guidelines on how to record progress
• **Retained Logic** and **Progress Override**	Open the **General Schedule Options** form by selecting **Tools, Schedule...** and clicking the ▷ Advanced... button.
• Setting the **Current Data Date** and **Scheduling** the project	Open the **Schedule** form by: • Selecting **Tools, Schedule...**, or • Pressing the **F9** key, or • Clicking the 🔯 button.

15.1 Understanding Date Fields

Primavera has many more date fields for the current schedule than P3, SureTrak or Microsoft Project. This section explains how these date fields calculate.

There is very little documentation available on how these dates are calculated and the author has ascertained the information following by trial using an unresourced schedule.

After you understand these fields, you should look again at the **Bar Timescale** options in the **Bars** form. It will be easier to understand how the bar formatting works.

• Early Start and Early Finish	These are always the earliest dates that unstarted activities or the incomplete portions of in-progress activities may start or finish based on calendars, relationships and constraints. • **Early Start** is set to the **Data Date** after an activity has commenced. • The **Early Finish** is set to the **Data Date** when the activity is complete. **NOTE:** Other software sets the **Early Dates** to the **Actual Dates** after an activity has commenced or has been completed. This is the reason why the **Early Bar** is not displayed by default in the Gantt Chart, as the **Early Bar** will not display Actual progress in the same way as other software.
• Late Start and Late Finish	The latest dates that unstarted activities or the incomplete portions of in-progress activities may start or finish based on calendars, relationships and constraints.
• Actual Start and Finish	These dates are manually applied, representing when an activity started or finished, and override constraints and relationships. These dates should be set in the past in relation to the **Data Date**.
• Start	These are set to the **Early Start** when the activity has not started and the **Actual Start** when it has started. • An "A" is placed after the date when an **Actual Start** has been set, & • An "*"is placed after the date when a start constraint has been applied to the activity.
• Finish	These are set to the **Early Finish** when the activity has not started or is in-progress and the **Actual Finish** when it is complete. • An "A" is placed after the date when an **Actual Finish** has been set & • An "*"is placed after the date when a finish constraint has been applied to the activity.
• Planned Dates	The **Planned Finish** is calculated from the **Planned Start** plus the **Original Duration**. These fields are always linked, therefore: • A change to the **Planned Start** will change the **Planned Finish** via the **Original Duration**, • A change to the **Planned Finish** will change permanently the **Original Duration,** and • A change to the **Original Duration** will change the **Planned Finish**. When a task has **NOT** started: • They **ARE** linked to the **Start** and **Finish** when a task has not started, • They are **NOT** linked to the Early Dates. • A **Planned Start** may be manually edited and as the **Start** date is linked it is also changed, but the **Early Start** is **NOT** changed. The **Planned Start** and

	Start are reset to the Early Dates when a project is rescheduled.
	• The **Planned Finish** may be edited and is linked to the **Finish** date and the **Original Duration**. A change to the **Planned Finish** will change the **Finish** date and **Original Duration**. Rescheduling will recalculate the schedule using the new **Original Duration** and set the **Planned Finish**, **Finish** and **Early Finish** to the same date.
	• Thus a change to the **Planned Start** is reversed by rescheduling, but a change to the **Planned Finish** affects the **Original Duration** and is not reversed by rescheduling.
	When a task is in-progress:
	• The **Planned Start** remains unchanged when an **Actual Start** of a date different from the original **Planned Start** is set. Therefore the **Planned Start** remains the same as the **Start Date** before the **Actual Start** was set.
	• The **Planned Finish** is calculated from the **Planned Start Date** plus the **Original Duration**.
	• After a task has commenced, the **Remaining Duration** may be edited independently from the **Original Duration**. The **Planned Finish** may have a different date from the **Finish**, which is now set to equal the **Early Finish**.
	When a task is complete:
	• The **Planned Dates** are unlinked from all other date fields.
	NOTE: The **Original** and **At Completion** durations are **ONLY** linked when an activity has not started and when **Link Budget and At Completion for not started activities** box in the **Projects Window**, **Calculations** tab is checked.
• Remaining Early Start and Finish	These are the earliest dates that the incomplete portions of unstarted or in-progress activities may start and finish.
	• They are blank when an activity is complete.
	• They may be edited in the same way as Planned Dates.
	➢ When a **Remaining Early Start** is edited to a later than scheduled date, there is an option for constraining the **Remaining Early Start** with a **Start on or After Constraint**. If this is not set then the task will move forward to its original position when scheduling.
	➢ When a **Remaining Early Start** is edited, the **Remaining Duration** is also edited and the change is permanent. Scheduling does not take the schedule back to the original position.
• Remaining Late Start and Finish	These are the latest dates that the incomplete portions of activities may start and finish.
	• They are blank when an activity is complete and may not be edited.
	• They may not be displayed as a bar.
	• They are set to equal the **Late Dates**.

15.2 Setting the Baseline

Setting the Baseline makes a complete copy of a project, including relationships, notebook entries and codes. Up to 50 baselines per project may be saved in a database in earlier versions but in Version 6.0 an unlimited number may be saved.

- The number of baselines that may be saved is set up in the **Admin Preferences** form by selecting **Admin**, **Admin Preferences…**, **Data Limits** and setting the number in the **Maximum baselines per project** box.

- Up to four baselines, one **Project Baseline** and three **User Baselines**, may be displayed and compared to the current project. **NOTE:** If another user opens the project, they will only see the one **Project Baseline** and not the other **Users Baseline**.

- A baseline project may be restored back into a database as a normal project. It may be edited and resaved as a baseline project.

After the Baseline is set, it is possible to compare the progress with the original plan. You will be able to see if you are ahead or behind schedule and by how much. The Baseline schedule should be established before you update the schedule for the first time.

15.2.1 Saving a Baseline

To save a Baseline, select **Project**, **Maintain Baselines…** to display the **Maintain Baselines** form:

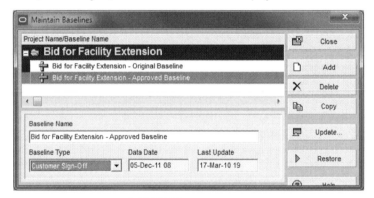

- To create a new baseline click the [☐ Add] button to open the **Add New Baseline** form:

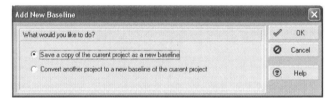

- Select either of the two options in the form:
  - ➢ **Save a copy of the current project as a new baseline** will make a copy of the currently open project, adds a - B1, B2 etc after the name and return you to the **Baselines** form, or
  - ➢ **Convert another project to a new baseline of the current project** will open the **Select Project** form where another project may be selected to be a baseline. This project will then move from the current projects window into the **Maintain Baselines** form and is not available to be opened from the **Projects Window**.

- Assign a **Baseline Type** from the drop down box. Baseline Types are defined in the **Admin**, **Admin Categories** form, **Baseline Type** tab.

15.2.2 Copy a Baseline when Saving a Baseline

A new baseline may be created in Primavera P6 Version 7 with a new function which allows the copying an existing baseline in the **Project**, **Maintain Baselines** form:

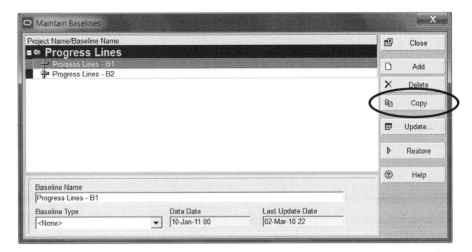

This new baseline may then be updated using the **Update** function or Restored so they may be edited or reviewed.

15.2.3 Deleting a Baseline

To delete a project baseline from the database:

- Open the **Baselines** form by selecting **Project**, **Maintain Baselines...**,
- Select the baseline project to be deleted, and
- Click on the ☒ Delete button.

15.2.4 Restoring a Baseline to the Database as an Active Project

To restore a project back to the database so it may be edited or used as a current project:

- Open the **Maintain Baselines** form by selecting **Project**, **Maintain Baselines...**,
- Ensure the baseline is not assigned as a project baseline in the **Baselines** form,
- Select the baseline project to be restored, and
- Click on the ▷ Restore button.

15.2.5 Setting the Baseline Project

The baselines are assigned from the **Project**, **Assign Baselines...** form:

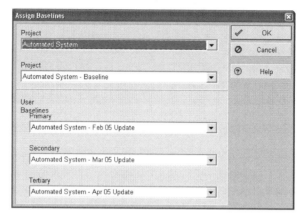

- Select from the drop down box under **Project** which of the open projects is to have a baseline set.

- The **Project Baseline** may be used for calculating **Earned Value**. See **Admin**, **Admin Preferences...**, **Earned Value** tab for other Earned Value options. This Baseline is seen by any User that opens the project.

- Select which from the drop down boxes under **User Baselines** which are to be the **Primary**, **Secondary** and **Tertiary** User Baseline. User Baselines are only seen by the User that has set the Baseline.

- Earned Value calculations may be performed using either the **Primary Baseline** values or the **Baseline** values, the values from the current project. Select the **Settings** tab in the **Projects Window**. This is similar to the P3 option **Tools**, **Options**, **Earned Value**.

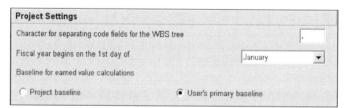

15.2.6 Understanding the <Current Schedule> Baseline

Because **Planned Dates** are difficult to understand and may lead to misinterpretation of the schedule baselines, it is important that you understand the following points:

- The **Planned Dates** are used by the <**Current Schedule**> **Baseline**.

- The <**Current Schedule**> **Baseline** is the default baseline for both the **Project Baseline** and **Primary User Baseline**.

- When **NO** baseline has been set by a user then the <**Current Schedule**> **Baseline** and therefore the **Planned Dates** are displayed as the **Baseline Bars**.

- The <**Current Schedule**> **Baseline** is not a true baseline and may change each time a schedule is updated.

- The term **Current Schedule** is normally used to describe the activities as they are currently scheduled and the term <**Current Schedule**> **Baseline** is confusing as it is not the **Current Schedule** but the **Planned Dates** that may be different to the **Current Schedule**.

The following picture have three bars:

- The upper bar represents the Start and Finish dates:
  - ➢ The **Start** date is set to the **Early Start** when an activity has not started and **Actual Start** when the activity has started.
  - ➢ The **Finish** date is set to the **Early Finish** when an activity has not finished and **Actual Finish** when the activity is complete.
- The middle bar is the **<Current Schedule> baseline**, the **Planned Dates** and
- The lower bar is a proper baseline made by copying the un-progressed project.

With no progress all bars are the same:

Activity ID	Activity Name	Original Duration	Start	Finish	February 2010			
					31	07	14	21
A1010	Activity 1	5d	01-Feb-10	05-Feb-10				
A1020	Activity 2	5d	08-Feb-10	12-Feb-10				
A1030	Activity 3	5d	15-Feb-10	19-Feb-10				

With Activity 1 complete, the un-started activities in the **<Current Schedule> baseline** have changed their dates:

Activity ID	Activity Name	Original Duration	Start	Finish	February 2010			
					31	07	14	21
A1010	Activity 1	5d	02-Feb-10 A	09-Feb-10 A				
A1020	Activity 2	5d	10-Feb-10*	16-Feb-10				
A1030	Activity 3	5d	17-Feb-10	23-Feb-10				

With Activity 2 in-progress and delaying Activity 3, Activity 2 holds the previous period **<Current Schedule> baseline** and Activity 3 has changed its **<Current Schedule> baseline** dates a second time in the **<Current Schedule> baseline**.

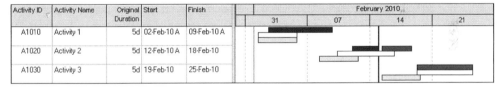

Activity ID	Activity Name	Original Duration	Start	Finish	February 2010			
					31	07	14	21
A1010	Activity 1	5d	02-Feb-10 A	09-Feb-10 A				
A1020	Activity 2	5d	12-Feb-10 A	18-Feb-10				
A1030	Activity 3	5d	19-Feb-10	25-Feb-10				

 When no Baseline is set by the user, the project will **DISPLAY** the **<Current Schedule> baseline** bar (from the Planned Dates, not the Current Schedule) as the Baseline bars and, in effect, all un-started activities are "re-baselined" at each update. This is generally not accepted as a good practice.

There are some significant issues here that need to be carefully managed:

- If no Baseline is set and a layout that displays a baseline bar is applied, then a baseline bar that the user did not set will be displayed. This may create confusion and these bars may change on each schedule update.
- If one user sets a Primary Baseline, which is a User Baseline and therefore only seen by that user, and a different user opens a project, then this second user will see only the **<Current Schedule> baseline** and not the other user's Primary Baseline. This will result in one user seen something different to another user when two users open a project.

You may wish to restrict the access to a project schedule to prevent the **<Current Schedule> baseline** being displayed inadvertently.

15.2.7 Update Baselines

The new Primavera Version 5.0 **Update Baseline** function is similar to the P3 function and enables the Baseline schedule to be updated with data from the current schedule or activities deleting that are no longer in the current schedule without restoring the Baseline schedule:

- Select **Project**, **Maintain Baselines…** and select the [⊞ Update…] button to open the **Update Baseline** form:

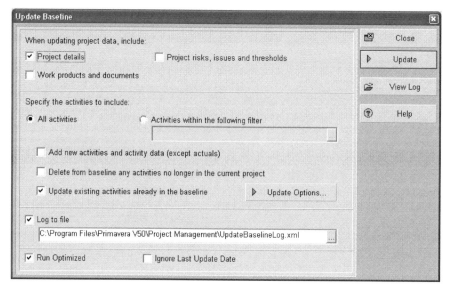

- When **Run Optimized** is not checked then an error log is kept during the updating process.
- **Ignore Last Update Date** may be used when a project has is updated at different times and the last Baseline Update may not be valid for the current schedule although the Baseline has been updated with more recent data.

- Select [▷ Update Options…] to open the **Update Baseline Options** form to select which data items are updated.

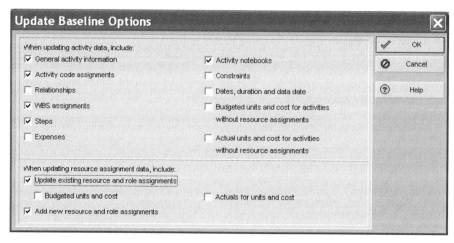

There was also a new project privilege introduced in Primavera Version 5.0 allowing a user to run Update Project Baselines.

15.2.8 Copying a Project with Baselines

Primavera Version 6.0 introduced the option of being able to copy baselines when a project is copied in the **Projects Window** using Copy and Paste.

NOTE: You must manually reassign the baseline after the project has been copied.

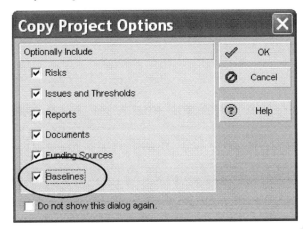

If you are using Version 5.0 or earlier then the Baselines need to be restored copied and reset as baselines.

15.2.9 Displaying the Baseline Data

The Baseline Dates may be displayed by:

- Displaying the **Baseline** columns:

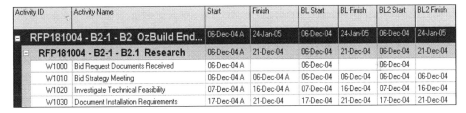

- Showing a baseline bar on the Bar Chart by selecting the appropriate bars in the **Bars** form:

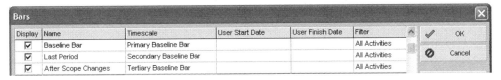

15.3 Practical Methods of Recording Progress

Normally a project is updated once a week, bi-weekly, or monthly. Very short projects could be updated daily or even by the shift or hour. As a guide, a project would typically be updated between 12 and 20 times in its lifetime. A high risk project should be updated more often than a low risk project. Progress is recorded on or just after the **Data Date** and the scheduler updates the schedule upon the receipt of the information.

The following information is typically recorded for each activity when updating a project:

- The activity start date and time if required,
- The number of days/hours the activity has remaining or the date and time the activity is expected to finish,
- The percentage complete, and
- If complete, the activity finish date and time.

A printout of the schedule may be used for recording the progress of the current schedule is often produced prior to updating the project. Ideally progress should be recorded by a physical inspection of the work or by a person who intimately knows the work, although that is not always possible. It is good practice to keep this marked-up record for your own reference. Ensure that you note the Data Date of the mark-up and, if relevant, the time.

Often a Status Report or mark-up sheet, such as the following illustration which has a 4-week look ahead filter applied, is distributed to the people responsible for marking up the project progress. The marked-up sheets are returned to the scheduler for data entry into the software and then filed for dispute resolution.

A page break could be placed at each responsible person's band from the **Page Setup**, **Options** tab, and when the schedule is printed each person could have a personal listing of activities that are either in-progress or due to commence. This is particularly useful for large projects.

Activity ID	Activity Name	Original Duration	Start	Actual Start	Activity % Complete	Remaining Duration	Finish	Actual Finish	Early Start
▬ **Estimation**		21d	12-Dec-03 A	12-Dec-03		6d	09-Jan-04		02-Jan-04
A1040	Request Component Bids	3d	05-Jan-04*		0%	3d	07-Jan-04		05-Jan-04
A1060	Draft Technical Details S...	11d	12-Dec-03 A	12-Dec-03	70%	3d	07-Jan-04		02-Jan-04
A1070	Compile Costs from Com...	2d	08-Jan-04		0%	2d	09-Jan-04		08-Jan-04
▬ **Proposal**		9d	12-Jan-04			9d	23-Jan-04		12-Jan-04
A1080	Draft Bid Document	3d	12-Jan-04		0%	3d	14-Jan-04		12-Jan-04
A1090	Meeting to Review the D...	1d	15-Jan-04		0%	1d	15-Jan-04		15-Jan-04
A1100	Design Presentation	1d	16-Jan-04		0%	1d	16-Jan-04		16-Jan-04
A1110	Edit Proposal Draft Bid D...	1d	19-Jan-04		0%	1d	19-Jan-04		19-Jan-04
A1120	Negotiate Component W...	3d	19-Jan-04		0%	3d	21-Jan-04		19-Jan-04
A1130	Final Review of Bid Doc...	1d	22-Jan-04		0%	1d	22-Jan-04		22-Jan-04

Other electronic methods, discussed next, may be employed to collect the data. Irrespective of the method used, the same data needs to be collected.

There are several methods of collecting data for the project status:

- By sending a printed sheet to each responsible person to mark up by hand and return to the scheduler.
- By cutting and pasting the data from Primavera into another document, such as Excel, and emailing the document to them as an attachment.
- By giving the responsible party direct access to the schedule software to update it. This approach is not recommended, unless the project is broken into subprojects. By using the multiple projects with one scheduler accessing each project or assigning assess through WBS Nodes, thus only one person updates each part of the schedule.
- When the Primavera timesheets have been implemented this process may be used to update the activities.

Some projects involve a number of people. In such cases, it is important that procedures be written to ensure that the update information is collected:

- In a timely manner,
- Consistently,
- Complete, and
- In a usable format.

 It is important for a scheduler to be aware that some people have great difficulty in comprehending a schedule. When there are a number of people with different skill levels in an organization, it is necessary to provide more than one method of updating the data. You even may find that you have to sit down with some people to obtain the correct data, yet others are willing and comfortable to e-mail you the information.

15.4 Understanding the Concepts

There are some terms and concepts used in scheduling and some that are specific to Primavera that must be understood before updating a project schedule:

15.4.1 Activity Lifecycle

There are three stages of an activity lifecycle:

- **Not Started** – The **Early Start** and **Early Finish** dates are calculated from the **Predecessors**, **Constraints** and **Activity Duration**.

- **In-Progress** – The activity has an **Actual Start** date but is not complete.
  - ➢ Assigning an **Actual Start** date overrides the **Start Constraints** and **Start Relationships** which are used to calculate the **Early Start**.
  - ➢ The end date may be calculated from the **Remaining Duration** or a **Finish Constraint** or a **Finish Relationship**.

- **Complete** – The activity is in the past, the **Actual Start** and **Actual Finish** dates have been entered into Primavera, and they override all logic and constraints.

15.4.2 Actual Start Date Assignment of an In-Progress Activity

This section will explain how Primavera assigns the **Actual Start** of an **In-Progress** activity. These activities have been started but not completed since the last update.

- When an **Actual Start** date is assigned in the **Actual Start** field by checking the **Started** check box, or entering a date in the **Actual Start** column, this date overrides the **Early Start date**.

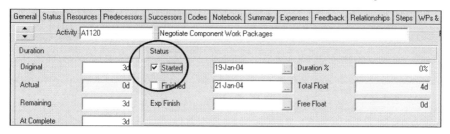

- The activity **Actual Start** date is set to equal the **Early Start** date when this box is checked.

- The **Actual Start** date calendar is opened by clicking on the ⬚ button to the right of the **Started** check box and a different start date may be assigned. This date should not be in the future of the project Data Date. It would not be logical to have an activity start in the future.

15.4.3 Calculation of Durations of an In-Progress Activity

Durations

The Primavera has many durations, we will discuss four durations now:

- An activity **Original Duration** is the duration from the **Early Start** to the **Early Finish** calculated over the **Activity Calendar** and is calculated when an activity has not yet started. When an **Actual Start** is entered, this duration is no longer recalculated or directly used for scheduling, but may be edited.

- The **Actual Duration** is the activity's worked duration and is either the duration from:
  - ➢ The **Actual Start** to the **Data Date** of an **In-progress** activity, or
  - ➢ The **Actual Start** to the **Actual Finish** of a **Completed** activity.

- The **Remaining Duration** is the unworked duration of an **In-progress** activity and is the duration from the **Data Date** to the **Early Finish** date of an activity.

- The **At Completion Duration** = **Actual Duration** + **Remaining Duration**. Before an activity has begun, the **Actual Duration** is zero and the **Remaining Duration** equals the **Original Duration**.

- The **Original Duration** is linked to the **Remaining Duration** when an activity is unstarted and **Link Budget and At Completion for not started activities box** in the **Calculations** tab of the **Projects Window** is checked.

- The Remaining bar is based on the **Remaining Duration**, and the Remaining Duration may commence a period of time after the **Data Date** so there is often a gap between the **Data Date** and the **Remaining Start** of an in progress activity.

 The in-built proportional link between **Original Duration**, **Actual Duration**, **Remaining Duration** and **% Complete** that exists in Microsoft Project does not exist in Primavera.

Percent Complete

As discussed in the **Adding Activities and Organizing Under the WBS** chapter, this section is repeated for completeness of this chapter.

The **Percent Complete** type should be understood if it is intended to be used to update (status or progress) the schedule. In Primavera this option may be set for each activity individually and the default for new activities is set in the **Percent Complete Type** drop down box. Primavera has many Activity Percent Complete fields that may be displayed in columns and we will discuss four of them now:

- **Activity % Complete**, which is displayed on the **% Complete Bar**, may be linked to one only of the three % Complete fields following:
- **Physical % Complete**
- **Duration %Complete**
- **Units % Complete**

There are three percent complete options; each new activity is assigned the project default **Percent Complete Type** and then this may be edited for each activity as required.

Therefore if the option of **Physical % Complete** is selected for an activity then the **Activity % Complete** and the **Physical % Complete** are linked and a change to one will change the other.

Default % Complete

The **Default % Complete Type** for each new activity in each project is assigned in the **Defaults** tab of the **Details** form in the **Project Window**:

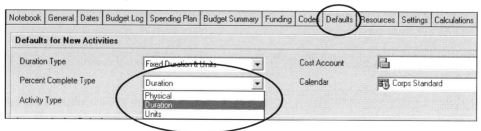

- Each new activity **Percent Complete Type** is set to the **Default Percent Complete** and may be changed at any time.

Percent Complete Types

- **Duration % Complete** – This field is calculated from the proportion of the **Original Duration** and the **Remaining Duration** and they are linked and a change to one value will change the other. When the **Remaining Duration** is set to greater that the **Original Duration** this percent complete is always zero. This is similar to the way P3 and SureTrak calculates the % Complete when the **Link Remaining Duration and Percent Complete** option is selected

- **Physical % Complete** – This field enables the user to enter the percent complete of an activity and this value is independent of the activity durations. This is similar to the way P3 and SureTrak calculates the % Complete when the **Link Remaining Duration and Percent Complete** option is NOT selected.

- **Units % Complete** – This is where the percent complete is calculated from the resources Actual and Remaining Units, a change to one value will change the other and when more than one resource is assigned then all the Actual Units for all resources will be changed proportionally. This will be covered further in The **Updating Resources** chapter. This is similar to the Microsoft Project % Work Complete.

Activity % Complete

This field is linked to the **% Complete Type** assigned to an activity in the **General** tab of the **Details** form in the **Activities Window** or the **% Complete Type** column:

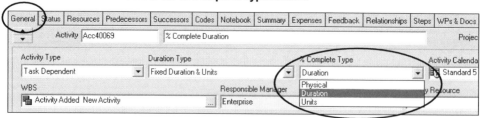

The **Activity % Complete** is linked to the **% Complete** field assigned the **% Complete Type** and the **% Complete Bar**. Therefore only the **Activity % Complete** column needs to be displayed and this value is represented on the **% Complete** Bar.

Percent Complete Type	Original Duration	Remaining Duration	Activity % Complete	Duration % Complete	Physical % Complete	Units % Complete	Actual Labor Units	At Completion Labor Units	Oct 24	Oct 31	No
% Co...	10d	6d		40%		33.33%	5	15			
Duration	10d	6d	40%	40%	5%	0%	0	0			
Physical	10d	6d	12%	40%	12%	0%	0	0			
Units	10d	5d	33.33%	50%	5%	33.33%	5	15			

15.4.4 Retained Logic and Progress Override

There are three options for calculating the finish date of the successor when the successor activity has started before the predecessor activity is finished. The selected option is applied to all activities in a schedule when it is calculated. Open the **Advanced Schedule Options** form by selecting **Tools, Schedule...** and clicking on the ▷ Advanced... button where the options are found under **When scheduling progressed activities use**:

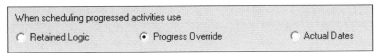

The status of the activities before updating the schedule is:

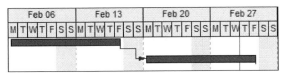

- **Retained Logic.** In the example following, the relationship is maintained between the predecessor and successor for the unworked portion of the activity (the Remaining Duration) and continued after the predecessor has finished. In the following example the relationship forms part of the critical path and the predecessor has no float:

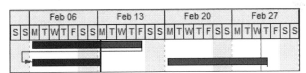

- **Progress Override.** In the example following, the Finish-to-Start relationship between the predecessor and successor is disregarded, and the unworked portion of the activity (the Remaining Duration) continues before the predecessor has finished. The relationship is not a driving relationship and DOES NOT form part of the critical path in the example following. The predecessor in the following example has float:

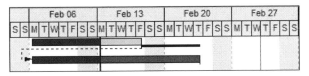

- **Actual Dates.** This function operates when there is an activity with Actual Start Dates in the future, which is not logical. With this option the remaining duration of an in-progress activity is calculated after the activity with actual start and finish in the future:

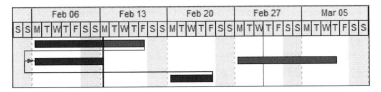

When there are no Actual Dates in the future this option calculates as Retained Logic.

This may happen when there are two project open together and they have different Data Dates.

Retained Logic and Progress Override are not terms used by Microsoft Project but are used in P3 and SureTrak and operate in the same way in Primavera. Retained Logic produces a more conservative schedule (a longer duration schedule) and is more likely to place an out of progress relationship on the critical path and adjustments may be made as required.

If your schedule has Actual dates in the future of the Data Date (which may occur when the update information is collected at different times and the earlier date is used as the Data Date or multiple projects are open) then the use of Actual Dates would calculate the most conservative schedule.

15.4.5 Actual Finish Date

An **Actual Finish** date overrides an **Early Finish** date and finish date constraints and finish relationships are ignored.

15.4.6 Summary Bars Progress Calculation

Summary bars such as WBS Node bars may not be updated, as in Microsoft Project, as they are virtual activities with their data created from summarizing the activities in the band.

15.4.7 Understanding the Current Data Date

The **Current Data Date** is also known as the **Data Date**, **Update Date**, **Status Date**, **Progress Date**, **As At Date**, **Time Now**, **Report Date** and the **Project Data Date**. Microsoft Project has several dates for the one **Current Data Date** but Primavera has one date, which is the same as for P3 and SureTrak.

The Primavera **Current Data Date** is displayed as a vertical line on the schedule; this Data Date vertical line may be formatted in later versions of Primavera in the **Bars** form.

In scheduling software the function of the **Current Data Date** is to:

- Separate the completed parts of activities from incomplete parts of activities.
- Calculate or record all costs and hours to date before the data date, and to forecast costs and hours to go after the data date.
- Calculate the **Finish Date** of an in-progress activity from the **Current Data Date** plus the **Remaining Duration** over the **Activity Calendar**.

15.5 Updating the Schedule

The next stage is to update the schedule by entering the mark-up information against each activity.

When dealing with large schedules it is normal to develop a look-ahead schedule by creating a filter to display incomplete and un-started activities commencing in the near future only.

The schedule may be updated using the following methods:

- Using the fields in the **Status** tab of the **Details** form in the lower pane, or
- Displaying the appropriate tracking columns by:
  - ➢ Creating your own layout, or
  - ➢ Inserting the required columns in an existing layout.

15.5.1 Updating Activities Using the Status Tab of the Details Form

Open the **Status** tab:

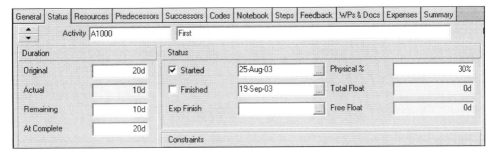

Updating a **Complete** activity:

- Check the **Started** box and enter the actual **Start Date and Time** if different from the displayed date.

- Check the **Finished** box and enter the actual **Finish Date and Time** if different from the displayed date.

Updating an **In-progress** activity:

- Check the **Started** box and enter the actual **Start Date and Time** if different from the displayed date.

- When the **Duration Type** is **% Duration** the **% Duration Complete** and **Remaining Duration** are linked, either:

  ➤ The **Remaining Duration** is edited and the **% Complete** is calculated, or
  ➤ The **% Complete** is entered and the software calculates the **Remaining Duration**, or
  ➤ A **Remaining Duration** greater than the **Original Duration** may be entered and the **% Duration** will remain at zero, until the **Remaining Duration** is less than the **Original Duration**.

  Irrespective of the method used to calculate the **Remaining Duration**, after the schedule is recalculated the end date of the activity is calculated from the **Current Data Date** plus the **Remaining Duration** over the **Activity Calendar**.

Updating an activity that has not started:

- The **Original Duration**, **Relationships** and **Constraints** of an un-started activity should be reviewed.

15.5.2 Updating Activities Using Columns

An efficient method of updating activities is by displaying the data in columns. This may be achieved by:

- Inserting the required columns in an existing layout, or better

- Create a Layout with the required columns and update the schedule using these columns.

15.6 Progress Spotlight and Update Progress

Primavera Version 5.0 introduced a new function for highlighting the activities that should have progressed in the update period. The user then has the option of selecting some or all of the activities that should be updated and updating them as if they progressed exactly as they were **Planned**. It is sometimes easier to **Automatically update** a project with functions like **Progress Spotlight** and then adjust the Actual dates and Remaining Durations as a second step in the updating process, especially if the project is going to plan.

This function is similar to the P3 Progress Spotlight function; however, it does not have the additional SureTrak features of reversing progress and not updating the resources.

The Spotlight may be moved to reflect the new Data Date by either:

- Dragging the Data Date, or
- Using the Spotlight Icon

 Unlike P3 and SureTrak, this Primavera **Update Progress** facility uses the **Planned Start** and **Planned Finish** dates (not the **Early Start** and **Early Finish**) for setting the **Actual Start** and **Actual Finish** dates of in-progress activities.

Thus, when the **Planned Dates** of an in-progress activity are different from the **Actual Start** and **Early Finish** dates and the task is Automatically updated to be complete, then both these dates are set to the **Planned** dates and the **Actual Start** may be changed and the **Actual Finish** not set to the original **Early Finish**.

The following picture displays the Early bar (the upper bar) and the Current Project set as a Baseline (the lower bar) which therefore reflects the Planned Dates:

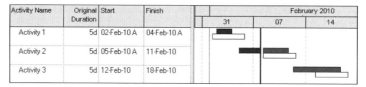

The following picture shows the effect of applying **Update Progress** to the schedule above. The Actual Start of Activity 2 has been changed and the Actual Finish of Activity 2 set to the Planned Dates, which is not the same as the original Early Finish.

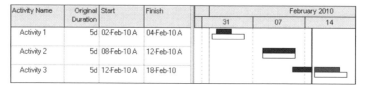

NOTE: You should not use this facility when you wish your activities to be Automatically updated to the Early dates (as in P3, SureTrak and Microsoft Project) and not the Planned dates. You may consider using a Global Change to set the Planned Dates to the Start and Finish dates before running Progress Spotlight, but this will change the Original Duration and the % Duration will not calculate correctly.

15.6.1 Highlighting Activities for Updating by Dragging the Data Date

To highlight activities that should have been progressed in the last period by dragging the Data Date:

- Hold the mouse arrow on the Data Date line and display the double-headed arrow ↔ , and
- Press the left mouse button and drag the Data Date line to the required date.
- All the activities that should have been worked in the time period are highlighted.

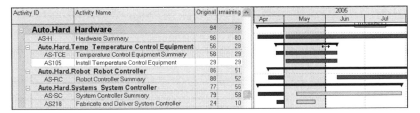

15.6.2 Spotlighting Activities Using Spotlight Icon

The Spotlight facility highlights all activities that should have progressed in one minor time period of the timescale settings. To use **Progress Spotlight**:

- Set the Timescale to be the same as your Update Periods. If you are updating weekly then set the time period to weeks in the **Timescale** form.
- Select **View**, **Progress**, **Spotlight** or click the 🔦 icon and the next period of time (one week if your scale is set to one week) will be highlighted.
- Click the **Progress Spotlight** 🔦 icon a second time to return the Spotlight back to the Data Date.

You are now ready to update progress.

15.6.3 Updating a Project Using Update Progress

To update a schedule using the **Update Progress** form, select **Tools**, **Update Progress**.

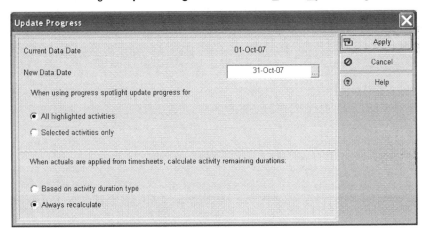

There are two options for setting the **New Data Date**:

- You may use the highlight facility before opening the **Update Progress** form and the **New Data Date** will be set to the highlighted Data Date; or
- You may select the **New Data Date** when opening the form.

Either all the activities that are Spotlighted may be updated or if some were selected before opening the form then just the selected ones may be updated.

- To update all the activities, select the **All highlighted activities** radio button, or

- To update selected activities, highlight the activities (hold the **Ctrl** key and click the ones you wish to status) before selecting **Tools**, **Update Progress…** and then clicking on the **Selected activities only** radio button.

The option **When actuals are applied from timesheets, calculate activity remaining durations:** decides how the Remaining Duration is calculated:

- **Based on the activity duration type** will take into account activity type and hours to date and reschedule the Remaining Duration in accordance with the activity Duration Type.

- **Always recalculate** will override the activity Duration Type and calculate the activity Remaining Durations and Hours as if the activity were a Fixed Units and Fixed Units/Time activity.

- Click [🖫 Apply] and the schedule will be updated as if all activities were completed according to the schedule.

15.7 Suspend and Resume

The Primavera Version 5.0 Suspend and Resume function enables the work to be suspended and the activity resumed at a later date. Open the **Activity Details** form **Status Details** tab and enter the **Suspend** and **Resume** dates. This function works in a similar way to the P3 and SureTrak function and enables only one break in an activity.

The following example shows an activity suspended from 30 Apr 05 to the 10 May 05.

- This feature works when a task has commenced and normally the Suspend date is in the past and the Resume date in the future.

- The activity must have an actual start date before you can record a suspend date.

- Only Resource Dependent and Task Dependent activities may be Suspended and resumed.

- The suspended period is not calculated as part of the task duration and resources are not scheduled in this period.

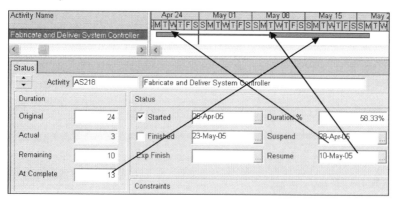

 The Suspend and Resume time may be set at 00:00, the start of the day, when set without the time hidden. Therefore you may wish to display the time when setting Suspend and Resume dates to ensure that are correct.

15.8 Scheduling the Project

At any time, but usually after all the activities have been updated, the project is scheduled :

- Open the **Schedule** form:
  - ➤ Select **Tools**, **Schedule…**, or
  - ➤ Press the **F9** key, or
  - ➤ Click on the 🗓 button.

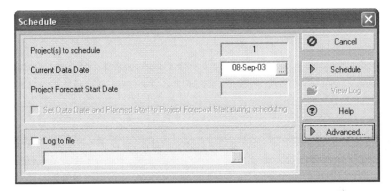

- Select the revised **Current Data Date** from the box and click the ▷ Schedule button.
- The software will recalculate all the early finish dates from the remaining durations and the new **Current Data Date**, taking into account the relationships and the **Retained Logic/Progress Override Options**.

15.9 Comparing Progress with Baseline

There will normally be changes to the schedule dates and more often than not there are delays. The full extent of the change is not apparent without having a Baseline bar to compare with the updated schedule.

To display one or more of the **Baseline Bars** in the **Bar Chart** you must open the **Bars** form and check the **Display** box of one or more baseline bar.

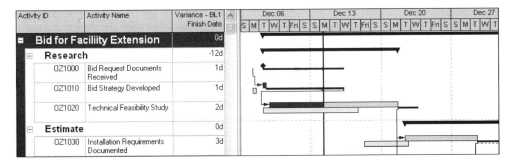

If you want to see the Start and Finish Date variances, they are available by displaying the **Variance - Start Date** and **Variance - Finish Date** columns. These variance columns use the **Primary Baseline** data.

 When a **Project Baseline** or a **Primary User Baseline** bar is displayed without a baseline being set the **Current Schedule** which is based on the **Planned Dates** will be displayed and the **Current Schedule** is not a true Baseline.

15.10 Progress Line Display on the Gantt Chart

This is a new feature to Primavera P6 Version 7.

A progress line displays how far ahead or behind activities are in relation to the Baseline. Either the Project Baseline or the Primary User Baseline may be used and there are four options:
- Difference between the Baseline Start Date and Activity Start Date,
- Difference between the Baseline Finish Date and Activity Finish Date,
- Connecting the progress points based on the Activity % Complete,
- Connecting the progress points based on the Activity Remaining Duration.

There are several components to displaying a Progress Line:
- Firstly the progress line is formatted using the **View, Bar Chart Options** form, **Progress Line** tab, which may also be opened by right clicking in the Gant Chart area:

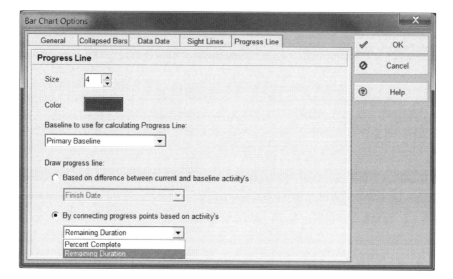

- Selecting **View, Progress Line** to hide or display the **Progress Line**.
- If you use either of the options of Percent Complete or Remaining Duration then you must display the appropriate Baseline Bar that has been selected as the **Baseline to use for calculating Progress Line:**.
- The picture below shows the option highlighted above of **Percent Complete**:

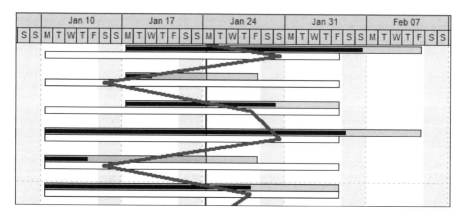

15.11 Corrective Action

Date slippage occurs when an activity is rescheduled to finish later than originally planned. There are two courses of action available:

- The first is to accept the slippage. This is rarely acceptable, but it is the easiest answer.
- The second is to examine the schedule and evaluate how you could improve the end date.

Solutions to return the project to its original completion date must be cleared with the person responsible for the project.

Suggested solutions to bring the project back on track include:

- Reducing the durations of activities on, or near the critical path. When activities have applied resources, this may include increasing the number of resources working on the activities. Changing longer activities is often more achievable than changing the length of short duration activities.
- Changing calendars, say from a five-day to a six-day calendar, so that activities are being worked on for more days per week.
- Reducing the project scope and deleting activities.
- Changing activity relationships so activities take place concurrently. This may be achieved by introducing negative lags to Finish-to-Start relationships, which maintain a Closed Network. A negative lag will allow the successor activity to start before the predecessor is complete, which is often what happens in reality.
- Replacing Finish-to-Start relationships with Start-to-Start relationships. Activities are now progressing in parallel and therefore at the same time. This has the potential of creating an open network as the predecessor activity may no longer have a finish date successor and an extension in the duration of this activity may not affect the critical path. Should maintaining the critical path be important then this option should be avoided or a successor added to complete a closed network.
- Changing the plan and therefore change the logic to reduce the overall length of the critical path.

15.12 Workshop 13 - Progressing and Baseline Comparison

Background

At the end of the first week you have to update the schedule and report progress and slippage.

Assignment

Open your **OzBuild Bid** project file and complete the following steps:

1. Select **Project**, **Maintain Baselines...** and save a copy of the current project as a Baseline and title it **Bid for Facility Extension - Baseline**.
2. Assign an appropriate Baseline Type, the options may vary depending on your database.
3. Select **Project**, **Assign Baselines...** and make this your **Project Baseline** and **Primary Baseline** and close the **Assign Baselines** form. This ensures that any baseline bar will show a real baseline and not the Planned Dates.
4. Apply the **OzBuild 11 – With Float** layout and save this as a new layout titled **OzBuild Workshop 13 – Baseline**.
5. Create if required and display:
   - The Primary Baseline Bar, a thick bar in yellow and in row 2.
   - The Primary Baseline Bar milestones in Row 2.
   - The % Complete bar in Row 1.
   - Move the Primary Baseline Bar and Milestones so they are below the other bars which will place the relationships on the Current schedule bars.
   - For clarity ensure all the text is removed from the all bars.
   - In order that completed activities do not show a total Float Bar edit this bar filter so it is only displayed for **Not Started** and **In Progress bars** by opening the Bars form and formatting the Filter field as per the picture below:

Display	Name	Timescale	User Start Date	User Finish Date	Filter	Preview
☑	Float Bar	Float Bar			Not Started or In Progress	▬▬▬

6. Show the following columns:
   - Activity ID
   - Activity Name
   - Activity % Complete
   - Original Duration
   - Remaining Duration
   - Start
   - Finish
   - Total Float
   - Variance BL1 – Finish Date
7. Make sure the Timescale is daily or weekly
8. Show the time in 24 hour format, but do not show the minutes by selecting **Edit, User Preferences**, **Time Units** tab.
9. We are now going to update the schedule as at the end of the first week.

Continued....

10. Update the project activities in the **Activities**, bottom pane **Status** tab with the following information:

Activity ID	Activity Name	Actual Start	Actual Finish	Rem Dur	Act % Comp
Bid for Facility Extension					
Technical Specification					
0Z1000	Approval to Bid	06-Dec-11 08		0d	100%
0Z1010	Determine Installation Requirements	06-Dec-11 08	08-Dec-11 16	0d	100%
0Z1020	Create Technical Specification	08-Dec-11 08		6d	60%

11. Reschedule the project by pressing **F9** to open the **Schedule** form:
   ➢ Check the data date to 12-Dec-11 08:00, that will be Monday morning,
   ➢ Open the **Schedule Options** form by clicking on the [▷ Options...] button and ensure **Retained Logic** is selected,
   ➢ Close the **Schedule Options** form,
   ➢ Click on the [▷ Schedule] to reschedule,
   ➢ Check the answer in the following pictures.

Activity ID	Activity Name	Act % Comp	Orig Dur	Rem Dur	Start	Finish	Total Float	Variance - BL Project Finish Date
Bid for Facility Extension								
Technical Specification								
0Z1000	Approval to Bid	100%	0d	0d	06-Dec-11 08 A			-1d
0Z1010	Determine Installation R...	100%	4d	0d	06-Dec-11 08 A	08-Dec-11 16 A		0d
0Z1020	Create Technical Specif...	60%	5d	6d	08-Dec-11 08 A	19-Dec-11 16	5d	-2d
0Z1030	Identify Supplier Compo...	0%	2d	2d	20-Dec-11 08	21-Dec-11 16	5d	-2d
0Z1040	Validate Technical Spe...	0%	2d	2d	22-Dec-11 08	23-Dec-11 16	7d	-2d
Delivery Plan								
0Z1050	Document Delivery Met...	0%	4d	4d	28-Dec-11 08	03-Jan-12 16	7d	-2d
0Z1060	Obtain Quotes from Sup...	0%	8d	8d	03-Jan-12 08*	12-Jan-12 16	0d	0d
0Z1070	Calculate the Bid Estimate	0%	3d	3d	13-Jan-12 08	16-Jan-12 16	0d	0d
0Z1080	Create the Project Sche...	0%	3d	3d	17-Jan-12 08	19-Jan-12 16	0d	0d
0Z1090	Review the Delivery Plan	0%	1d	1d	20-Jan-12 08	20-Jan-12 16	0d	0d
Bid Document								
0Z1100	Create Draft of Bid Doc...	0%	6d	6d	04-Jan-12 08	11-Jan-12 16	7d	-2d
0Z1110	Review Bid Document	0%	2d	2d	23-Jan-12 08	24-Jan-12 16	0d	0d
0Z1120	Finalise and Submit Bid ...	0%	2d	2d	25-Jan-12 08	26-Jan-12 16	0d	0d
0Z1130	Bid Document Submitted	0%	0d	0d		26-Jan-12 16*	0d	0d

Continued.....

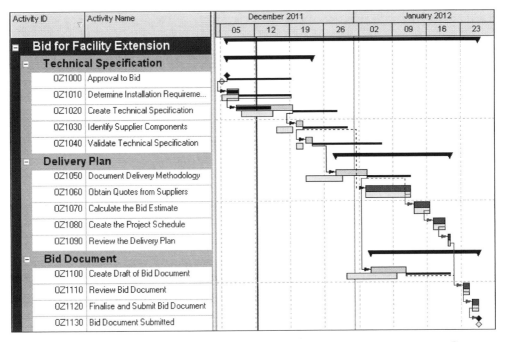

NOTE: The lower bar is the Baseline and delays to activities created by the late scheduling of the **Create Technical Specification** activity is clear in the picture above.

12. Open the **General tab** of the **Create Technical Specification** activity and change the % Complete Type to **Duration**. Reschedule and the **% Complete** will change to 0%. A link is now established between the % Complete and Remaining Duration and the % Complete and Remaining Duration may not be entered independently from the Activity % Complete. The Activity % Complete Value is zero because the Remaining Duration is greater than the original duration.

Activity ID	Activity Name	Act % Comp	Orig Dur	Rem Dur	December 2011
Bid for Facility Extension					
Technical Specification					
0Z1000	Approval to Bid	100%	0d	0d	
0Z1010	Determine Installation Requireme...	100%	4d	0d	
0Z1020	Create Technical Specification	0%	5d	6d	

13. Enter 20% Complete against the **Create Technical Specification** and you will notice the link between the Activity % Complete and Remaining Duration.

Activity ID	Activity Name	Act % Comp	Orig Dur	Rem Dur	December 2011
Bid for Facility Extension					
Technical Specification					
0Z1000	Approval to Bid	100%	0d	0d	
0Z1010	Determine Installation Requireme...	100%	4d	0d	
0Z1020	Create Technical Specification	20%	5d	4d	

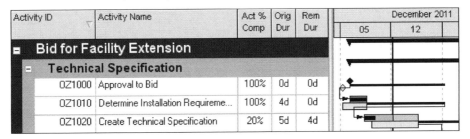

Continued.....

14. Now change the % Complete to 50%.
15. Reschedule.
16. Show the Duration Sub Unit of Hours by opening the **Edit, User Preferences…, Time Unit** tab and check the **Duration Format Sub-unit Hours** box and check **Show Unit label**.
17. This has resulted in the Remaining Duration no longer being whole days and now activities which are two days long now span three days.

Activity ID	Activity Name	Act % Comp	Orig Dur	Rem Dur	Start	Finish	Total Float	Variance - BL Project Finish Date
Bid for Facility Extension								
Technical Specification								
0Z1000	Approval to Bid	100%	0d	0d	06-Dec-11 08 A			-1d
0Z1010	Determine Installation …	100%	4d	0d	06-Dec-11 08 A	08-Dec-11 16 A		0d
0Z1020	Create Technical Spe…	50%	5d	2d 4h	08-Dec-11 08 A	14-Dec-11 12	8d 4h	1d 4h
0Z1030	Identify Supplier Comp…	0%	2d	2d	14-Dec-11 12	16-Dec-11 12	8d 4h	1d 4h
0Z1040	Validate Technical Sp…	0%	2d	2d	16-Dec-11 12	20-Dec-11 12	10d 4h	1d 4h
Delivery Plan								
0Z1050	Document Delivery M…	0%	4d	4d	20-Dec-11 12	28-Dec-11 12	10d 4h	1d 4h
0Z1060	Obtain Quotes from Su…	0%	8d	8d	03-Jan-12 08*	12-Jan-12 16	0d	0d
0Z1070	Calculate the Bid Esti…	0%	3d	3d	13-Jan-12 08	16-Jan-12 16	0d	0d
0Z1080	Create the Project Sch…	0%	3d	3d	17-Jan-12 08	19-Jan-12 16	0d	0d
0Z1090	Review the Delivery Pl…	0%	1d	1d	20-Jan-12 08	20-Jan-12 16	0d	0d
Bid Document								
0Z1100	Create Draft of Bid Do…	0%	6d	6d	28-Dec-11 12	06-Jan-12 12	10d 4h	1d 4h
0Z1110	Review Bid Document	0%	2d	2d	23-Jan-12 08	24-Jan-12 16	0d	0d
0Z1120	Finalise and Submit Bi…	0%	2d	2d	25-Jan-12 08	26-Jan-12 16	0d	0d
0Z1130	Bid Document Submitt…	0%	0d	0d		26-Jan-12 16*	0d	0d

18. This situation is often not desirable and may be prevented by using Physical % Complete and entering the remaining duration in whole days.

16 USER AND ADMINISTRATION PREFERENCES AND SCHEDULING OPTIONS

This chapter will look at the following topics:

- User Preferences,
- The Admin menu items,
- Admin Preferences, a multi tab form under the Admin menu,
- Advanced Scheduling Options, and
- Admin Categories.

16.1 User Preferences

Select **Edit**, **User Preferences…** to open the **User Preferences** form. This form is used to set up a number of user-defined parameters, which will determine how data is displayed.

The **User Preferences** form may also be opened by right-clicking in the right side of the bottom views when the **Resource Usage Spread Sheet** or **Resource Usage Profile** are being displayed.

16.1.1 Time Units Tab - Version 6.2 and Earlier

- The **Units Format** section of the tab is used to define the format of the **Unit of Time** that resource assignments are displayed with, e.g. days or hours.

- The **Durations Format** section of the tab is used to define the format of the **Unit of Time** that activity durations are displayed with, e.g. days or hours.

NOTE: The Units Format and Durations Format apply to every Layout, Window and project. These factors will have to be continually changed when there are a number of projects and a number of resource analysis layouts with different display requirements.

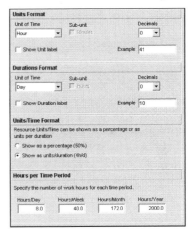

The **Units/Time Format** section of the form enables the Microsoft Project-type formatting options of **Resource/Time Format** to show Resource utilization as a percentage (50%) or as units per duration (4h/d).

The **Hours per Time Period** is an option new to Primavera Version 5.0 and removed in Version 7 enables the user, when assigned the rights, to specify how durations in days, week, months and years are calculated. The default setting and the option to enable users to set their own **Hours per Time Period** are set in the **Admin**, **Admin Preferences…**, **Time Periods** form.

16.1.2 Time Units Tab - Version 7

The **Units Format** section of the tab is used to define the format of the **Unit of Time** that resource assignments are displayed with, e.g. days or hours.

The **Durations Format** section of the tab is used to define the format of the **Unit of Time** that activity durations are displayed with, e.g. days or hours.

The **Units/Time Format** section of the form enables the Microsoft Project-type formatting options of **Resource/Time Format** to show Resource utilization as a percentage (50%) or as units per duration (4h/d).

16.1.3 Dates Tab

The **Dates** tab is self-explanatory and is used to format the display of dates and time.

NOTE: it is not possible to display the years with 2 characters or hide the year and there always has to be a date separator leading to wider date columns than otherwise could be achieved. It is also not possible to display the days in characters such as Mon or Monday.

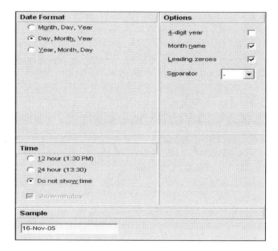

16.1.4 Currency Tab

The **Currency Options** tab selects the currency symbol used to display costs.

The **Currencies** form, available from the **Admin** menu item, is used to define the Base Currency. All costs are stored in the **Base Currency** and all other **Currencies** are calculated values using the **Base Currency** value and conversion rate.

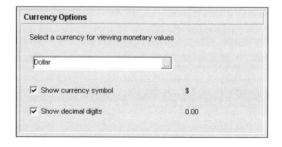

It is possible to have two currencies with the same symbol and if a User selects a different currency then all costs displayed by the user will be converted to a different value. This option must be carefully monitored and if you do not need multiple currencies then it is suggested that you should delete them all, to avoid any possible problems. If you are using multiple currencies then make sure that all have a different sign so there is no confusion.

16.1.5 E-Mail Tab

The **E-Mail Protocol** tab sets up the current user's e-mail system.

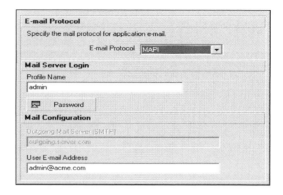

16.1.6 Assistance Tab

The **Assistance** tab specifies which Wizards are run when creating **Resources** and **Activities**.

NOTE: It is suggested to turn both off as it is quicker to type the information straight into the required fields when you know how to use the software.

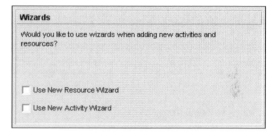

16.1.7 Application Tab

The **Application** tab:

- **Startup Window** specifies which dialog boxes are displayed when the software is started.
  - ➢ If you work in the same project all the time then set this to **Activities** and do not close the project when closing Primavera. The next time you open Primavera you will be take to your project in the Activities Window.
  - ➢ If you work in different projects all the time then select **Projects** and you will be taken to the **Projects Window**.
- **Application Log File** creates a log of all data entries titled ERRORS LOG. This would be used by support staff.

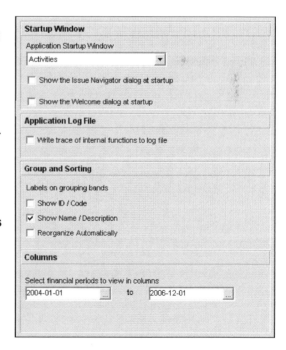

- **Group and Sorting** specifies what information is displayed in the bands; one or both options of Description or Code may be selected. This setting is effective in situations where a Group and Sort form is not available, such as the **Predecessor** and **Successors** forms.

- Primavera Version 5.0 introduced a function titled **Reorganize Automatically**, when the **Reorganize Automatically** box is checked, all views will reorganize automatically when data fields are changed that are used in the layout such as Grouping and Sorting. To reorganize a view when unchecked, select **Tools**, **Reorganize Now** or **Shift+F2**.

- **Columns** - Primavera Version 5.0 introduced **Financial Periods** and this is where the periods that may be displayed in columns is specified.

When many Financial Periods have been created and if you do not want to scroll down hundreds of rows to find a data field when searching for a column you should limit the number of Financial Periods that are displayed

16.1.8   Password Tab

The **User Password** tab is used to change the user password.

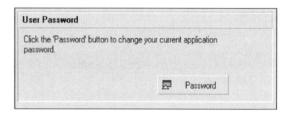

16.1.9   Resource Analysis Tab

The **Resource Analysis** tab has two sections:

- The **All Projects** option specifies which projects are used to calculate the Resources Remaining Values in **Resource Usage Profiles**.

- **Time-Distributed Data**.
  - ➢ It is possible to drag a project forward or backwards in time in the **Tracking Window** or **Portfolio Analysis**. This action creates a new set of dates titled **Forecast** dates. The **Resource Usage Profile** and **Resource Usage Spreadsheet** may be calculated using either the Current Schedule by checking **Remaining Early Dates** or the revised **Forecast Dates**.

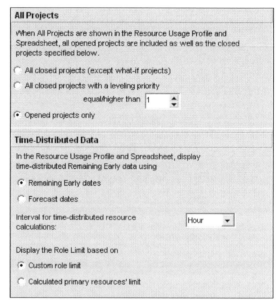

- ➢ **Interval for time-distributed calculations:** This option determines the time increment for displaying the Resource Usage Profile and Resource Usage Spreadsheet data.
- ➢ **Display the Role limit based on** – Primavera introduces **Role Limits** in Version 6.0 and this enables options for displaying the **Role Limits** in **Resource Profiles**.

The **Interval for time-distributed calculations:** must be equal to or smaller than the timescale or the resource data will be displayed in the first time increment of the timescale and not distributed over the whole time period.

16.1.10 Calculations Tab

IT IS IMPORTANT TO UNDERSTAND THIS OPTION.

The **Calculations** tab has two options:

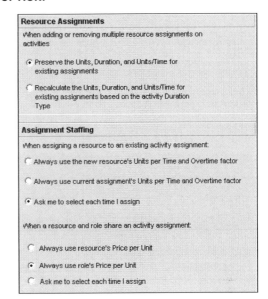

- **Preserve the Units, Duration, and Units/Time for existing assignments**. With this option, as Resources are added or deleted the total number of hours assigned to an Activity increases or decreases. The hours assigned for each resource are calculated independently.

- **Recalculate the Units, Duration, and Units/Time for existing assignments based on the activity Duration Type**. The total number of hours assigned to an activity will stay constant as second and subsequent resources are added or removed from an Activity, except when the Activity Type is **Fixed Duration and Units/Time**.

This is similar to making an activity Effort Driven in Microsoft Project. There is no similar function in P3 and SureTrak.

Note: This function does not work when the Activity Type is **Fixed Duration and Units/Time**.

- **Assignment Staffing** are new functions to Primavera Version 5.0 options available on the **Calculations** tab of the **User Options** form allowing the user to set the defaults for:
  - ➢ Selecting the Units per Time when assigning a substitute resource to an existing resource assignment.
  - ➢ Selecting the Price per Unit for a resource which is being assigned to a Role.

The options are to select the existing resource, the new resource or to be prompted each time a resource/role is substituted.

16.1.11 Setup Filters Tab

The **Setup Filters** option enables the selection of filters for Resources, Roles, OBS, Activity Codes and Cost Accounts, which may be applied to the current project or to all data.

You may find when you open up a window such as the Resources window and no data is displayed. This is due to the settings in this tab.

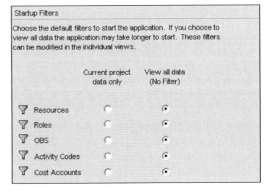

16.2   Admin Menu

The links between Users, OBS and Projects is covered in more detail in the **Managing the Enterprise Environment** chapter.

The **Admin** command opens the **Admin** form.

Depending on how Primavera has been installed and your access rights set, you may or may not have access to all these menus.

16.2.1   Users

The **Users** form is used to add and delete system users. The following information may be recorded:

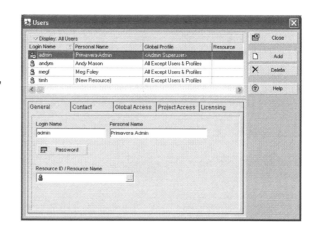

- **General** tab: The Personal Name (the person's name), Login Name, Password and the Users Resource ID in the Resources Window.

- **Contact** tab: The person's telephone number and e-mail.

- **Global Access** tab: The Global information a user may change is specified here by assigning a **Global Profile**.

NOTE: The resources a user may see in the **Resource Window** is set in this specifies here.

- **Project Access** tab: This is where the **User** is assigned to one or more OBS Nodes and may only access Projects associated with those OBS Nodes and access to is projects controlled by the **Security Profile**.

- **Licensing** tab: This is where a person is assigned a license. A license needs to be assigned before the person may operate the system.

The User may also be assigned to an OBS Node in the **Organizational Breakdown Structure** form.

16.2.2 Security Profiles

The **Security Profiles** form is used to set up security.

- **Global Profile** and **Project Profiles** may be established in this form.

- **Global Profiles are** created and/or edited to enable access to specific Enterprise functions and are assigned to users.

- **Project Profiles** are created and/or edited to enable access to specific Project functions.

- A **Project Profile** is assigned to a user when they are assigned to one or more **Organization Breakdown Structure** Nodes.

- A different **Project Profile** may be assigned to a user for different OBS Nodes and Projects are assigned to one OBS Node

16.2.3 Currencies

The **Currencies** form is used to define system currencies. Currency fields are:

- **Currency ID**
- **Currency Name**
- **Currency Symbol**
- **Exchange Rate**

To make the Base currency into your countries currency you will need to edit the **Currency ID** and **Currency Symbol** as the first currency is permanently checked.

NOTE: See the warning under the Currency earlier in this chapter. Delete all unwanted currencies and make all Currency Symbols Unique.

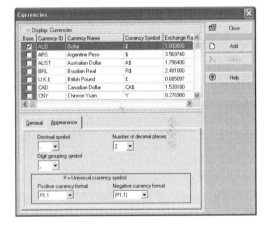

16.2.4 Financial Periods

This is where the Financial Periods associated with Storing Period Performance are created.

For details on this function see the section on Store Period Performance in the **Updating a Resourced Schedule** chapter.

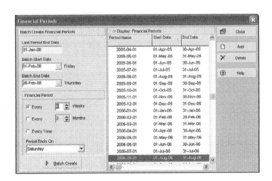

16.2.5 Purge Deletes

This function removes all deleted data from the database and was removed from the Admin menu in Version 6.0 . Deleted data was read by some external applications resulting in incorrect data reading.

16.2.6 Timesheet Dates

The **Timesheet Periods** are chosen in the **Timesheet Dates Administration** form.

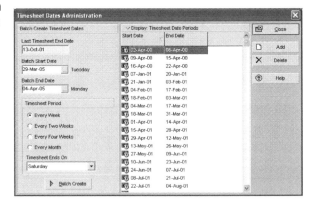

16.3 Miscellaneous Defaults

16.3.1 Default Project

Select **Set Default Project...** from the **Project** menu to open the **Set Default Project** form. When multiple projects are opened the default project's settings are used to:

- Schedule and level all open projects.

- New data items, such as issues, are assigned to the default project when they are added to the database.

 When multiple projects are scheduled all the scheduling options of all the projects are changed to the **Default Project**. This is issue must be well thought through by the Database Administrator and is covered in more detail in the **Multiple Project Scheduling** chapter.

16.3.2 Set Language

Select **Tools**, **Set Language...** to open the **Set Language** form and select the language that the column headers and menu items are displayed in.

16.4 Admin Preferences

This form sets the default preferences for Primavera.

The **Admin Preferences** form has a number of tabs, which will be covered in more detail in the next section of this chapter.

If you do not have access to the **Admin Preferences**, then these options would have been set up by the system administrator for your organization.

Some preferences may only be changed in this form. Items described as **defaults** may be changed in other Windows.

Select **Admin**, **Admin Preferences…** to open the **Admin Preferences** form.

Click on the [✎ Wizard] button to run the **Admin Preferences Wizard**, which will assist in the setting up of the essential Administrators preferences.

16.4.1 General Tab

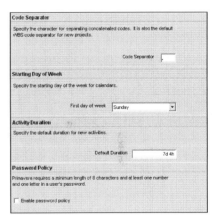

- **Code Separator** sets the default separator for new project WBS Codes and other codes such as Cost Accounts.
- **Starting Day of the Week** sets the day of the week that is shown on the timescale and the left column of calendars.
- **Activity Duration** sets the default duration for new activities.
- **Password Policy** introduced in Version 6.2 and allows the requirement for a password of a minimum of 8 characters including a letter and number.

16.4.2 Timesheets Tab

The **Timesheets** tab enables specification of the default setup options when **Timesheets** are being used and is beyond the scope of this publication. There are two sections:

- **Entering Timesheets**
- **Timesheet Approval Level**

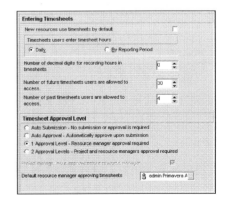

16.4.3 Timesheet Privileges Tab

The **Timesheet Privileges** tab is beyond the scope of this publication. It has two sections:

- **Default time window to access activities**
- **Privileges for logging hours on timesheets**

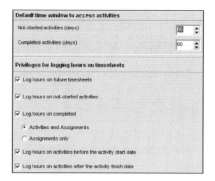

16.4.4 Data Limits Tab

The **Data Limits** tab specifies:

- The maximum number of levels allowed in all hierarchical code structures,
- The maximum number of Activity Codes per project, and
- The maximum number of Baselines per project.

Primavera Version 6.0 added the **Maximum baselines copied with project**.

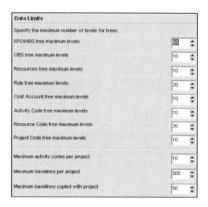

16.4.5 ID Lengths Tab

The **ID Lengths** tab specifies the maximum number of characters in the Code ID fields, not the Code Description.

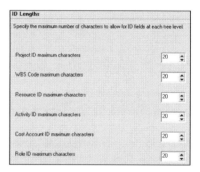

16.4.6 Time Periods Tab

- **Hours per Time Period** values are used to convert from one time period Unit to another, for example, from days to hours. Therefore, a 5-day activity would be calculated as 40 hours with the setting displayed in the picture.

- **NOTE:** It is important that these conversions are understood, please refer to the **Calendar** chapter for more details.

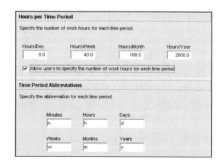

- Checking **Allow users to specify the number of work hours for each time period** enables users to edit the **Hours per Time Period** in the **Edit, User Preferences…, Time Units** form.
- **Time Period Abbreviations** are used to indicate the display durations.

16.4.7 Earned Value Tab

This tab sets the defaults for calculating Earned Value and may be changed for each WBS.

- The **Technique for computing performance percent complete** selects the formula for calculating the Earned Value.

- The **Technique for computing Estimate to Complete (ETC)** selects the formula for calculating the ETC. The ETC is a calculated field and is independent of the **At Completion Fields** but may contain the same value.

- **Earned Value Calculations** selects some options for calculating the Earned Value.

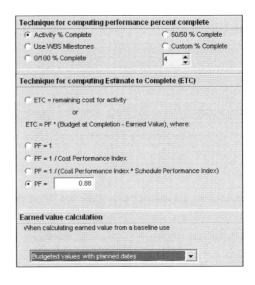

16.4.8 Reports Tab

The **Report Headers and Footers** form sets the default labels for reports.

These may also be accessed in printouts.

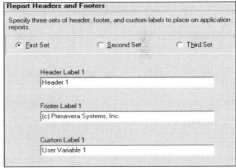

16.4.9 Options Tab

- The **Specify the interval to summarize and store resource spreads** tab sets the time period, such as week or month, for storing summarized activity data at WBS and Resource/Role Assignment Levels.

- The **Project Architect** check box enables the use of Project Architect to import methodologies.

- **Purge Deletes** removes data from the database that the **Undo** function could restore when exiting the system. (Removed in Version 6.0)

- Primavera **Web Access Server URL** is required to allow access to timesheet approval and the web server.

- **Link to Contract Management Module** (originally called Expedition) enable linking to this module when installed.

16.4.10 Rate Types Tab

Primavera has five resource rates types and the **Resource Rate Types** form enables you to rename the titles of the rates. You may have, for example, rates for:

- Internal consulting,
- External consulting,
- Preparing evidence, and
- Giving evidence.

16.5 Scheduling Options

When a project is rescheduled there are some options available in the **Schedule Options** form which is opened by selecting **Tools, Schedule...,** ▷ Options... .

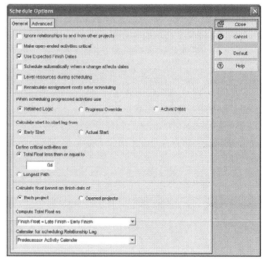

16.5.1 General Tab

- **Ignore relationships to and from other projects** – Check this to ignore relationships with other projects that are currently not open. These relationships may be created between two projects when two or more projects are opened together. This option will also ignore **External Dates**; which are the **External Early Start** and **External Late Finish** dates. These are constraints created when a project is exported from a Primavera Contractor and/or another P5/6 database and imported P6. They act like Early Start and Late Finish Constraints and are used to represent the relationships that would provide the Early Start and Late Finish dates to the CPM calculations of the imported schedule. These dates can be very confusing if one is not aware that they have been created or how they operate. The negative float in the picture below is created by these dates after an activities duration was increased by 34 days:

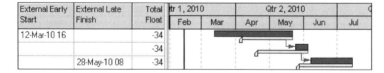

- **Make open-ended activities critical** – An open-ended activity is an activity without a successor and which has float to the end of the project. Checking the box makes these activities critical with zero total float when they do not have a successor.

- **Use Expected Finish Dates** – Expected finish dates may be chosen in the Timesheets; check this box to use this date to calculate the activity finish date. This is always checked by default. This option will also disable or enable Expected Finish constraints assigned in the **Status** tab of the **Activities Details** tab.

- **Schedule automatically when a change affects dates** – This is similar to automatic recalculation in other products. It recalculates the schedule when data that affects the timing of the schedule is changed.

- **Level resources during scheduling** – This levels the project resources each time it is scheduled. **NOTE:** Not recommended as it can take a lot of time to execute.

- **Recalculate resource costs after scheduling** – This option recalculates resource costs after scheduling. Use this option when resources are assigned rates in the **Units & Prices** tab of the **Resources Window** which change over time.

- **When scheduling progressed activities use** –This decides how original logic applies to the remaining work of a partially completed activity with an incomplete predecessor. There are three options for calculating this relationship:
  - ➢ **Retained Logic**
  - ➢ **Progress Override**
  - ➢ **Actual Dates**

  Refer to the **Tracking Progress** chapter paragraph on **Retained Logic and Progress Override in the** for further details.

- **Calculate start-to-start lag from** – The successor of an activity with a Start-to-Start and positive lag would start after the lag has expired. When the predecessor commences out of sequence the lag may be calculated from the predecessor calculated Early Start or the Actual start.

  - ➢ The Actual Start gives a less conservative schedule:

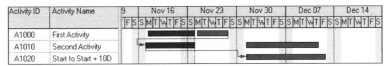

  - ➢ The Early Start gives a more conservative schedule:

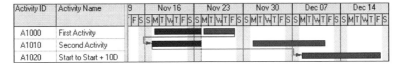

- **Define critical activities as**. These options are used for analyzing schedules that utilize multiple calendars which may result in activities on the critical path possessing float.

  - ➢ **Total Float less than or equal to** – Activities may be marked as critical and with a chosen float value. Sometimes a small positive value is used to isolate the near critical activities on schedules or displaying the full critical path on multiple calendar schedules.
  - ➢ **Longest Path** – This option isolates the longest chain of activities in a schedule and should be used when multiple calendars are in use and some activities which form part of the critical path still have float when the successor is assigned a calendar with fewer or different working days.

- **Calculate float based on either** – This is a new function to Version 6.2. When more than one project is opened the Total Float may be calculated based on each individual project or the longest project, see the **Multiple Project Scheduling** chapter in the **Administrators Workshop** book for more details.

- **Compute Total Float as** – There are three options for this calculation:
  - ➢ Start Float = Late Start – Early Start
  - ➢ Finish Float = Late Finish – Early Finish
  - ➢ Smallest of Start Float and Finish Float

  The computed value may be different with Level of Effort Activities, but Finish Float is normally used.

- **Calendar for scheduling Relationship Lag** – There are four calendar options for the calculation of the lag for all activities:
    1. **Successor Activity Calendar** is the default, or
    2. **Predecessor Activity** Calendar, or
    3. **24 Hour,** or
    4. **Project Default Calendar**.

 P3 and SureTrak use the predecessor calendar and Microsoft Project 2000 and 2002 uses the Project Base calendar and Microsoft Project 2003 to 2007 use the successor calendar. Microsoft Project also has the option of an Elapsed lag duration. Asta Powerproject does not assign lags to the relationship but a relationship may have a lag on the predecessor activity and a lag on the successor activity.

- **Default** – Reapplies the Primavera default settings.

16.5.2 Advanced Tab

This tab selects the options for calculating multiple critical paths and is covered in detail in the **Utilities** chapter.

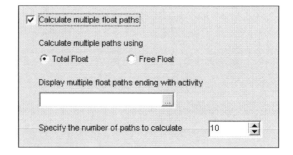

16.6 Admin Categories

The **Admin**, **Admin Categories** form is where the global data items are defined. This form is self-explanatory and will not be explained in detail. The following categories are defined:

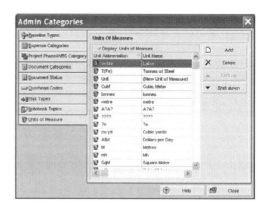

- Baseline Types
- Expense Categories
- Project Phase/WBS Categories
- Document Categories
- Document Status
- Overhead Codes
- Risk Types
- Notebook Topics
- Units of Measure

The Baseline Type allow a predefined set of codes that may be assigned to WBS Nodes allowing the WBS structure to be reorganized under a different set of codes.

17 CREATING ROLES AND RESOURCES

Traditionally, planning and scheduling software defines a **Resource** as something or someone that is required to complete the activity and sometimes has limited availability. This includes people or groups of people, materials, equipment and money.

Primavera is able to assign Costs, a Calendar, one or more Roles and some personal information to a **Resource**.

Primavera a has a function titled **Roles**. A Role is normally used at the planning stage of a project and represents a skill or position. Later, and before the activity begins, a Role would be filled by assigning a specific individual who would be defined as a resource. Roles may be assigned to both Resources and Activities. A search by Role may be conducted on all the Resources when it is required to replace an Activity Assigned Role with an individual from the Resource pool. Primavera allows rates to be assigned to Roles.

There are a large number of resource functions available in Primavera. Without getting into too much detail, this publication will outline the important resource-related functions that will enable you to create and assign Roles and Resources to your schedules.

This chapter will concentrate on:

Topic	Menu Command
Creating **Roles**	Select **Enterprise**, **Roles...** to open the **Roles** form.
Creating **Resources**	Open the **Resources Window**: • Select **Enterprise**, **Resources**, or • Click on the ▣ button on the **Directory** toolbar, or • Select **Resources** from the **Home** Window.
Editing **Resource Calendars**	Select **Enterprise**, **Calendars...** to open the **Calendars** form.

The following steps should be followed to create and use resources in a Primavera schedule:

- Create the resources in the **Resource Window**.
- Create the **Roles**, if required, in the **Roles** form.
- Assign Resources to Roles from either the **Resource Window** or the **Roles** form.
- Manipulate the Resource Calendars if resources have special timing requirements.
- Assign resources to Activities and review the resource loading.

17.1 Understanding Resources

There are typically two methods of using the Resource function for resource planning:

- Individual Resources, and
- Group Resources

17.1.1 Individual Resources

These resources are individual people who are often responsible for completing the activity or tasks associated with activities to which they have been assigned.

This is typically work undertaken in an office environment, such as an IT development project, where timesheets are often completed by the people undertaking the work and the timesheet system is directly linked to the scheduling system.

In this situation, the updating of Activities that are in-progress is completed by the person assigned as a Resource to an Activity, often via the timesheet system, and the scheduler has a review function in the project updating.

17.1.2 Group Resources

These resources represent groups of people, such as trades or disciplines on a construction site. On very large projects gangs or crews, which would be made up of equipment and a number of different trades, could also be considered. The person responsible for the work is not a resource assigned to an activity and individual people doing the work will not be assigning their timesheets directly to activities in the schedule.

Also, in this environment the scheduler normally updates the activities and the resources. In this situation it is recommended that a minimum number of resources be assigned to activities. This is because every resource added to the schedule will need to be updated and as more resources are added, the scheduler's workload will increase.

Resource minimization simplifies a schedule and makes it easier to manage large schedules. This is achieved by not cluttering the schedule with resources that are in plentiful supply or are of little importance, and by grouping trades or disciplines into crews and gangs on large projects.

When Group Resources are used the Role function tends to become redundant but could be used to plan the contractor type or the actual contractor that is planned to be used on the project.

17.1.3 Input and Output Resources

When you create your resources, you may also consider them within the context of the following headings:

- **Input Resources** – These resources are required to complete the work and represent the project costs:
  - ➢ Individual people by name.
  - ➢ Groups of people by trade, discipline or skill.
  - ➢ Individual equipment or machinery by name.
  - ➢ Groups of equipment or machinery by type.
  - ➢ Groups of resources such as Crews, Gangs or Teams made up of equipment and machinery.
  - ➢ Materials.
  - ➢ Money.

- **Output Resources** – These could be the project deliverables or outcomes and could have a direct relationship to the project income:
  - ➢ Specifications completed.
  - ➢ Bricks laid.
  - ➢ Tonnes of material loaded with an excavator.
  - ➢ Lines of code written.
  - ➢ Tests completed.

  This type of resource is often used in the mining environment where the output in tones/tonnes or volume is scheduled and/or leveled.

The analysis of and difference between the Input and the Output resources' value and timing may be used to represent the Cash Flow, Cash Position and Project Profit (or loss).

The type of contract that the work is being conducted under would often determine if the client is more interested in the Input or Output Resources.

17.2 Creating Roles

Roles are created, edited and deleted in a similar method as WBS's.

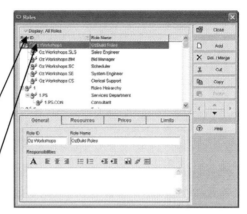

To create, edit or delete a **Role** select **Enterprise**, **Roles...** to open the **Roles** form:

The following formatting, filtering and sorting functions are available in the **Roles** form:

- Click on **Display: All Roles** and then the **Filter By** tab to open a menu where the roles can be filtered by **All Roles** or **Current Projects Roles**.

- Click on the **Role ID** title or the **Role Name** title to sort the Roles by **Role ID** or **Role Name.**

- **Roles** may also be displayed by the **Chart View**. The **Roles** form will have to be resized to use this function effectively.

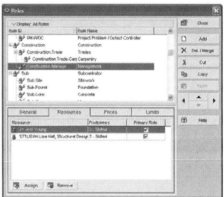

- The **Find** function (or Ctrl+F) enables a Role name to be searched.

- The **Print** function opens the **Print Preview** form allowing the printing of the current list of Roles.

In the **General** tab each Role may be assigned:

- **Role ID**, a code used to assign the Role to an Activity.
- **Role Name**, the Name of the Skill or Trade.
- **Responsibilities**, where you may enter text, hyperlinks and pictures about the Role Responsibility.

In the **Resources** tab each Role may be assigned:

- To one or more Resources.
- The Resource is assigned by default a **Proficiency** of "3-Skilled" which may then be changed to any of the options shown in the list.
- The Resource may be assigned a **Primary Role** which would represent the task or job they would normally be assigned.

Primavera supports **Rates for Roles**. Up to 5 rates (the same number of rates as resources) may be assigned to roles which may be used for estimating and cash flow forecasting of projects before the actual resource completing the work is assigned to the activity. Click on the **Prices** tab to edit the Role Price/Unit. **NOTE:** These may not be varied over time but Resources may be.

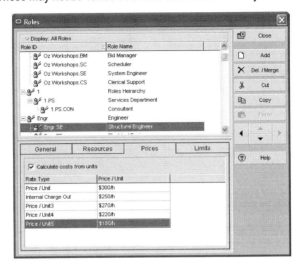

All data columns in this form may be sorted by clicking on the column titles.

The default rate for a project is selected when a project is created and may be changed in the **Projects Window**, **Resources** tab, **Assignment Details** area:

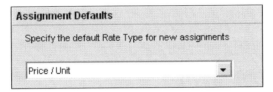

Different rates may be required for different clients such as an internal project rates and rates for different types of external clients.

 Five resource and role rates may not be sufficient when a company has a number of clients. There are some options which include creating a new set of resources for each project or a new database for each project or not selecting the option of linking costs and units and manually assigning the rate for each resource in each project.

17.3 Creating Resources and the Resources Window

To create, edit or delete resources open the **Resources** Window:

- Select **Enterprise**, **Resources...**, or
- Click on the button on the **Directory** toolbar, or
- Select **Resources** from the **Home Window**.

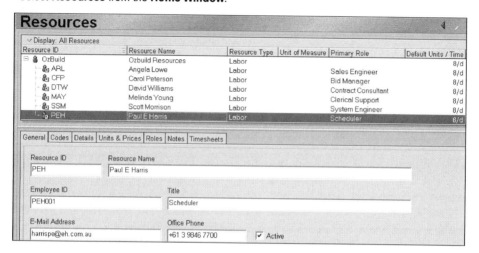

17.3.1 Resource Breakdown Structure - RBS

Resources may be added and organized hierarchically in a similar method to creating a WBS.

The OzBuild resources in the picture above are listed under a higher-level node titled **OzBuild Resources**. Primavera Systems calls this structure a **Resource Breakdown Structure** or **RBS**.

17.3.2 Formatting the Resources Window

The menu under the **Display: All Resources** has many functions that are similar to other forms:

- The **Details** check box displays or hides the **Details** form in the lower pane.

- **Chart View** displays the resources as a Chart. To use this format **Group and Sort By** must be set as **Default** or have the **Customize...** option grouped by Resources.

- **Columns**, **Table Font and Row...**, **Filter By** and **Group and Sort By** options work in a similar way to the formatting of the **Activities Window**. Click on the menus to see the options available with each.

- When the **Resources** are organized hierarchically, the **Expand All** and **Collapse All** options work in a similar way to other Windows and rolls up the Resources.

17.3.3 Adding Resources

New Resources are added and deleted in a similar method to adding Activities in the **Activity** Window. Use the **Insert** key, right-click and select **Add**, or use the **Command** toolbar by clicking on the button.

17.3.4 General Tab

The fields in this tab are self-explanatory:

- The **Resource ID** and **Resource Name** are mandatory,
- The **Employee ID**, **E-Mail Address**, **Title** and **Office Phone** are optional, and
- When the **Active** box is unchecked, the Resource is inactive and indicates that the resource is not available. When assigning Resources to Activities there is a filter to display only active Resources.

17.3.5 Codes Tab

Resource Codes are assigned to Resources allowing additional facilities to sort and report on them in the **Resource Usage Spreadsheet**:

- **Resource Codes** may be defined in the **Resource Code Definition** form, which is opened by selecting **Enterprise**, **Resource Codes…** and clicking on the [Modify…] button.
- Individual **Resource Code Values** may be added to a **Resource Code** in the **Resource Codes** form by selecting **Enterprise**, **Resource Codes…**.
- Resource Codes may then be selected in a layout to sort and group Resources.

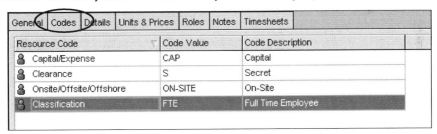

17.3.6 Details Tab

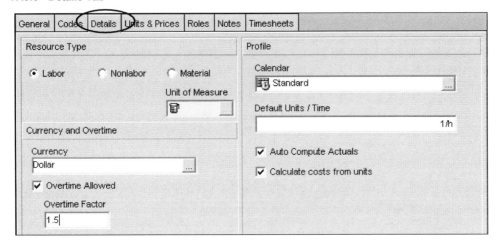

Resource Types

There are three types of Resource:

- **Labor**, intended for people
- **Nonlabor**, intended for equipment used to perform project work
- **Material**, intended for materials/supplies.

Material Resources may be leveled and have the following differences from other resources:

- They may be assigned a **Unit of Measure**, which is created in the **Admin**, **Admin Categories...**, **Unit of Measure** tab. This is not available to Labor and Nonlabor resources.
- They may not be assigned a Role.
- They may not log Overtime.

Currency

An alternative **Currency** may be associated with a resource. This will not affect how the Resource Unit Rates costs are entered but provides a further tagging mechanism for sorting and reporting. The costs are stored in the default currency but are displayed using the conversion rate in the currency selected for the resource.

Overtime

A **Labor Resource** may be allowed to record **Overtime** in the **Primavera timesheet** system when the **Overtime** box is checked and the costs derived from the **Unit Rates** are multiplied by the **Overtime** Factor.

Calendar

The Resource is assigned a **Global** or **Resource Calendar** in this form. Unlike Microsoft Project, P3 and SureTrak, each resource does not by default have its own calendar. A Resource Calendar may be created and assigned to more than one Resource. This topic is covered in more detail in the next section of this chapter.

NOTE: This calendar is used to display the resource limits.

Default Units/Time

The **Default Units/Time** is the value that a resource adopts when it is first assigned to an activity. In a similar way to Microsoft Project, the **Units per Time Period** may be displayed as a **Percentage** or in **Units/Time**.

- Select **Edit**, **User Preferences**, **Time Units** tab and select the preferred display from the **Units/Time Format** section:

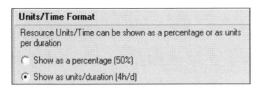 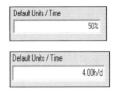

Resource and Activity Auto Compute Actuals

When this option is checked, Primavera calculates the Actual Units and Remaining Units using the Budgeted Units and Activity % Complete. When unchecked, the work for this resource may be read from the Primavera Timesheet system or manually entered.

There are several places where the Resource **Auto Compute Actuals** field in Primavera is displayed:

- Against each resource in the **Resources Window**, **Details** tab,
- In a column in the **Resources Window**, when displayed, and
- Against each resource after it has been assigned to an activity and is displayed in the **Resources** tab of the bottom window in the **Activities Window**.

The option may only be switched on or off in the **Resources Window**.

The Activity **Auto Compute Actuals** field may be displayed as a column. When this option is checked, all Resources Auto Compute Actuals irrespective of how they are checked in the **Resources Window**.

Calculate Costs from Units

With this option checked, the costs for a resource are calculated from the **Resource Unit/Time** when a resource is assigned to an activity. When unchecked, the costs remain at zero when a resource is assigned to an activity.

When a resource has been assigned to an activity, there is a Resource Assignment field available in the Resources tab of the **Activities Window** titled **Cost Units Linked**. This is checked to match the **Calculate Costs from Units** field in the **Resources Window**.

The **Activities Window** field titled **Cost Units Linked** is not linked to the **Calculate Costs from Units** field in the **Resources Window** and only adopts the setting when a resource is assigned to an Activity.

The following picture shows a resource with the **Cost Units Linked** field unchecked; therefore, the costs are not calculated from the **Resource Unit Rate**.

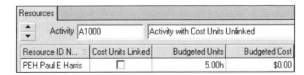

17.3.7 Units and Prices Tab

Effective Date and Rates

Each Resource may have up to five rates (Price/Unit) and these rates may be varied over time.

- To display the other rates their columns should be displayed.
- The Column Titles may have their description formatted to suit their intended purpose.
- When a rate is added the effective date is the date from which the rate is applied.

Shifts

Resource Shifts are used when leveling and should not be assigned unless they are being used. **Resource Shifts** will are covered in the **Leveling** chapter:

- **Resource Shifts** are created in the **Resource Shifts** form which is opened by selecting **Enterprise**, **Resource Shifts...**,
- The **Resource Shifts** and the number of shifts a resource works is assigned in the **Units and Prices** tab, **Shifts Calendar:**.

17.3.8 Roles Tab

- A Resource may be assigned more than one role, and their **Proficiency** for the Role, in this tab.
- When multiple Roles are assigned, one is assigned as the **Primary Role**.

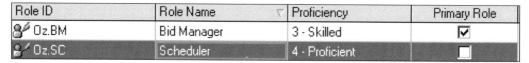

Role ID	Role Name	Proficiency	Primary Role
Oz.BM	Bid Manager	3 - Skilled	☑
Oz.SC	Scheduler	4 - Proficient	☐

17.3.9 Notes Tab

Notes may be added here in the similar way as with Activities but there are no Notebook topics available.

17.3.10 Timesheets Tab

Originally called **Progress Reporter** tab, when Timesheets are implemented, the user must be added as a system user in **Admin**, **Users...**, **Users** form where he or she is also assigned to a Resource, thus providing the link from the timesheet user to the Primavera resource. This was covered in the **Admin Menu**, **Users** section.

For timesheets to operate, the **Uses Timesheets** box in the **Progress Details** tab must also be checked and the **Timesheet Approval Manager** selected.

17.4 Editing Resource Calendars

Each resource when created is assigned a **Resource Calendar** inherited from the resource that is highlighted when it is created.

- The resource calendar is acknowledged when the **Activity Type** is set to **Resource Dependent** in the **Activities Window**, **General** tab.
- The resource calendar is always used to display the resource availability in Resource Spreadsheets and Resource Profiles.

Select **Enterprise**, **Calendars...** to open the Calendar form.

- **Resource Calendars** are edited the same way as other calendars.
- A **Resource Calendar** may be assigned to more than one resource or a resource may be assigned its own calendar.
- It is important to create a coding system for Resource Calendars to easily identify shared and individual Resource Calendars. This guarantees that the edits to calendars may be made with confidence and that the edits will affect the intended resources.

17.5   Workshop 14 - Adding Resources to the Database

Background

This workshop will only use Resources and these must now be added to the database.

We have updated our current project, but we need an project that has not been updated for the next task of assigning resources. Therefore, we will have to restore a copy of the Baseline schedule saved prior to updating the current schedule to provide an unprogressed schedule for this exercise.

NOTE: If you are working in a database with other people completing this workshop then each persons' Resource ID will have to be unique, say by adding your Initials at the end of each Resource ID. A training course leader or database administrator should advise here.

Assignment

1. Select **Project**, **Assign Baselines...**and remove all project Baselines by setting the Baselines to the <Current Project>.
2. Restore the project using **Project**, **Maintain Baselines...**.
3. Go to the Projects window where the restored baseline file will be visible.
4. Rename the restored Baseline project **Bid for Facility Extension - Resourced Schedule** and change the Project ID to **OZB-R**.
   NOTE: Users sharing a database will need to use unique Project IDs.
5. Open the restored project.
6. Open the **User Preferences** form, set the **Calculations** and **Time Units** tab as per in the following picture.

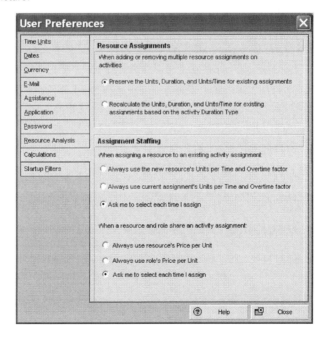

Continued.....

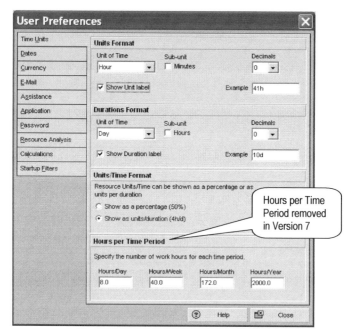

7. Now open the **Resource Window**.

8. If no resources are displayed then select all resources from the Display Resources menu:

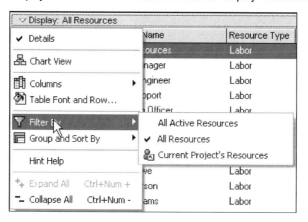

9. Format the columns in the Resources window as in the following picture.

Continued...

10. Add the resources as in the following picture:

NOTE: If you are working in a database with other people completing this workshop then each persons' Resource ID will have to be unique, say by adding your Initials at the end of each Resource ID.

Resource ID	Resource Name	Resource Type	Price / Unit	Unit of Measure
☐ 👤 OBR	OzBuild resources	Labor	$0/h	
👤 PM	Project Manager	Labor	$120/h	
👤 SE	Systems Engineer	Labor	$90/h	
👤 PS	Project Support	Labor	$80/h	
👤 PO	Purchasing Officer	Labor	$70/h	
👤 CS	Clerical Support	Labor	$50/h	
🔶 RB	Report Binding	Material	$100/ea	Each

11. You may need to use the arrows to move the resources to the correct indent location.
12. Set the **Default Units/Time** to 8 hours per day for all the resources.
13. Set the calendar for all resources to be the **Standard 5 Day Workweek**.
14. Check **Calculate Costs from units** and **Auto compute actuals** for each resource.

18 ASSIGNING ROLES, RESOURCES AND EXPENSES

During the planning stage, **Roles** may be assigned to Activities to gain an understanding of the resources requirements and they are later replaced by a **Resource** when it is known who will be undertaking the work. A Resource may be assigned:

- Directly to an Activity, or
- To a Role which has been assigned to an Activity.

There are three types of resources, **Labor**, **Nonlabor** and **Material**, and as discussed in the previous chapter. A Labor Resource has additional functionality including Overtime, Resource Calendars, Shifts and user-defined Autocost rules. The **Labor** and **Nonlabor** resources are similar to the Microsoft Project **Work Resources**. A **Material** resource is similar to Microsoft Project **Material Resources**.

Primavera also has a function titled **Expenses**, where costs may be assigned to activities without resources and may be assigned a quantity and the default quantity is one. This function is similar to the **Costs** function in Microsoft Project but with far more functionality. As the project progresses Actual and To Complete Units and Costs may be assigned to Expenses in the same way as resources.

This chapter will cover the following topics:

- Understanding Resource Calculations and Terminology
- Project and Activity Window Resource and Role Preferences
- Details Status Form
- Activity Types and Duration Types
- Assigning and Removing Roles and Assigning Resources
- Resource and Activity Duration Calculation and Resource Lags
- Expenses
- Suggested Setup for Assigning Resources

Topic	Menu Commands
• Set **Units/Time Format** and **Resource Assignments**	Select **Edit**, **User Preferences…** to open the **User Preferences** form and select the **Time Units** tab and **Calculations** tab.
• Set **Default Duration Type** and **Default Activity Type**	Set these defaults in the **Defaults** tab in the **Projects Window**.
• Assign a **Role** to an Activity	Select the **Resources** tab in the **Activity Details** form and Click on the [Add Role] button to open the **Assign Roles** form.
• To assign a **Resource** to a **Role** that has been assigned to an activity	Select the Role to be assigned a Resource from the **Resources Details** tab and click the [Assign by Role] button to open the **Assign Resources By Roles** form.
• To assign a **Resource** to an activity without a **Role**	Select the Activity to be assigned the Resource and click the [Add Resource] button to open the **Assign Resource** form.

18.1 Understanding Resource Calculations and Terminology

A Resource has three principal components after it has been assigned to an Activity:

- **Quantity**, in terms of **Work** in hours or days or **Material** quantities required to complete the activity, which are referred to as **Units** by Primavera,
- The **Resource Unit Rate** is termed **Price/Unit** in Primavera and
- **Cost**, which is calculated from the **Resource Unit Rate** x **Units**.

Each Resource and Expense has the same four fields for **Costs** and **Units**: **Budget**, **Remaining**, **Actual** and **At Completion**. The relationship among these fields changes depending on whether the activity is Not Started, In-Progress or Complete.

- When an activity is Not Started and the % Complete is zero then:
  - ➢ **Budget** may be linked to **Remaining** and **At Completion** and therefore a change to one will change the other two and they will always be equal, and
  - ➢ **Actual** will be zero.
- When the activity is marked Started and would normally be In-Progress and the % Complete is between 1% and 99% then:
  - ➢ **Budget** becomes unlinked from **Remaining** and **At Completion**, thus allowing progress and the **At Completion** value to be compared to the **Budget**, and
  - ➢ **At Completion** = **Actual** + **Remaining** and have a link to **% Complete** and a change value to one will result in a change to other values.
- When the activity is Complete and the % Complete is 100% then:
  - ➢ **Remaining** is set to zero, and
  - ➢ **At Completion** = **Actual**.

In summary, the Budget values for Costs and Units are linked to the At Completion values until:

- An Activity has been marked as Started or has a % Complete, or
- The **Link Budget and At Completion for not started activities** in the **Project Window Calculations** tab is unchecked, see the following picture.

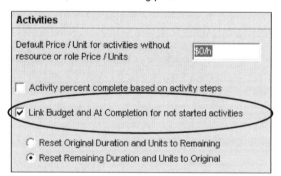

One would normally unlink **Budget and At Completion** when a project has been approved and a re-estimate is required while maintaining the Budget.

This function also unlinks the **Original Duration** from the **At Completion Duration** for un-started activities.

18.2 Project Window Resource Preferences

Preferences set in the **Activity Window** decide how each individual activity and resource is calculated and are covered in the next section.

Preferences and defaults (which may be changed for each resource assignment) that affect how all resources in a project are calculated are set in the **Project Window** and pertain to all activities and resources.

18.2.1 Resources Tab

The **Resources** tab in the Projects Window:

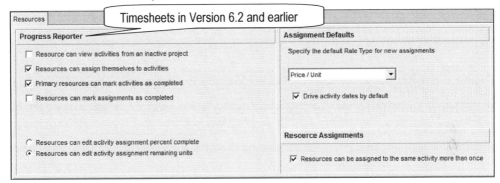

- **Progress Reporter (Timesheets in Version 6.2 and earlier)**. This sets the defaults for the Timesheet, if it has been implemented
- **Resource Assignment Defaults**. There are five Resource Rates available in Primavera ; one rate may be set as a project default. After assignment to an activity, the Resource Rate may be changed using the **Rate Type** field in the Resources tab of the Activities Window.
- **Drive activity dates by default** is covered in more detail in the next section.
- **Resource Assignments**. Checking the **Resources can be assigned to the same activity more than once box** enables a resource to be assigned to an activity more than once. This is useful if it is required to assign a resource at the beginning of an activity and later at the end of an activity with a lag.

18.2.2 Understanding Resource Option to Drive Activity Dates

A resource has the following fields that are linked and a change to the **Original lag** or **Original Duration** will make a change to one or both dates:

- **Original Lag**. The duration from the Activity Start Date to the Resource Start Date, which is the date the resource commences work.
- **Original Duration**. The duration that a resource is working.
- **Start**. The Resource Start Date =Activity Start Date + the Resource Original Lag.
- **Finish**. This date is calculated by the addition of the Activity Start Date + Original Lag + the Original Duration.

When this option is switched off it is possible for a resource to calculate outside the activity duration. In the following example the activities are 5 days long and the resources assigned to each activity are working for 10 days. This has resulted in resource being overloaded. The Resources acknowledge the activity Start date but not the Finish Date.

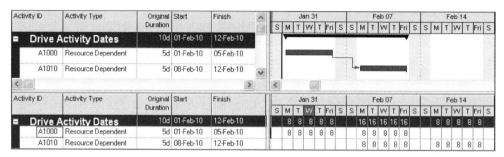

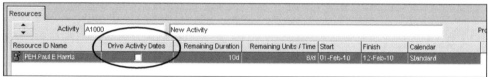

Now the **Drive Activity Dates** option has been checked against each activity, the activities are now 10 days long and the resource is not overloaded.

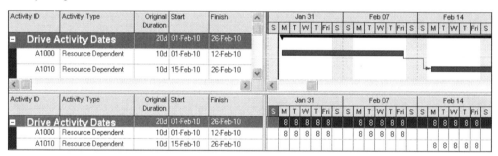

It is recommended that the **Drive activity dates by default** box is always checked, thus Resources will be assigned as **Drive Activity Dates** and this ensures that all work is contained within the duration of an activity.

The Activity Start is controlled by the Activity Calendar, therefore it is important to set an Activity Calendar that will allow the resource to start work when it is required to start. Thus if there is a morning shift starting at 4:00am in the morning, the Activity Calendar should start at 4:00am or earlier.

This function works in a similar way in P3 and SureTrak when a Lag and/or Duration is assigned to a non driving resource but there is no equivalent in Microsoft Project.

18.2.3   Calculations Tab

The **Calculations** tab in the **Projects Window:**

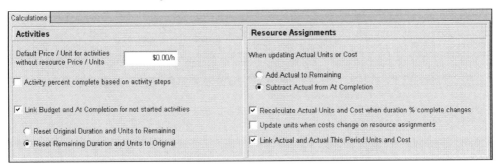

- **Activities – Default Price/Unit for activities without resource Price/Units**. This rate is also used to calculate the resource costs when an activity is not assigned roles or resources but is assigned a quantity in the in the **Activities** Window, **Status** tab.
- The other functions in this tab affect the updating of resourced activities and are covered in the **Updating a Resourced Schedule** chapter.

18.3   User Preferences Applicable to Assigning Resources

Select **Edit**, **User Preferences…** to open the **User Preferences** form:

18.3.1   Units/Time Format

Select the **Time Units** tab. The **Units/Time Format** enables Microsoft Project style formatting of **Resource/Time Format** showing Resource utilization as a percentage or as units per duration.

> **Units/Time Format**
> Resource Units/Time can be shown as a percentage or as units per duration
> ○ Show as a percentage (50%)
> ⦿ Show as units/duration (4h/d)

18.3.2   Resource Assignments

The **Calculations** tab has two **Resource Assignment** options:

> **Resource Assignments**
> When adding or removing multiple resource assignments on activities
> ⦿ Preserve the Units, Duration, and Units/Time for existing assignments
> ○ Recalculate the Units, Duration, and Units/Time for existing assignments based on the activity Duration Type

- **Preserve the Units, Duration, and Units/Time for existing assignments**. With this option, as Resources are added or deleted the total number of hours assigned to an activity increases or decreases. Each Resource's hours are calculated independently.

- **Recalculate the Units, Duration, and Units/Time for existing assignments based on the activity Duration Type**. The total number of hours assigned to an activity will stay constant as second and subsequent resources are added or removed from an activity.
  Note: This function does not work when the Activity Type is **Fixed Duration and Units/Time**.

This function is similar to the Microsoft Project Effort Driven function and the **Recalculate the Units, Duration, and Units/Time for existing assignments based on the activity Duration Type** is the same as Effort Driven.

There is no similar function in P3 and SureTrak.

It is recommended that **Preserve the Units, Duration, and Units/Time for existing assignments** is used as a default as the resource assignment does not change as resources are added or removed from n activity.

18.3.3 Assignment Staffing

The **Assignment Staffing** option are self explanatory and should be considered carefully when resources and roles have different rates. If they are not understood and set correctly the resource may end up with the incorrect unit rate when assigned to a Role or existing Resource.

When two users have different settings this may result in a schedule having two different rates for the same resource.

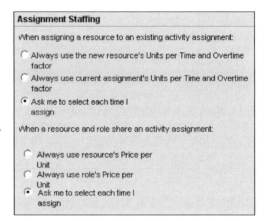

18.4 Activity Window Resource Preferences and Defaults

18.4.1 Details Status Form

This form has a section titled **Labor Units** at the right side as seen in the following picture. The drop down menu enables you to select which data is to be displayed in this section of the form.

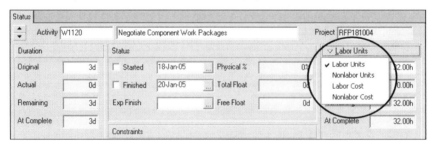

There is a link between the entries in this form and the values that are assigned to resources:

- The values in this form are the sum of the values assigned to Resources and Roles.
- When these values are edited, they will change the values assigned to Resources and Roles.

Note: It is possible to enter a **Labor Unit** value in the **Status** tab and not assign a resource. When a resource is assigned the resource will adopt this value in the **Status** tab. This rate is set in the **Calculations** tab in the **Projects Window:**, in the **Activities – Default Price/Unit for activities without resource Price/Units**.

18.4.2 Activity Type

There are five **Activity Types** assigned in the **General tab** in the **Activities Window**:

Activity Type	Notes
Task Dependent	Activities assigned as Task Dependent acknowledge their **Activity Calendar** when scheduling and the Finish Date is calculated from the Activity Calendar.
Resource Dependent	Activities assigned as Resource Dependent acknowledge their **Resource Calendar** when being scheduled. This is similar to an Independent Activity Type in P3 and SureTrak and the resources work independently and do not have to be available at the same time.
	The Activity Finish Date is calculated based on the longest Resource Duration when the resource option of **Drive Activity Dates** is checked against the resource assignment.
	The activity start date calculated on the activity calendar is acknowledged.
Level of Effort (LOE)	This Activity Type spans other Activities. Therefore the Start Date, Finish Date and Durations may change as the start or finish date of activities that it is dependent on change during scheduling or updating. LOE Activity Type is similar to a Hammock in P3 and SureTrak, but more relationships may control the Start and Finish Dates. There is no equivalent in Microsoft Project.
	This type of activity does not create a critical path irrespective of the float calculations that are displayed.
	The Start Date is controlled by the following relationships:
	• Finish-to-**Start** predecessors
	• Start-to-**Start** predecessors
	• **Start**-to-Finish successors
	• **Start**-to-Start Successors
	The Finish Date is controlled by the following relationships:
	• Finish-to-**Finish** predecessors
	• Start-to-**Finish** predecessors
	• **Finish**-to-Start successors
	• **Finish**-to-Finish successors
	Resources assigned to a Level of Effort activity are not considered in calculations when a schedule is **Leveled**.
	Level of Effort activities may not be assigned a **Constraint**.
	When creating a **LOE** activity and the bar is not displayed, check the **Bars** form to ensure a LOE bars has been created and is being displayed.

Activity Type	Notes
Start Milestone	This Activity Type is used to indicate the commencement of Phase, Stage or a major event in a project. It has only a Start Date and no Duration or Finish Date. It may only have **Start Constraints** assigned. It may not have time dependent resources assigned but may have a **Primary Resource** assigned to indicate who is responsible for the activity.
Finish Milestone	This Activity Type is used to indicate the completion of Phase, Stage or a major event in a project. It has only a Finish Date and no Duration or Start Date. It may only have **Finish Constraints** assigned. It may not have time dependent resources assigned but may have a **Primary Resource** assigned to indicate who is responsible for the activity.
WBS Summary Activity	The new Primavera Version5.0 **WBS Summary Activity** is an activity that spans the duration of all activities which are assigned exactly the same WBS Code and unlike a Level of Effort Activity it does not have any predecessors or successors. Therefore a WBS activity will change duration when either the earliest start or latest finish of activities that it spans is changed. This may happen as the project progresses and activities do not meet their original scheduled dates, or the duration of an activity is changed, or logic is changed, or the schedule is leveled. This function calculates the WBS Activity Duration in the same way as WBS activities in P3 or SureTrak, Topic activities in SureTrak. It is similar to the way Summary activity durations are calculated in Microsoft Project, except the activities do not need to be demoted below the detailed activities in as in Microsoft Project. WBS activities may be used for: • Reporting at summary level by filtering on WBS activities, • Entering estimated costs at summary level for producing cash flow tables while the detailed activities are used for calculating the overall duration for the WBS and day to day management of the project and • Recording costs and hours at summary level when is it not desirable or practicable to record at activity level, especially when the detailed activities are liable to change.

18.4.3 Duration Type

The Duration Type becomes effective after a resource has been assigned to an activity.

The **Duration Type** is set in the **Defaults** tab in the **Projects Window** and all new activities are assigned this Duration Type.

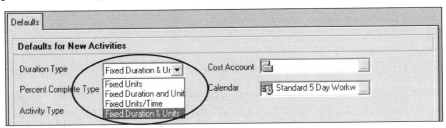

The **Duration Type** for each new activity may be changed in the **General** tab in the **Activities Window** or by displaying the **Duration Type** column:

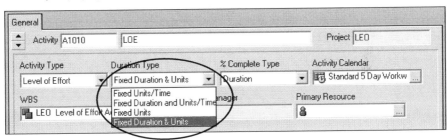

The Duration Type determines which of the following variables change when one of the others is changed in the equation:

- Resource Units = Resource Units per Time Period x Duration

For example, a 40-hour activity with 2 people working 8 hours per day will take 20 hours or 2.5 days:

- 40 hours of work = 2 people per hour x 20 hours

When an activity is in-progress this equation is modified to:

- Remaining Resource Units = Resource Units per Time period x Remaining Duration

Primavera has four options for Duration Type, Microsoft Project has three options, and P3 and SureTrak have two options (which are a lot easier to understand).

The Primavera terminology that describes the way the software treats the relationship between Durations, Resource Units and Resource Units/Time Period is different from Microsoft Project, P3 and SureTrak. Primavera has more options than all the other products and this gives the product more flexibility. The following table should clarify these options.

Purposes of the Duration Types

Duration Type	Purpose
• **Fixed Units/Time**	This option is used when the same number of people are required to complete an activity irrespective of the activity duration.
	For example, if a machine requires two people to operate and therefore a Resource is assigned to the Activity at 200%, changing either the Units or the Duration will not change the Units/Time and there will always be two people operating the machine.
• **Fixed Duration & Units/Time**	This **Duration Type** disables the **User Preferences**, **Calculations** tab option **Recalculate the Units, Duration, and Units/Time for existing assignments based on the activity Duration Type**.
	Option 1
	This option is used when the Duration of an activity should not change when Resources are added or removed or Units/Time changed.
	For example, when the time to complete an activity is fixed, the resources may be manipulated until a satisfactory resource loading is established without the activity duration changing.
	Option 2
	A change in the Duration will change the Units; however, the Units/Time will remain constant.
	For example, when there are two people assigned to an activity and the activity is increased in duration, there will still be two people working but for a longer period of time.
• **Fixed Units**	This option is used when the amount of work required to finish an activity is constant.
	For example, if there are 8,000 bricks to be laid and a bricklayer is able to lay 100 bricks per hour, there are 80 hours of work for one bricklayer, 40 hours for 2 bricklayers and 20 hours for 4 bricklayers. Changing the Duration or the Units/Time will not change the number of hours required to complete the activity.
• **Fixed Duration & Units**	**Option 1**
	This option is used when the Duration of an activity should not change when Resources are added or removed or Units/Time changed.
	For example, when the time to complete an activity is fixed, the resources may be manipulated until a satisfactory resource loading is established without the activity duration changing.
	Option 2
	A change to the Duration will change the Units/Time; however, the Units will remain constant.
	It one person is assigned to an activity for 8 hours per day and the activity is doubled in duration, there will be now be one person working on the activity for 4 hours per day and the activity will require the same number of hours to complete.

The following table displays what happens to the relationship in each of the four options when one variable is changed and

- The **User Preferences**, **Calculations** tab option **Recalculate the Units, Duration, and Units/Time for existing assignments based on the activity Duration Type** is selected:

Duration Type	Labor Units Change in Status Tab	Activity Duration Change	Resource Units Change	Units/Time Period Change	Add or Remove Resources
Fixed Units/Time	Duration Change	Units Change	Duration Change	Duration Change	Activity Units Change, Resource Units Constant, Duration Constant
Fixed Duration & Units/Time	Units/Time Change	Units Change	Units/Time Change	Units Change	Activity Units Change, Resource Units Constant, Duration Constant
Fixed Units	Duration Change	Units/Time Change	Duration Change	Duration Change	Activity Units Change, Resource Units Constant, Duration Constant
Fixed Duration & Units	Units/Time Change	Units/Time Change	Units/Time Change	Units Change	Activity Units Change, Resource Units Constant, Duration Constant

The following table displays what happens to the relationship in each of the four options when one variable is changed and

- The **User Preferences**, **Calculations** tab option **Preserve the Units, Duration, and Units/Time for existing assignments** is selected:

Duration Type	Labor Units Change in Status Tab	Activity Duration Change	Resource Units Change	Units/Time Period Change	Add or Remove Resources
Fixed Units/Time	Duration Change	Units Change	Duration Change	Duration Change	**Activity Units Constant**, **Resource Units Change**, **Duration Change**
Fixed Duration & Units/Time	Units/Time Change	Units Change	Units/Time Change	Units Change	Activity Units Change, Resource Units Constant, Duration Constant
Fixed Units	Duration Change	Units/Time Change	Duration Change	Duration Change	**Activity Units Constant**, **Resource Units Change**, **Duration Change**
Fixed Duration & Units	Units/Time Change	Units/Time Change	Units/Time Change	Units Change	**Activity Units Constant**, **Resource Units Change**, Duration Constant

- Bold descriptions in the right column on the table above indicate the differences to the table above.
- The **User Preferences**, **Calculations** tab option **Preserve the Units, Duration, and Units/Time for existing assignments** will not freeze the Activity Units when the **Duration Type** of **Fixed Units** is selected.

18.5 Assigning and Removing Roles

To assign a Role to an activity:

- Select the one or more activity to be assigned the Role,

- Select the **Resources** tab in the **Activity Details** form,

- Click on the [Add Role] button to open the **Assign Roles** form,

- Use the **Display:**, **Filter By** menu to select either:

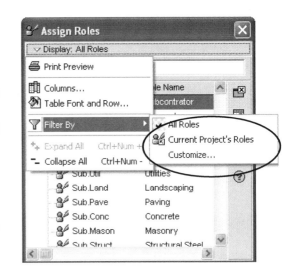

  - ➢ **All Roles**, which will display all Roles in the database,
  - ➢ **Current Project's Roles**. This option will only display Roles that have been assigned to this project, or
  - ➢ **Customize**, which opens a **Filter** form enabling the user to limit the number of displayed Roles by creating a filter.

- Select one or more Roles to be assigned to an activity using the Ctrl-click function,

- Then to assign a Role:

  - ➢ Click on the [icon] button, or

Double-click one of the Roles. To achieve the following picture you may need to format the columns in the **Resources Details** form.

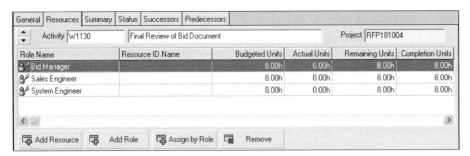

At this point, the Roles hours and costs may be edited as required.

Costs may be assigned to Roles but these costs are not calculated, as a Role Rate is not available from the database.

To remove a Role:

- Select the Role, and

- Click on the [Remove] button.

18.6 Assigning and Removing Resources

Resources may be assigned directly to:

- An activity that has an Assigned Role, or
- An Activity without a Role.

18.6.1 Assigning a Resource to an Assigned Role

To assign a Resource to a Role assigned to an activity:

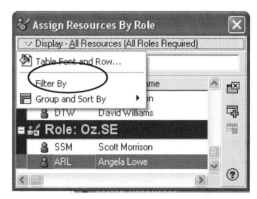

- Select the activity to be assigned a Resource,
- Select the Role to be assigned a Resources from the **Resources Details** tab,
- Click on the [Assign by Role] button to open the **Assign Resources By Roles** form,
- Click on the **Display:** menu and select **Filter By** to open the **Filter By** form,
- Select which Resources you wish to have displayed in the **Assign Roles** form from the **Filter By** form,

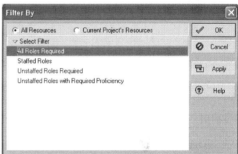

- Select [Apply] to return to the **Assign Resources By Role** form,
- From the **Assign Resources By Role** form click the Resource you wish to assign,
- To assign the Resource either:
  - ➤ Double-click the Resource, or
  - ➤ Click on the [image] button.

18.6.2 Assigning a Resource to an Activity Without a Role

To assign a Resource to an activity:

- Select the activity to be assigned the Resource,
- Click on the [Add Resource] button to open the **Assign Resource** form,
- Click on the **Display:** menu and select **Filter By** and then select from the three options which resources you wish to display in the **Assign Resources** form,
- To assign the Resource either:
  - ➢ Double-click the Resource, or
  - ➢ Click on the button.

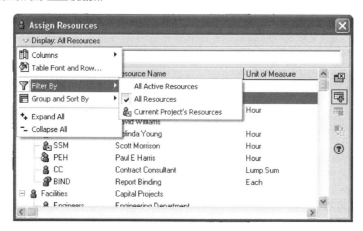

You may now edit the hours or Units/Time Period for each resource.

18.6.3 Removing a Resource

Before you remove a Resource from an activity that has more than one resource assigned to it, you must be aware of your **Resource Assignment** preferences. These preferences determine if the total number of Units assigned to the activity (or work) will be reduced or remain constant.

To remove a resource, select the Resource in the Bottom Pane Resource tab and either:

- Strike the **Del** key, or
- Click on the [Remove] button.

18.6.4 Assigning a Resource to an Activity More Than Once

The option in the **Projects Window Resources** tab under the **Resources Assignments** heading enables a resource to be assigned more than once to an activity. A resource could be assigned to work at the start of an activity and then in conjunction with **Resource Lag** work again at the end of an activity.

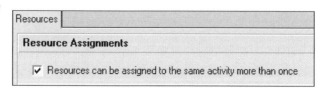

18.6.5 Resource and Activity Duration Calculation and Resource Lags

18.6.6 Activity Duration

An Activity Duration (or Activity Remaining Duration of an In-Progress Activity) is adopted from the longest Resource Duration (or Resource Remaining Duration of an In-Progress Activity) when more than one resource has been assigned to an activity.

In a situation where more than one Resource has been assigned to an activity with different Units and/or Units/Time, the Resources many have different durations.

In the following example the Activity Duration is 10 days, which is calculated from David William's **Resource Original Duration** of 10 days:

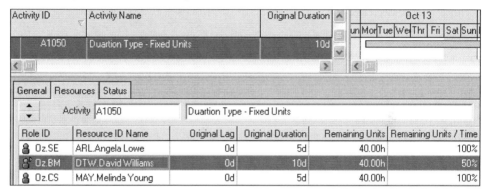

This is calculated in a similar way to P3 and SureTrak when all Resources are set to Driving.

18.6.7 Resource Lag

A Resource may be assigned a Lag, the duration from the start of the activity to the point at which the Resource commences work.

In the following example the Activity Duration is 12 days, which is calculated from Angela Lowe's **Resource Original Lag** of 7 days and **Resource Original Duration** of 5 days:

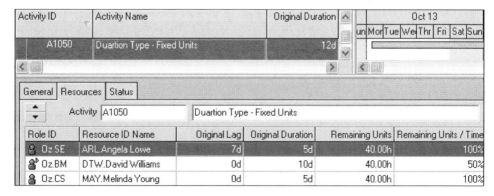

18.7 Expenses

Expenses are intended to be used for one off non-resource type costs and could include:

- Purchase of office equipment to set up a project office,
- Travel costs,
- Payment for a consultant's report,
- Insurance costs, and
- Training courses.

Expenses may be created using the:

- **Expenses Window** and assigned to an activity, or
- Created in the **Expenses** tab of an activity.

18.7.1 Expenses Window

The **Expenses Window** is opened by:

- Clicking in the [▦] button on the **Directory** bar, or
- Selecting **Project, Expenses**.

Creating a new **Expense** is similar to creating a new activity:

- Select **Edit, Add**, or
- Strike the **Ins** key.
- The **Select Activity** form will then be displayed and the activity the expense is to be associated with is selected.

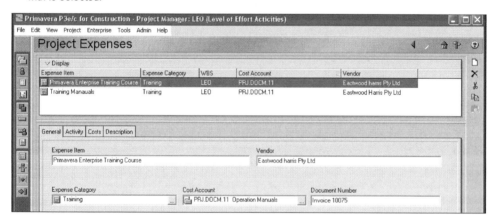

Enter the following Information in the tabs in the bottom window:

- **General Tab**
  - ➢ **Expense Item** – A free form field to enter the description of the Expense.
  - ➢ **Vendor** – A free form field to enter the vendor or supplier name.
  - ➢ **Expense Category** – Select the Expense Category, these are created in the **Admin Categories** form.

> **Cost Account** – Select a Cost Account should you wish to see or report the costs against a Cost Account. Costs accounts are created in a similar method to other hierarchical structures in Primavera, such as the WBS, by selecting **Enterprise**, **Cost Accounts**....

> **Document Number** – A free form field to enter the document number that could represent the Purchase Order, Contract or Invoice Number.

- **Activity** tab displays information mainly adopted from an activity, the Accrual Type, is editable:

> **Accrual Type** – this enables you to select if the costs are accrued or cash flowed at the beginning, end, or uniformly over the duration of the activity.

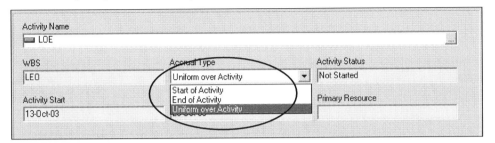

- **Costs** tab is mainly self-explanatory. The following information is entered:

> **Budgeted Units** – the quantity of the Expense item,

> **Price/Unit** – the cost per Expense item,

> **Unit of Measure** – the units of the Expense; for example, each, foot, meter, etc.

> Check **Auto Compute Actuals** to allow the software to calculate the Actual and Remaining Costs and Units (quantities) based on the **Activity % Complete**,

> The remainder of the fields are used when the activity is progressed.

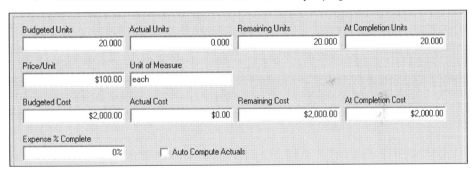

- **Description** tab is where you enter an extended description of the Expense item.

18.7.2 Expenses Tab in the Activities Window

This tab may have all the columns of data available in the **Expenses Window** displayed. All the fields may be edited from this tab:

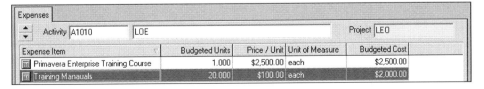

18.8 Suggested Setup for Creating a Resourced Schedule

The order that topics are introduced in this chapter is also a satisfactory order of actions that should be considered when preparing to assign resources to activities.

The simplest calculation options should be used as a default, and more complex options considered only when there is a specific scheduling requirement.

The table following lists process and suggested options that could be considered when creating a resourced schedule. It is important to set all the parameters before the activities are added otherwise a lot of time is wasted changing parameters on a number of activities. These are not intended to suit every project but are a starting point for less experienced users.

Step	Suggested Settings
• Set the **Units/Time** format by selecting **Edit**, **User Preferences...** to open the **User Preferences** form and select the **Time Units** tab.	There is a choice of **percentage (50%)** or **units/duration (4h/d)**. This should be set on personal preference. The author prefers **(4h/d)** as this reduces typing.
• Set the **Resource Assignments** option by selecting **Edit**, **User Preferences...** to open the **User Preferences** form and select the **Calculations** tab.	It is suggested that the **Preserve the Units, Duration, and Units/Time for existing assignments** is selected. With this option as Resources are added or deleted the total number of hours assigned to an Activity increases or decreases. Each Resource's hours are calculated independently. The options under **Assignment Staffing** need to be carefully considered and understood so that when Resources are assigned to Roles and resource assignments are changed that the user understands which Unit Rate and which Unit Cost will remain against the activity.
• In the **Project Window**, **Defaults** tab set the default **Activity Type**.	It is suggested that **Task Dependent** is used as with this option Resource calendars are not used making the schedule simpler.
• In the **Project Window**, **Defaults** tab set the default **Duration Type**.	It is suggested that **Fixed Duration & Units** is used. With this option the Activity Duration does not change when resource assignments are altered, and when an Activity Duration is changed the Units do not change, so your estimate of hours and costs will not change.
• In the **Project Window**, **Defaults** tab set the default **Percent Complete Type**.	The author prefers to use **Physical** as this enables the Activity Percent Complete to be independent of the Activity Durations.
• In the **Project Window**, **Resource** tab set the default **Resource Assignment Defaults**.	Unless multiple Rates are being used then **Price / Unit** should be selected. Check **Drive activity dates by default**.

18.9   Workshop 15 - Assigning Resources and Expenses to Activities

Background
The Resources must now be assigned to their specific activities.

Assignment
Open the OzBuild with Resources project and complete the following steps.

1. Copy the **OzBuild Workshop 11 – Without Float** layout as **OzBuild Workshop 15 – Assigning Resources** layout.
2. In the **Activities Window** display the **Gantt Chart** in the top view and **Resources** and **Expenses** tab of the **Activities Details** form in the bottom view.
3. Assign an Expense to the **Create Technical Specification** activity as per the picture below:

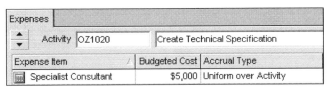

4. Format the **Resources** tab with the columns shown in the following picture:

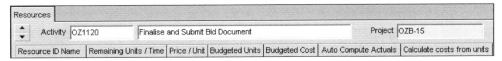

5. Add the **Resources** column to the Gantt Chart as per the picture over the page and save a layout **OzBuild Workshop 15 - Assigning Resources and Expenses to Activities**.
6. Assign the following Resources to the Activities using the [Add Resource] button:

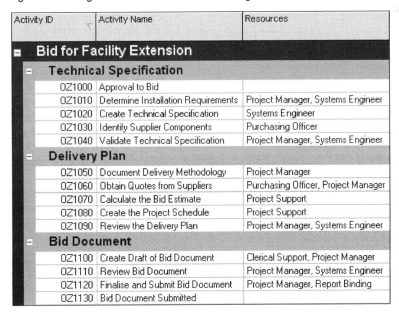

7. Enter 3 as the Budgeted Units and Quantity at Completion for the Report Binding.
8. Add the columns as per below and your answer should look like this:

Activity ID	Activity Name	Resources	At Completion Labor Units	At Completion Labor Cost	At Completion Material Cost	At Completion Expense Cost	At Completion Total Cost
Bid for Facility Extension			520h	$49,760	$300	$5,000	$55,060
Technical Specification			152h	$14,800	$0	$5,000	$19,800
0Z1000	Approval ...		0h	$0	$0	$0	$0
0Z1010	Determin...	Project Manager, Systems Engineer	64h	$6,720	$0	$0	$6,720
0Z1020	Create Te...	Systems Engineer	40h	$3,600	$0	$5,000	$8,600
0Z1030	Identify S...	Purchasing Officer	16h	$1,120	$0	$0	$1,120
0Z1040	Validate ...	Project Manager, Systems Engineer	32h	$3,360	$0	$0	$3,360
Delivery Plan			224h	$21,520	$0	$0	$21,520
0Z1050	Documen...	Project Manager	32h	$3,840	$0	$0	$3,840
0Z1060	Obtain Q...	Purchasing Officer, Project Manager	128h	$12,160	$0	$0	$12,160
0Z1070	Calculate ...	Project Support	24h	$1,920	$0	$0	$1,920
0Z1080	Create th...	Project Support	24h	$1,920	$0	$0	$1,920
0Z1090	Review t...	Project Manager, Systems Engineer	16h	$1,680	$0	$0	$1,680
Bid Document			144h	$13,440	$300	$0	$13,740
0Z1100	Create Dr...	Clerical Support, Project Manager	96h	$8,160	$0	$0	$8,160
0Z1110	Review B...	Project Manager, Systems Engineer	32h	$3,360	$0	$0	$3,360
0Z1120	Finalise a...	Project Manager, Report Binding	16h	$1,920	$300	$0	$2,220
0Z1130	Bid Docu...		0h	$0	$0	$0	$0

9. You will notice that there is no column to display the Materials quantity at completion.
10. The **At Completion Labor Units** change when the **User Preferences, Time Units, Units Format, Units per Time** are changed to Days:

Activity ID	Activity Name	Resources	At Completion Labor Units	At Completion Labor Cost	At Completion Material Cost	At Completion Expense Cost	At Completion Total Cost
Bid for Facility Extension			65d	$49,760	$300	$5,000	$55,060
Technical Specification			19d	$14,800	$0	$5,000	$19,800
0Z1000	Approval ...		0d	$0	$0	$0	$0
0Z1010	Determin...	Project Manager, Systems Engineer	8d	$6,720	$0	$0	$6,720
0Z1020	Create Te...	Systems Engineer	5d	$3,600	$0	$5,000	$8,600
0Z1030	Identify S...	Purchasing Officer	2d	$1,120	$0	$0	$1,120
0Z1040	Validate ...	Project Manager, Systems Engineer	4d	$3,360	$0	$0	$3,360
Delivery Plan			28d	$21,520	$0	$0	$21,520
0Z1050	Documen...	Project Manager	4d	$3,840	$0	$0	$3,840
0Z1060	Obtain Q...	Purchasing Officer, Project Manager	16d	$12,160	$0	$0	$12,160
0Z1070	Calculate ...	Project Support	3d	$1,920	$0	$0	$1,920
0Z1080	Create th...	Project Support	3d	$1,920	$0	$0	$1,920
0Z1090	Review t...	Project Manager, Systems Engineer	2d	$1,680	$0	$0	$1,680
Bid Document			18d	$13,440	$300	$0	$13,740
0Z1100	Create Dr...	Clerical Support, Project Manager	12d	$8,160	$0	$0	$8,160
0Z1110	Review B...	Project Manager, Systems Engineer	4d	$3,360	$0	$0	$3,360
0Z1120	Finalise a...	Project Manager, Report Binding	2d	$1,920	$300	$0	$2,220
0Z1130	Bid Docu...		0d	$0	$0	$0	$0

NOTE: In a multi user environment it is important that all users have the same User Preferences otherwise each person may display different Quantities at completion.

11. Now create a new activity under the **Delivery Plan** WBS Node, Activity ID **OZ1150** titled **WBS Activity** and assign it an **Activity Type** of **WBS Summary** using the **Activities** window, **General** tab.

12. Schedule to see how it operates.

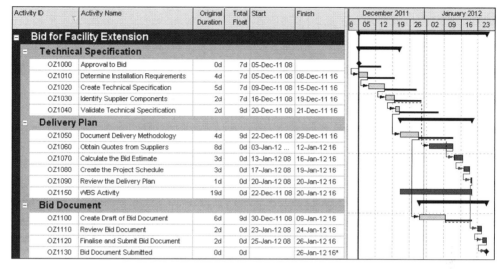

13. Drag from WBS Node to another WBS Node and schedule to see how it operates.
14. Change the **Activity Type** to a **Level of Effort** and rename it to **LOE Activity**,
15. Open the Bars form and ensure LOE bars are displayed,
16. Drag it to the **Delivery Plan** WBS Node,
17. Add OZ1060 SS OZ1150 and OZ1150 FF OZ1070 relationships and see how it calculates.

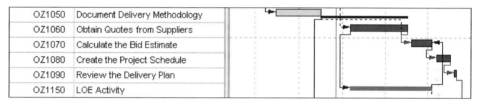

18. Add OZ1050 SS OZ1150 and OZ1150 FF OZ1110 relationships and see how it calculates.

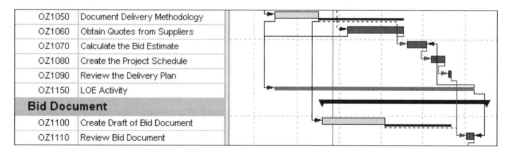

19. Delete the LOE activity.

19 RESOURCE OPTIMIZATION

The schedule may now have to be resource optimized to:

- Reduce peaks and smooth the resource requirements, thus reducing the mobilization and demobilization costs, or to reduce the demand for site facilities, or

- Reduce resource demand to the available number of resources, or

- Reduce demand to an available cash flow when a project is financed on income.

19.1 Reviewing Resource Loading

There are a number of facilities for reviewing resource loading which consist of either displaying a Layout or running a report. The Timescale interval affects the displays. Layouts will not be covered in detail, as they are self-explanatory.

19.1.1 Activity Usage Profile

This is displayed by clicking on the [icon] button and displays the total resource histogram for selected or all activities, right-click the Histogram for the display options:

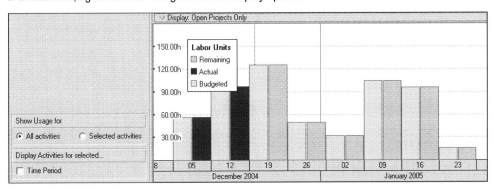

19.1.2 Resource Usage Spreadsheet

This is displayed by clicking on the [icon] button. The units are formatted using the **User Preferences**, **Time Units** tab. If the minimum time unit is an hour, ensure that the **User Preferences**, Resource Analysis **Interval for time-distributed resource** calculations is set to one hour; otherwise, the data will not be displayed correctly.

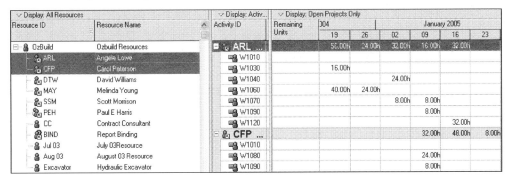

19.1.3   Resource Usage Profile displaying a Resource Histogram

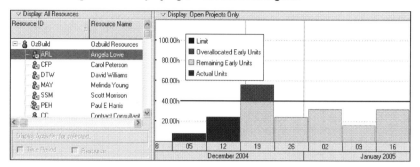

Note: The resource availability is displayed using the Resource Calendar when the **Activity Type** is set to **Task Dependent** and the activity is scheduled using the Task Calendar.

19.1.4   Resource Usage Profile displaying S-Curves

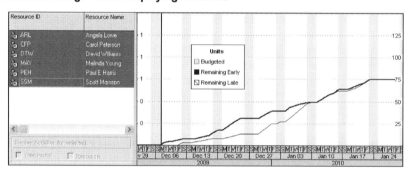

19.1.5   Activity Usage Spreadsheet

The units are formatted using the **User Preferences**, **Time Units** tab. If the minimum time unit is an hour, ensure the **User Preferences**, Resource Analysis **Interval for time-distributed resource** calculations is set to one hour; otherwise, the data will not be displayed correctly.

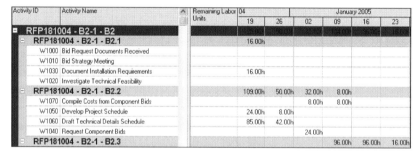

You must be prepared to experiment with the formatting menus by right-clicking in each of the windows of the above displays to understand all the many options, which include:

- Roles or Resources,

- All Resources, All Active Resources and Current Projects Resources only,

- Options to show period and cumulative values, or an average by dividing by a number,

- Options to filter, and

- Options to Group and Sort.

19.2   Methods of Resolving Resource Peaks and Conflicts

Methods of resolving resource overload problems are:

- **Revising the Project Plan**. Revise a project plan to mitigate resource conflicts, such as changing the order of work, contracting work out, or using off site pre-fabrication, etc.
- **Duration Change**. Increase the task duration to decrease the resource requirements, so a 5-day activity with 10 people could be extended to a 10-day task with 5 people.
- **Resource Substitution**. Substitute one resource with another available resource.
- **Increase Working Time**. Accelerate the working time of a project task, which may release the resource for other tasks.
- **Split an activity around peaks in demand**. Some software enables the splitting of activities, which in turn enables work to be split around peaks in resource demand. This function is not available in Primavera but an activity may be split into two to allow the work to cease in times of peak demand.
- **Leveling the schedule**. This technique delays activities until resource(s) are available.
- **Resource Curves** or **Manually Editing the Resource Spreadsheet** may assist in some instances.

19.3   Resource Leveling

19.3.1   Methods of Resource Leveling

After resource overloads or inefficiencies have been identified with Resource and Tables, the schedule may now have to be leveled to reduce peaks in resource demands. Leveling is defined as delaying activities until resources become available. There are several methods of delaying activities to level a schedule:

- **Turning off Automatic Calculation and Dragging Activities**. This option does not maintain a critical path and reverts to the original schedule when recalculated. This option should not be used when a contract requires a critical path schedule to be maintained, as the schedule will no longer calculate correctly.
- **Constraining Activities**. A constraint may be applied to delay an activity until the date that the resource becomes available from a higher priority activity. This is not a recommended method because the delay of the higher priority activity may unlevel the schedule.
- **Sequencing Logic**. Relationships may be applied to activities sharing the same resource(s) in the order of their priority. In this process, a resource-driven critical path is generated. If the first activity in a chain is delayed then the chain of activities will be delayed. But the schedule will not become unleveled and the critical path will be maintained. In this situation, a successor activity may be able to take place earlier and the logic will have to be manually edited.
- **Leveling Function**. The software Resource Leveling function levels resources by delaying activities without the need for Constraints or Logic, and finds the optimum order for the activities based on user defined parameters. Again, as this option does not maintain a critical path developed by durations and relationships, it should not be used when a contract requires a critical path schedule developed in this way. The Leveling function may be used to establish an optimum scheduling sequence and then Sequencing Logic applied to hold the leveled dates and to create a critical path.

The Resource Leveling function enables the optimization of resource use by delaying activities until resources become available, thus reducing the peaks in resource requirements. This feature may extend the length of a project.

The leveling function should be used by novices with extreme caution.

- It requires the scheduler to have a solid understanding of how the software resourcing functions calculate.

- Leveling increases the complexity of a schedule and requires a different approach to building a schedule. In principal, the sequencing logic is replaced by Priorities but a Closed Network should still be maintained.

Your ability to understand how the software operates is important for you to be able to utilize the leveling function with confidence on larger schedules. It is recommended that you practice with small simple schedules to gain experience in leveling and develop an understanding of the leveling issues before attempting a complex schedule.

19.4   Resource Leveling Function

This chapter outlines the software Resource Leveling functions including:

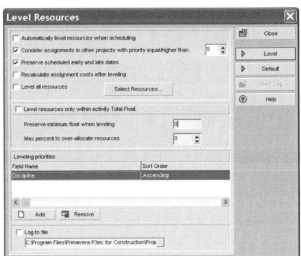

- **Level Resources** form,

- Leveling Examples, including Resource Shifts,

- Guidelines on Leveling, and

- What to look if resources are not leveling.

19.4.1   Level Resources Form

The **Level Resources** form enables you to assign most of the Leveling prerequisites. Select **Tools**, **Level Resource...** to open the **Level Resources** form:

- **Automatically level resources when scheduling** – levels the schedule each time the schedule is recalculated.

- **Consider assignments in other projects with priority equal/higher than**. – levels resources and at the same time considers the demands of other projects. The leveling priority is set in the **Projects Window**, **General** tab.

- **Preserve scheduled early and late dates** – in simple terms, when unchecked enables the option of **Late Leveling**. This is explained in more detail in the following paragraphs as the computations are a little more complicated. **Late Leveling** pushes forward in time activities from their late dates to meet the resource availability and provides the latest dates the activities may be started and finished without delaying the finish date of the project.

- **Recalculate assignment costs after leveling** – is used with the resource **Effective date** and **Price/Unit**. These facilities allow a change in the cost of a resource over time. The Resource Costs are recalculated based on the resource **Price/Unit** if an activity is moved into a different price bracket when this check box is marked.

- **Level all resources** – if checked, the schedule levels all the resources; if unchecked, enables the **Select Resources** form to be opened and one or more resources selected for leveling.

- **Level resources only within activity Total Float**

  ➤ When checked, the leveling process will not generate negative float but may not completely level a schedule. Thus, the activities will only be delayed until all float is consumed and leveling will not extend the finish date of the project. This option will also check the **Preserve scheduled early and late dates** option.

  ➤ When unchecked, leveling will allow activities to extend beyond a **Project Must Finish By date**, when assigned in the **Projects Window Dates** tab, or beyond the latest date calculated by the schedule and may create **Negative Float**..

  ➤ **Preserve minimum float when leveling** – works with **Level resources only within Total Float** and will not level activities if their float will drop below the assigned value.

  ➤ **Max percent to over-allocate resources** – works with **Level resources only within activity Total Float** and enables the doubling of the resource availability, although this is not displayed in the histograms.

- **Leveling priorities:** – sets leveling the priorities, and activities are assigned resources according to the Data item chosen in the first line. If two activities have the same value in the first line then the priority in the second line is used. The Activity ID is the final value used to assign resources. There are many options for leveling priority and the following are some to consider:

  ➤ **Activity Leveling Priority** is a field that may be set from 1 Top to 5 Lowest, the default is 3 Normal. Those with a priority 1 Top are assigned resources first.

  ➤ **Activity Codes** or **User Defined Fields** and many other data fields such as **Remaining Duration**, **Early Start**, **Total Float** and **Late Start** may be used to set the priority for leveling.

19.5 Leveling Examples

Two simple examples can assist you in understanding how the software works.

- The first will allow the schedule to level with positive float, and
- The second will NOT allow the schedule to level with positive float.

It is recommended that you set up a small schedule and try the various options until you understand what the software is doing and how it operates before trying your hand with a large schedule.

You should then look at leveling more complex schedules only after you have mastered leveling a small schedule like the examples in this chapter.

19.5.1 Leveling with Positive Float

The following picture displays the schedule unleveled:

- A project **Must Finish By Date** of 27 Feb has been set.
- The histogram shows both the Early and Late resource histogram is overloaded.
- The bars displayed are the **Remaining Early**, the **Late** and **Total Float**:

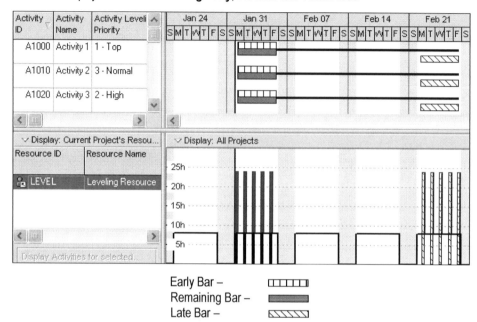

Early Bar –
Remaining Bar –
Late Bar –

After Leveling with all the Leveling options off:

- Early and Late leveling has taken place and the Early and Late histogram are leveled.
- The Early and Remaining Bars have the same dates and are leveled.
- The Total Float is the difference between the Late and Early Finish and provides a similar result if there is a relationship between the activities.

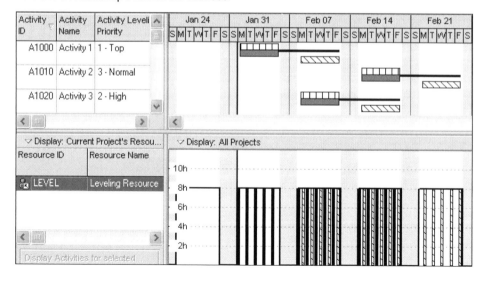

With **Preserve scheduled early and late dates** option checked:

- Early leveling of the Remaining dates has taken place and the Early histogram is leveled.
- Late leveling has NOT taken place and the Late histogram is NOT leveled.
- The Early and Late Bar have NOT been leveled.
- The Total Float is the difference between the Late and Remaining Finish dates and provides a similar result if there is NO relationship between the activities.

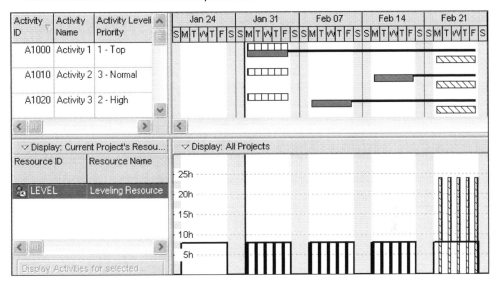

19.5.2 Leveling without Positive Float

The following picture displays the schedule unleveled:

- A project **Must Finish By Date** of 13 Feb has been set.
- The histogram shows both the Early and Late resource histogram are overloaded.

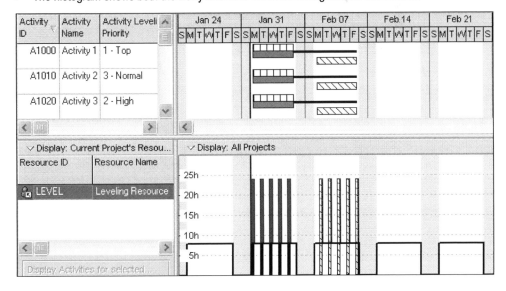

After Leveling with all the options off:

- Early and Late leveling has taken place and the Early and Late histogram is leveled.
- The Early and Remaining Bars have the same dates and are leveled and Negative Float developed.
- The Total Float is the difference between the Late and Early Finish and provides a similar result if there is a relationship between the activities.

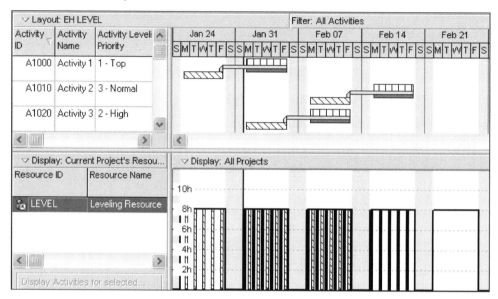

With **Preserve scheduled early and late dates** option checked:

- Early leveling has taken place and the Early histogram is leveled.
- Late leveling has NOT taken place and the Late histogram is NOT leveled.
- The Early and Late Bar have NOT been leveled
- The Remaining Bar has been leveled and Negative Float developed.

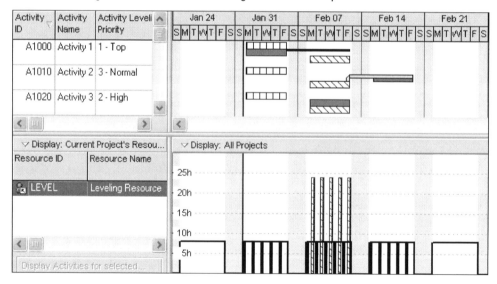

With **Preserve scheduled early and late dates** and the **Level resources only within activity Total Float option** checked:

- Early leveling on the Remaining dates has taken place as much as possible without creating Negative Float.
- Activity 2 with the lowest priority has been left on the Data Date.
- Late leveling has NOT taken place and the Late histogram is NOT leveled.
- The Early Bar has NOT been leveled

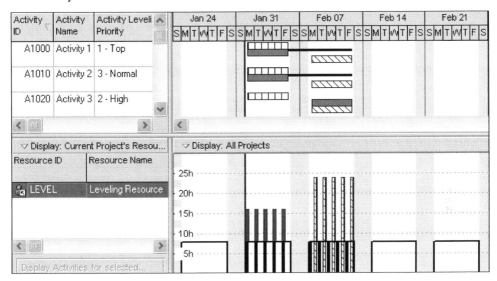

19.6   Resource Shifts

Resource shifts enable the modeling of resource availability when a different number of resources may be available on various shifts. Some key points are covered in the following text:

Resource shifts should be used with:

- Resource Dependent tasks, and
- Resources set to Drive Activity Dates after they have been assigned to activities.

Unlike other products, when a Task is made Resource Dependent the Activity Calendar is still acknowledged for the start of a Task, but not the finish.

Before attempting to use shifts, a user should have considerable familiarity with the software or work with someone experienced.

19.6.1 Creating Shifts:

Select **Enterprise**, **Shifts** to open the **Resource Shifts** form:

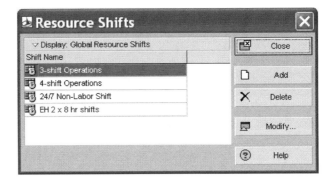

When a shift is added it must total 24 hours:

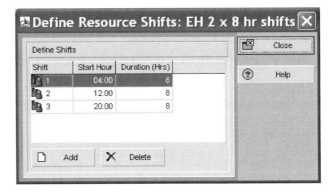

19.6.2 Assigning Shifts to Resources

A shift may be assigned to a resource in the **Resource Window Units & Prices** tab, with a different availability (**Max Units / Time**) and rate (**Price / Unit**) assigned for each shift.

This example shows there are no resources assigned to shift 3, therefore representing a two-shift environment.

A Resource will have a little arrow in a box pointing to its head when assigned to an activity of an open project:

19.6.3 Leveling With Shifts

Shifts are acknowledged when the leveling function is used. The following example shows activities on a 24-hour per day, 7-day per week activity calendar, with shifts set up as on the previous page, with all tasks set as Resource Dependent and Drive Activity Dates. The situation before leveling with the Resource Limit displayed according to shift availability:

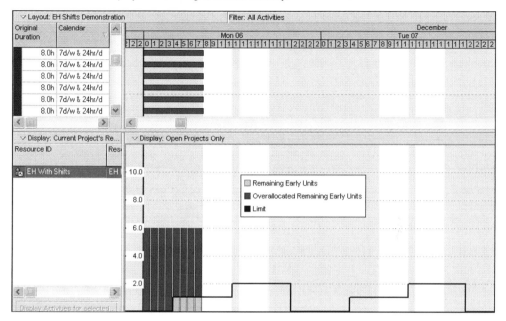

After Leveling with all leveling options **NOT** checked:

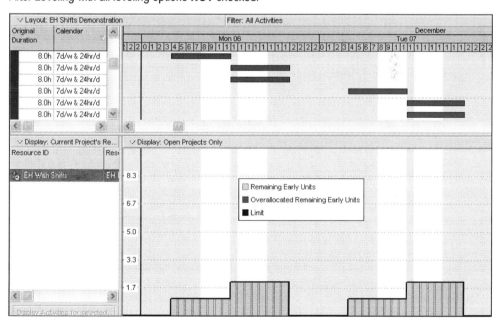

The following example has the activities on an 8-hour per day, 7-day per week calendar:

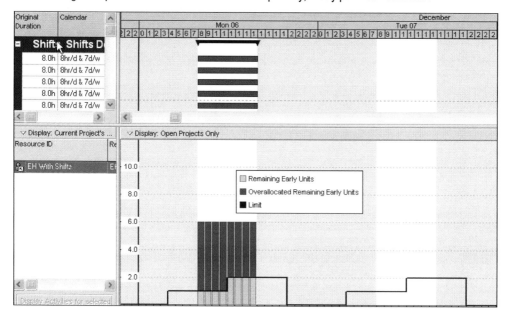

In this situation, the leveling takes into account the Activity Calendar for each Start of each activity and the Shifts operated after the activity Start time. Even though the activities are Resource Driven:

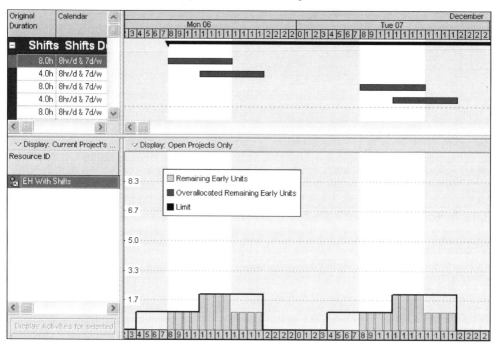

When the Resources are set to **NOT Drive Activity Dates** the resources still level, but:

- Work begins on the start date and time of the first activity, not at the start of the resource shift.
- The Activity Bars do not show when the work is taking place.
- The activities also do not begin on the shift start time when the **Default Calendar** is set 7 days per week, 24 hours per day.

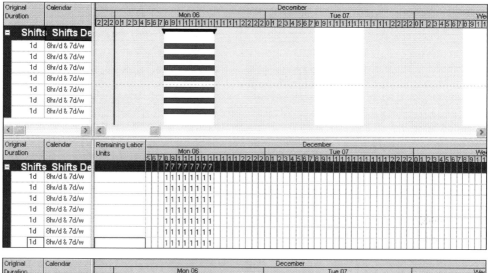

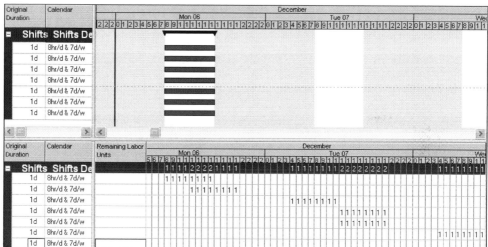

It appears the best option to make resources calculate correctly when using shifts is to:

- Put the activities on a calendar that has the same or greater working hours than the Resource Shifts, so the start of the resource work is not delayed,
- Set the resources to **Resource Driven**, to acknowledge the resource calendars,
- Set the resources to **Drive Activity Dates**, to ensure the Activity Bars move with the Leveled Resources,
- Create a small schedule and experiment to make sure the schedule is behaving the way you think it should and you understand what is happening.

19.7 Guidelines for Leveling

Leveling a schedule is a skill that is acquired through practice and experience and there are a few fundamentals that a user must bear in mind before attempting to level a complex schedule.

- If you are not an experienced scheduling software user then it is strongly suggested that you obtain some serious experience in using Primavera with resources before attempting to use leveling on a complex schedule, especially if you are trying to level a progressed schedule. You will need this experience to resolve some of the complex issues that are often present when leveling a schedule.

- You need to approach the structure of the schedule differently at the beginning of schedule construction. Without leveling, schedulers normally apply soft logic (sequencing logic) to prevent a number of activities occurring at the same time. If leveling is your method of scheduling, then soft logic should be omitted from the beginning of the construction of the schedule.

- All users and reviewers of the schedule must understand that a leveled schedule may dramatically change with the addition or removal or change to activities or change in priorities.

- There are some principles that should be considered when leveling:
  - ➢ Only level resources that are overloaded and that you are unable to supplement easily or that have an absolute limit.
  - ➢ Try leveling one resource at a time and view the histograms to ensure each resource is leveling. If a resource is not leveling and the histograms display overload, you will need to go through the check list on the next page and level again. This process often finds a driving overload resource and leveling that resource levels the whole project.
  - ➢ After all resources are leveling individually, you should start leveling with two resources and then three. Do not start leveling with all the resources at once, as the schedule will often do some drastic things and extend the project end date unrealistically.
  - ➢ Do not expect a perfect result; be satisfied with an average resource usage that meets your requirements over periods, such as months. Sort out small peaks in future resource requirement nearer to the start of the activity.

- Activities have the following options which affect how the duration is calculated:
  - ➢ Activity Types of Task, Independent or Meeting.
  - ➢ Resources assigned to Activities may be either Driving or Non-Driving.
  - ➢ Resources may have their own calendars.

To understand how leveling will delay or change durations of activities you will need to be aware of which of the above combinations you have employed in your schedule, and you will then need to understand how each combination calculates under a non-leveling environment.

19.8   What to Look For if Resources Are Not Leveling

It is very frustrating if you have a project that will not level, try some of these options when your schedule will not level:

- Have you selected a resource to level in the Select Resources form? The resources to be leveled must be selected in the Select Resources form.

- Have you set the Limits in the Resource Window? A resource needs a limit to level.

- A resource will not be leveled when you assign a resource to an activity with a Units per time period greater than value set in the resource dictionary. This may occur when:

    ➤ The **Resource Limit** in the **Resource Dictionary** is reduced, or

    ➤ An activity has been assigned a resource with a **Unit per Time Period** that is greater than the **Limit**, or

    ➤ When the activity has **Fixed Units** and the duration of an activity has been reduced, thus increasing the assigned **Units per time period** over the maximum available in the **Resource** form.

- Have you assigned a **Mandatory Constraint** to an unleveled activity? Activities with a Mandatory constraint will not be leveled.

- Have you checked **Level resources only within activity Total Float** option? This option enables activities without float to level.

19.9   Resource Curves

Resource Curves enable a non-linear assignment of resources to schedules in the same way as P3 and Microsoft Project. These are often used on long activities where there is not a requirement for a linear assignment of resources.

Resource curves are assigned in the **Curve** column in the **Resources** tab of the **Projects Window**:

The Electrical wiring activity in the following picture has a bell shaped Resource Curve assigned to it:

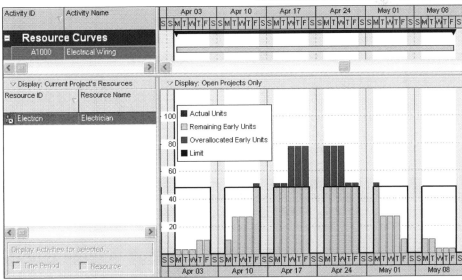

To create and use **Resource Curves**:

- Select **Enterprise**, **Resource Curves...** to open the **Resource Curves** form:

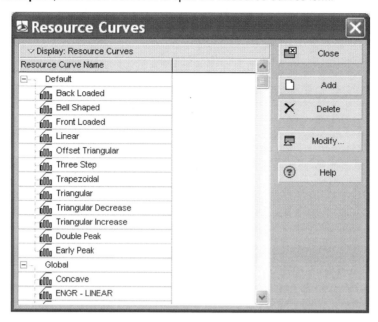

- **Default** curves may not be deleted or edited but may be copied in the **Modify Resource Curves** form.

- **Global** curves may be edited, copied or deleted.

- To create a new curve, select [Add] to open the **Select Resource Curve To Copy From** form and select a curve to copy.

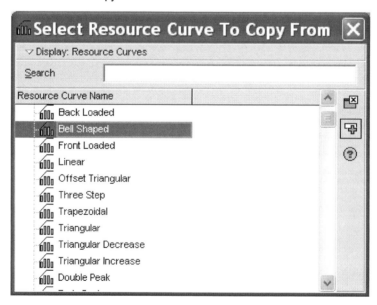

- You will be returned to the **Resource Curves** form where the title may be edited.

- Click the [⊞ Modify...] button to open the **Modify Resource Curves** form:

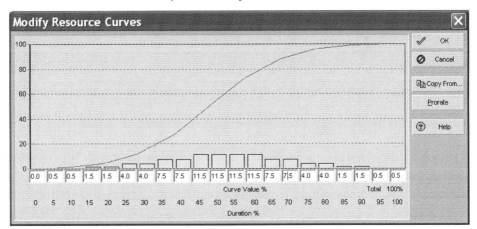

- Edit the percentages to achieve the desired shape:

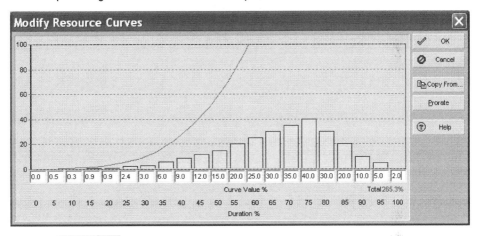

- Click on [Prorate] to make the percentages add to 100%:

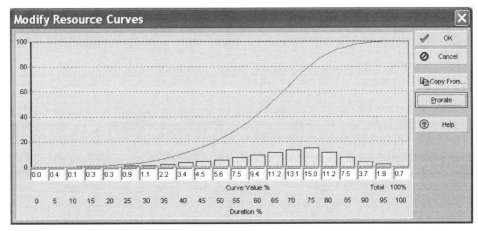

You may now assign this curve to an activity.

19.10 Editing the Resource Usage Spreadsheet – Bucket Planning

This new option in Primavera Version 6.0 enables resource assignment values to be manually edited. This enables more control over the assignment of resources that are working intermittently on an activity.

This is similar to editing a Microsoft Project Resource Usage table and making a resource assignment "Contoured." There is no P3 or SureTrak equivalent.

The following picture shows the edited values in the **Resource Usage Spreadsheet**.

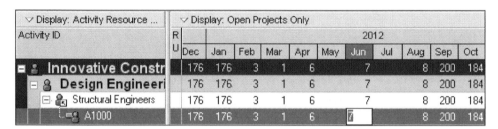

Each time period, therefore, may contain a different value.

It is recommended that you experiment with this function if you plan to progress Bucket Planned Resources as the author has found this process give some interesting results.

19.11 Workshop 16 - Resources Optimization

Assignment

1. Display the **Activity Usage Spreadsheet** by clicking on the 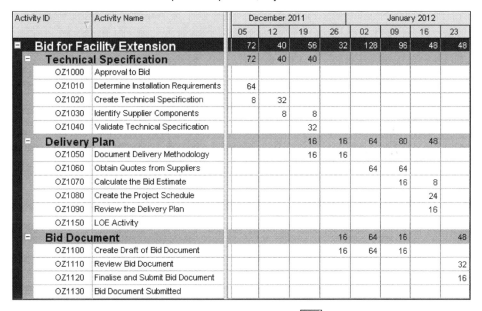 button, the following picture shows the number of hours per week per task, adjust the timescale to weeks:

Activity ID	Activity Name	December 2011				January 2012			
		05	12	19	26	02	09	16	23
Bid for Facility Extension		72	40	56	32	128	96	48	48
Technical Specification		72	40	40					
OZ1000	Approval to Bid								
OZ1010	Determine Installation Requirements	64							
OZ1020	Create Technical Specification	8	32						
OZ1030	Identify Supplier Components		8	8					
OZ1040	Validate Technical Specification			32					
Delivery Plan				16	16	64	80	48	
OZ1050	Document Delivery Methodology			16	16				
OZ1060	Obtain Quotes from Suppliers					64	64		
OZ1070	Calculate the Bid Estimate						16	8	
OZ1080	Create the Project Schedule							24	
OZ1090	Review the Delivery Plan							16	
OZ1150	LOE Activity								
Bid Document						16	64	16	48
OZ1100	Create Draft of Bid Document					16	64	16	
OZ1110	Review Bid Document								32
OZ1120	Finalise and Submit Bid Document								16
OZ1130	Bid Document Submitted								

2. Display the **Resource Usage Sheet** by clicking on the 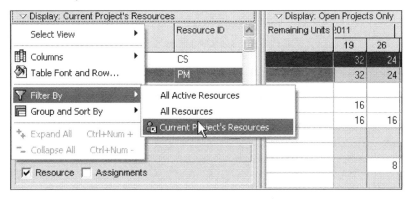 button.

3. Use the **Display, Filter** option in the bottom left window to display the **Current Project's Resources** only,

4. Select **Resource** for the option **Display Activities for selected...** (in the bottom left corner of the screen). Increase the timescale to a daily interval.

Continued.....

---

5. Select the **Projects Manager** (in the bottom left window), which will select the activities he/she is assigned,

6. The **Projects Manager** is overloaded (16 hours per day) on a number of days where he/she is working two activities at a time:

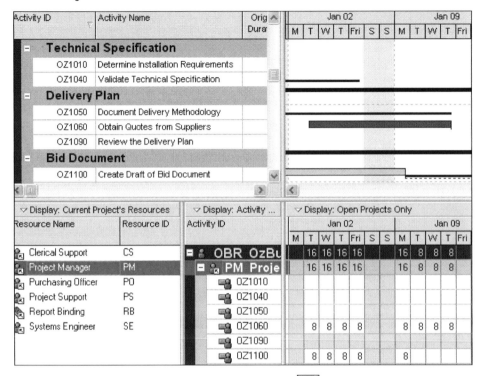

7. Display the **Resource Usage Profile** by clicking on the 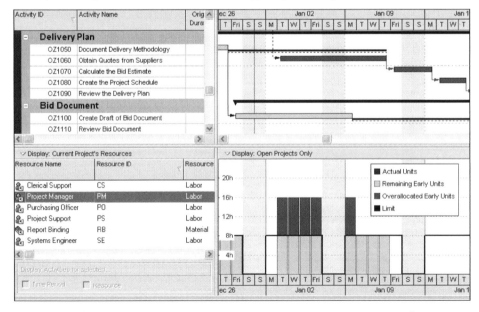 icon; you will also see that the Project Manager is overloaded on the week beginning 2 January.

Continued.....

8. Check the other resources, Project Support appears overloaded on Saturday 14 January, this is because some activities are on a 6 day per week and the resource calendar is a 5 day per week:

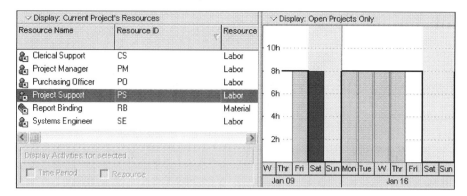

9. At this point in time resources may be optimized by a number of methods including:
   ➢ Assigning a different resource, or
   ➢ Reducing the assignment against the activities, or
   ➢ Adding sequencing logic to level the schedule, or
   ➢ Using the Primavera leveling function.
10. We will try using the leveling function now.
11. Firstly we will create and assign a baseline and display the Baseline bar by:
   ➢ Select **Project**, **Maintain Baselines…** and create a Baseline by saving a copy of the existing project,
   ➢ Select **Project**, **Assign Baselines…** and select this as both your **Project Baseline** and **Primary User Baseline**, thus ensuring and baseline bar will either be blank or display the **Baseline** and not the **Planned Dates**.
   ➢ Apply your **OzBuild Workshop 13 – Baseline** layout and the Baseline bar should be displayed.
   ➢ If there is a yellow vertical band then this is created by the **Progress Spotlight** line, drag the **Progress Spotlight** line back to the **Data Date**.
12. Display the **Resource Usage Profile:**
13. Click on the [icon] icon,
14. Select **Current Projects Resources**.
15. Increase the timescale to a daily timescale:

Continued.....

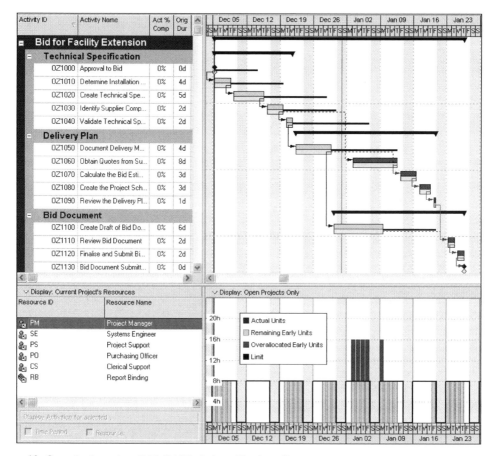

16. Save the layout as **OzBuild Workshop 16 – Leveling**.
17. Select **Tools**, **Level Resources**.
18. Switch off all options:

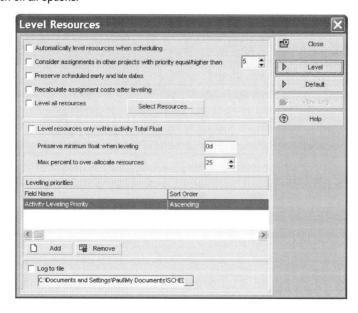

Continued.....

19. Click on the [Select Resources...] button and select only **Project Manager** to level:

20. Click on the [✔ OK] button to return to the **Level Resources** form,

21. Click on the [▷ Level] button to level **Project Manager's** resource assignment:

> ➤ The **Project Manager's** assignment will be leveled,

> ➤ There should be Negative Float as your schedule should have a **Late Finish Constraint** on the last activity, and

> ➤ There will be a Baseline variance.

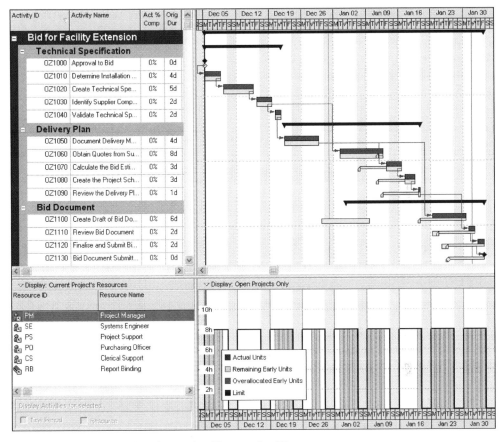

22. Reschedule and therefore un-level by pressing F9.

23. You may now wish to work through and recreate some of the other examples in this chapter.

24. At the end of the workshop, schedule the project so it is not leveled.

20   UPDATING A RESOURCED SCHEDULE

It is often considered best practice to update a project between 10 and 20 times in its lifecycle. Some companies update schedules to correspond with accounting periods, which are normally every month. This frequency is often too long for projects that are less than a year in duration, as too much change may happen in one month. Therefore, more frequent updating may identify problems earlier.

Updating a project with resources employs a number of preferences and options, which are very interactive and will require a significant amount of practice by a user to understand and master them.

After reading this chapter and before working on a live project, inexperienced users should gain confidence with the software by:

- Creating a new project and setting the **Defaults**, **Preferences** and **Options** to reflect the method you wish to enter information and how you want Primavera to calculate the project data.
- Creating two or three activities and then assigning two or three resources to each activity.
- Update the Activities and Resources as if you were updating a schedule and observe the results.
- Alter the preferences and defaults if you are not receiving the result you require. Re-update and note the preferences and defaults for future reference.

Some of these settings may have been set by your organization and you may not be assigned access rights to change the settings. You should still go through the updating process in a test project with dummy data similar to your real project data and be prepared to change those settings to which you do have access, as required.

Updating a project with resources takes place in two distinct steps:

- The dates, durations and relationships are updated using the methods outlined in the **Tracking Progress** chapter, and
- The Resource, Expenses Units (hours and quantities) and Costs, both the Actual to Date and To Complete, are then updated. These values may be automatically updated by Primavera from the % Complete or imported from accounting and timesheet systems or updated by the Primavera Timesheet system.

A decision needs to be made about what data is to be entered or imported into the schedule and what data is to be calculated by the software and the software options set appropriately.

This chapter covers the following topics:

- Understanding **Budget** data and **Baseline Projects**
- Understanding the **Current Data Date** with respect to resources
- Information required to update a resourced schedule
- Project and Activity Window Defaults
- Updating Resources and Expenses
- Reviewing the updated schedule

20.1   Understanding Budget Values and Baseline Projects

20.1.1   Cost and Units Budget Values

The Budget Values in Primavera are assigned to both Units and Costs for each Resource and Expense at the time the Resource or Expense is assigned to an Activity.

Budget Values reside in the current project and in all Baseline Projects.

The Budget values may be linked to the At Completion values when an activity has not commenced but after the activity is in-progress by being marked as Started or having a % Complete these values become unlinked.

Should you wish to re-estimate the cost of a project and compare it to a previous value when activities have not started you could either:
1. Create a Baseline Project before re-estimating the project and compare your revised costs to the Baseline, or
2. Uncheck the **Project**, **Project Properties**, **Calculations** tab and uncheck the **Link Budget and At Completion for non started activities** which will unlink Budget Costs from At Completion Costs, Budget Units from At Completion Units and Original Durations from At Completion Durations.

20.1.2   Baseline Project and Values

A Baseline project is a complete copy of a project including the relationships, resource assignments and expenses.

The creation and assignment of a Baseline Project was covered in the **Tracking Progress** chapter.

- **Baseline Dates** are also known as Target Dates and are normally considered to be the approved Project Early Start and Early Finish dates of an unprogressed project , which are recorded by saving a Baseline project.

- **Baseline Duration** is the original planned duration of an activity, calculated from the Early Start to the Early Finish of an Activity.

- **Baseline Costs** are also known as Budgets and represent the original project cost estimate. These are the figures against which the Actual Costs and Cost at Completion (or Estimate at Completion) may be compared.

- **Baseline Units** is also known as Budgeted Quantity and represents the original estimate of the project quantities. These are the quantities against which the consumption of resources may be compared.

The Baseline values are values against which project progress is measured. All these values may be read by and compared with the current project values and show variances from the original plan.

A Baseline would normally be created prior to updating a project for the first time.

The Primavera Variance columns use Baseline data from Baseline Projects to calculate variances.

20.2 Understanding the Current Data Date

The **Current Data Date** is a standard scheduling term. It is also known as the **Review Date**, **Status Date**, **Report Date**, **As of Date** and **Update Date**.

- The **Current Data Date** is the date that divides the past from the future in the schedule. It is not normally in the future but is often in the recent past due to the time it may take to collect the information required to update the schedule.

- **Actual Costs** and **Quantities/Hours** or **Actual Work** occur before the Data Date.

- **Costs** and **Quantities/Hours to Complete** or **Work to Complete** are scheduled after the Data Date.

- **Actual Duration** is calculated from the **Actual Start** to the **Current Data Date**.

- **Remaining Duration** is the duration required to complete an activity. It is calculated forward from the **Current Data Date** and the Early Finish date or an in-progress activity is calculated from the **Current Data Date** using the:

  - ➢ **Activity Calendar** when the Activity Type is Task Dependent or is Resource Dependent but no Resources have been assigned, or

  - ➢ **Resource Calendar** when the Activity Type is Resource Dependent and uses the longest Resource Duration.

 Primavera has one Data Date, the **Current Data Date,** which operates in the same way as the P3 and SureTrak Data Date. Microsoft Project has four dates associated with updating a schedule. The Microsoft Project Status Date is similar in function to the Primavera **Current Data Date**.

20.3 Information Required to Update a Resourced Schedule

A project schedule is usually updated at the end of a period, such as each day, week or month. One purpose of updating a schedule is to establish differences between the plan, which is usually saved as a Baseline, and the current schedule.

The following information is required to update a resourced schedule:

Activities completed in the update period:

- **Actual Start** date of the activity.

- **Actual Finish** date of the activity.

- **Actual Costs** and **Quantities** (Units) consumed or spent on **Labor Resources**, **Material Resources** and **Expense**. These may be calculated by the software or collected and entered into the software.

Activities commenced in the update period:

- **Actual Start** date of the activity.

- **Remaining Duration** or **Expected Finish** date.

- **Actual Costs** and/or **Actual Quantities**. These may be calculated by the software or collected and entered into the software.

- **Quantities to Complete** and **Costs to Complete**. These may be calculated by the software or collected and entered into the software.

Activities Not Commenced:

- Changes in Logic or Constraints, or
- Changes in Duration, or
- Changes in estimated **Costs**, **Hours** or **Quantities**.

The schedule may be updated after this information is collected.

Other Considerations

Primavera may calculate Actual Costs and the Costs to Complete by turning on a relationship between the Units and Resource Units. When this relationship is turned off costs may be entered manually. If the Actual Costs are to be calculated by Primavera then the Actual Costs do not need to be collected.

A marked-up copy of the schedule recording the progress of the current schedule is often produced prior to updating the data with Primavera. Ideally, the mark-up should be prepared by a physical inspection of the work or by a person who intimately knows the work, although that is not always possible. It is good practice to keep this marked-up record for your own reference. Ensure that you note the date of the mark-up (i.e., the data date) and, if relevant, the time.

Often a Status Report or mark-up sheet is distributed to the people responsible for marking up the project's progress. A page break could be placed at each responsible person's band, and when the schedule is printed, each person would have a personal listing of activities that are either in-progress or due to commence. This is particularly useful for large projects. The marked-up sheets are then returned to the scheduler for data entry into the software system.

Other electronic methods, such as the Primavera Timesheet system or an e-mail based system with spreadsheet or pdf attachments, may be employed to collect the data. Irrespective of the method used, the same data needs to be collected.

It is recommended that only one person update each schedule. There is a high probability for errors when more than one person updates a schedule.

20.4 Project Window Defaults for Updating a Resourced Schedule

The Project Window settings affect all activities in a project that are being updated. When more than one project is open, the settings of the **Default Project** are used to calculate all open projects when they are scheduled or leveled. The Default Project is set in the **Set Default Project** form opened by selecting **Project**, **Set Default Project....** NOTE: Read the **Multiple Project Scheduling** chapter for more details.

The **Calculations** tab in the **Projects Window** sets some important resource defaults:

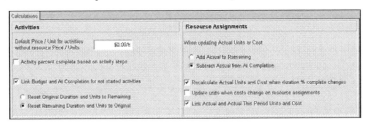

- **Activities**
  - ➤ **Default Price/Unit for activities without resource Price/Units**. When an activity is assigned a quantity in the **Activities**, **Status** tab but no resource is assigned, then this rate is used to calculate the cost against Labor and Nonlabor units.
  - ➤ **Activity percent complete based on activity steps**. The Primavera **Step** function enables activities to be broken down into elements called Steps. Each element earns a designated % Complete when the Step is marked as complete. Physical % Complete must be selected to use Steps.
  - ➤ Unchecking **Link Budget and At Completion for not started activities** enables the user to re-estimate the cost or quantities of unstarted activities while preserving the **Original Budget** of an activity. This also unlinks the **Original Duration** from the **At Completion Duration** for un-started activities. This is similar to the P3 Auto Cost Rule No 6 and was new to Primavera Version 4.1.
  - ➤ The next two options **Reset Original Durations and Units to Remaining** and **Reset Remaining Duration and Units to Original** determine how the Original Duration and Units are set when progress is removed from activities. This was new to Primavera Version 4.1.
- **Resource Assignments**
  - ➤ **When updating Actual Units or Costs**. There are two options, which is the same as the P3 Autocost Rule Number 3:
    - – **Add Actual to Remaining**. When Actual Costs are entered, the At Completion increases by the amount of the Actual Costs.
    - – **Subtract Actual from At Completion**. When Actual Costs are entered, the At Complete does not change and the To Complete is reduced by the value of the Actual. This is the author's preferred option, as the At Completion does not change until the At Completion is exceeded by the Actual.
  - ➤ **Recalculate Actual Units and Cost when duration % complete changes**. This option links the % Complete of **Duration Type** activities to the Actual and To Complete, thus an increase in % Complete will increase the Actual and decrease the To Complete values.
  - ➤ **Update units when costs change on resource assignments**.
    - – With this option checked a change in Costs will recalculate the Units.
    - – With this option unchecked, a change in costs may be made independently of units after units have been changed.

➢ **Link Actual and Actual This Period Units and Cost**. This is the same as the P3 Autocost Rule Number 6. With this option checked, when you enter an **Actual this period**, the **Actual to date** will be calculated by increasing the original value by the value of the **Actual this period**. Alternatively, you may enter the **Actual to date** and Primavera will calculate the **Actual this period**. When unchecked, the two fields are unlinked and you may enter any figure in each field. This option is grayed out if the project is not open and is used to fix errors in data entry.

20.5 Activity Window - Percent Complete Types

There are three **% Complete** types which may be assigned to each activity. The default is adopted from the setting in the **Defaults** tab in the **Projects Window**.

- **Physical**
- **Duration**
- **Units**

20.5.1 Assigning the Project Default Percent Complete Type

A project default **Percent Complete Type** is assigned in the **Defaults** tab of the Projects Window and is assigned to each new activity created in a project. This may be changed at any time and only affects new activities created from that time onward:

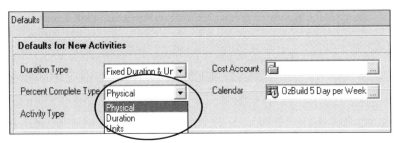

After an activity has been created, the **Percent Complete Type** may be changed in the **General** tab of the **Activities Window**:

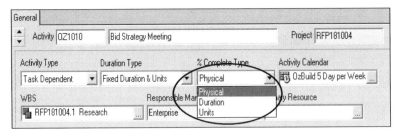

The Activity Percent Complete may be updated in the **Status** tab of the **Activities Window** where the **Percent Complete Type** is also displayed:

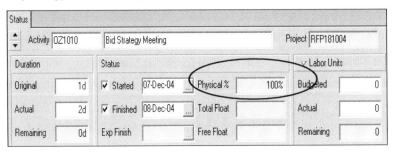

Each **Percent Complete Type** has its own data column. There is also an **Activity % Complete** column which is linked to and displays the value from the **Percent Complete Type** column that has been assigned to the activity. See the following picture:

Activity ID	Activity Name	Percent Complete Type	Activity % Complete	Physical % Complete	Duration % Complete	Units % Complete
AA1000	% Complete Physical	Physical	50% ⟷	50%	0%	0%
AA1010	% Complete Duration	Duration	50% ⟵	0% ⟶	50%	0%
AA1020	% Complete Type Units	Units	50% ⟵	0%	0% ⟶	50%

20.5.2 Physical Percent Complete Type

An activity assigned Physical Percent Complete Type may be entered in the **Physical % Complete** or the **Activity % Complete**. This field has no impact and is not linked to either the Resource Units or the Actual and Remaining Durations of the Activity.

Physical % Complete muct be used when **Steps** are being used to record progress.

The **Physical Percent Complete** type is used when the progress of an Activity is being measured outside Primavera. For example, an activity representing the installation cable that is measured by length of cable installed would have the percent complete calculated by:

- % Complete = Qty. of Cable Installed / Total Qty. of Cable to be Installed

For example, the activity may only have the installation labor assigned to it, and therefore the installation labor parameter may not be used for the measurement of the Activity % Complete. In addition, because the percent complete of the activity is based on the length of cable installed, the activity % Complete (the progress of the work) may be compared to the resource **Units % Complete** (the amount of labor used) which is calculated from the formula:

- Units % Complete = Actual Units / At Completion Units

This example is demonstrated in the following picture:

- The Activity Physical % Complete is set at 50%.
- The Activity Unit % Complete of 20% is calculated from the At Completion Units of 12.00 hrs and At Completion Units of 60.00 hrs and not the Budget Units of 48.00 hrs.

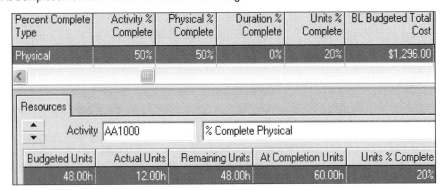

Percent Complete Type	Activity % Complete	Physical % Complete	Duration % Complete	Units % Complete	BL Budgeted Total Cost
Physical	50%	50%	0%	20%	$1,296.00

Resources

Activity AA1000   % Complete Physical

Budgeted Units	Actual Units	Remaining Units	At Completion Units	Units % Complete
48.00h	12.00h	48.00h	60.00h	20%

After a second resource is added, the Activity Units % Complete of 40% is calculated from the addition of the two resource Actual Units and At Completion Units:

- Activity Unit % Complete = Actual Labor Units / At Completion Labor Units
- Therefore, 40% = (12 + 36) / (60 + 60)

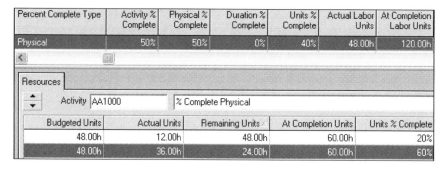

20.5.3 Duration Percent Complete Type

With Duration Percent Complete there is a link established between:

- **Duration % Complete**
- **Original Duration**
- **Remaining Duration**

A **Duration % Complete** may only be entered after an Actual Start Date has been assigned and should be in the past with respect to the Current Data Date.

A change in one parameter will change one other:

- A change in the **Duration % Complete** will change the **Remaining Duration,** and
- A change in the **Original Duration** or **Remaining Duration** will change the **Duration % Complete**:

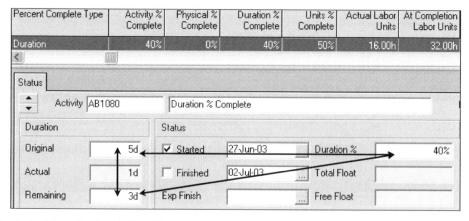

The **Actual Duration** is calculated from the duration of **Actual Start** to the **Current Data Date**.

The Activity **Units Percent Complete** is still calculated from the Resource Units.

20.5.4 Units Percent Complete Type

When **Units Percent Complete** type is selected:

- This option creates a link between the **Activity % Complete** and the activity **Units % Complete**, and

- The **Duration % Complete** is calculated from the relationship between the **Original Duration** and **Actual Duration**.

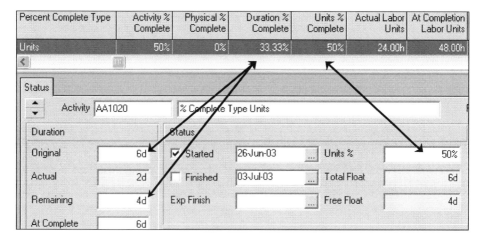

20.6 Using Steps to Calculate Activity Percent Complete

An activity percent complete may be defined by using steps. A Step is a measurable or identifiable task required to complete an activity. In summary to use steps:

- A Step template may be created by selecting **Enterprise**, **Activity Step Template....** to open the **Activity Step Templates** form.

- Add as many step as required and assign their weigh which will be used to apportion the percent complete of an activity.

- Check the **Activity percent complete based on steps** check box in the **Projects Window**, **Calculations** tab,

- Select the **Physical** in the **% Complete Type** for each activity that is to be measured by steps in the **General** tab of **Activity Window**,

- Select the **Steps** tab in the **Activity Window**,

- Format the columns you wish to display,

- Add the number of steps you require or import from a Step Template,

- Edit the descriptions as required,

- Edit the **Step Weight** so the **Step Weight Percent** reflects the desired value of the Step,

- Check the **Completed** check box as each step is completed and this will update the percent complete.

- The **Remaining Duration** may be updated from the **Step % Complete** via the **Physical % Complete** using a **Global Change**.

Step Name	% Complete	Step Weight	Step Weight Percent	Completed
Specify Document Composition	100%	10.0	10.0	☑
Document First Draft	100%	40.0	40.0	☑
Final Draft and Internal Approval	0%	25.0	25.0	☐
Client Approval	0%	25.0	25.0	☐

20.7   Updating the Schedule

20.7.1   Preferences, Defaults and Options for Updating a Project

The options to be considered and checked before updating a schedule:

Function	Discussion
• **% Complete Type**	It is the author's preference to use **Physical % Complete** when the resources are **Input** resources, i.e. those doing the work. This allows the % of deliverables complete to be measured independently of the resource(s) doing the work, thus allowing a comparison of the deliverables completed against the resources consumed.
• **Activity Type**	Activities with known durations should be set as **Task Dependent** and will use the Activity calendar (not the Resource Calendar) for calculating the finish date of the activity. **Resource Dependent** activities should only be used if there are resource availability issues which may only be resolved by the use of **Resource Calendars**. **Level of Effort** and **WBS** activities are useful but should be avoided by the novice user as these add an additional level of complexity that is not required.
• **Project Window Calculations tab**	The **Calculations** tab in the **Projects Window** sets some important resource defaults that should be reviewed, understood and set so the schedule calculates the desired way. The **Link Actual and Actual This Period Units and Cost** option found in the **Calculations** tab of the **Project Window** should be checked if it is intended to **Store Period Performance**.
• **Duration Type**	It is the author's preference to use **Fixed Duration and Units** because the estimate to complete is not altered by changing the Activity Duration or Units/Time. This duration type also sets the **Resource Assignments** option in the **User Preferences**, **Resource Analysis** tab to **Recalculate the Units, Duration, and Units/Time for existing assignments based on the activity Duration Type**.
• **Timesheets**	Timesheets may be used to update actuals for none, some, or all resources. Organizations using timesheets should have procedures managing their use. Timesheets are out of the scope of this publication but if they are being used the actual values should be carefully checked before being applied to ensure they are logical.

Function	Discussion
• **Resources Cost Calculation**	Resource Costs may be calculated from the Resource Unit Rates for each individual resource assignment.
	Each resource assignment has a field titled **Cost Units Linked**. When this is checked the resource costs are calculated from the resource units.
	The **Calculate costs from units** check box in the **Resource Window, Details** tab sets the default value for **Cost Units Linked** for new resource assignments.
	The two fields are not linked and the resource assignment setting may be changed at any time.
• **Resource Window Details Tab**	• **Auto Compute Actuals**
	This field is linked to all resources assignments. When this option is checked for a resource, Primavera calculates the Actual Units and Remaining Units using the Budgeted Units and Activity % Complete. This option may be overridden by applying the Activity **Auto Compute Actuals**.
	• **Calculate costs from units**
	There is a field available when a resource is assigned to an activity titled **Cost Units Linked.** With this option checked the costs for a resource are calculated from the **Resource Unit/Time** when a resource is added to an activity and whenever the Resource Units are changed.
• **Advanced Schedule Options**	One of the more important options to review is the **When scheduling progressed activities use** options, as these affect how out of progress sequence is handled. These options should be reviewed to ensure that when the schedule is recalculated you will understand what is happening.
	The author prefers **Retained Logic** as this gives a more conservative schedule and those relationships that need editing may be edited to reflect retained logic as required.
• **Steps**	Should it be decided to use Steps to update a schedule the **Projects Window Calculations** tab should have the **Activity percent complete based on activity steps** option checked and the Activity must be assigned **Physical % Complete Type** in the **General tab** of the **Activity Window** for each activity.

20.7.2 Updating Dates and Percentage Complete

The schedule should be first updated as outlined in the **Tracking Progress** chapter. In summary, this is completed by entering:

- The **Actual Start** and **Actual Finish** dates of **Complete** activities.
- The **Actual Start**, **% Complete** and/or **Remaining Duration** of **In-Progress** activities.
- Adjust **Logic**, **Constraints** and **Durations** of **Unstarted** activities.

Before updating the **% Complete**, the **% Complete Type** should be checked to ensure that the Actual and Remaining Durations, Costs and Units calculate as required. This ideally should be done by setting the project defaults at the time the project is created and adjusting the settings as activities are added and resources assigned.

20.8 Updating Resources

There are many permutations available for calculating resource data. Due to the number of options available in Primavera, it is not feasible to document all the combinations available for resource calculation.

Resource units and costs may be updated by either:

- Estimating Progress Automatically, a process titled **Applying Actuals**, or
- Entering the data using the **Resource** tab in the **Activities Window**, or
- Entering the data using the right section of the **General** tab in the **Activities Window**.

20.8.1 Resource Tab

The **Resources** tab may be used to update the resource **Units** (and Costs if the Units and Costs have been unlinked with the **Cost Units Linked** field). An updating layout could be created and the columns in the Resources tab formatted to your updating method, see the following picture:

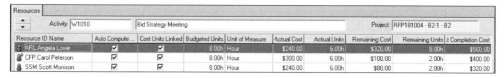

20.8.2 Status Tab

The right window may be used for updating the resources.

- When there is one resource there will be a direct link between this form and the values assigned to the resource.
- When there is more than one resource there will be a proportional change to all the resource values when a change is made in this form.

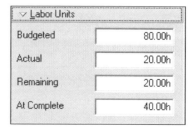

20.8.3 Applying Actuals

This function automatically:

- Statuses activities with resources as if they went according to the Planned Dates (this may changed Actual Dates and current schedule dates) and only updates activities in the period from the old to the New Data Date, or

- Apply actuals entered in the Primavera Timesheet system.

To Apply Actuals:

- Select **Tools**, **Apply Actuals...** to open the **Apply Actuals** form,

- Enter the **New Data Date** and click 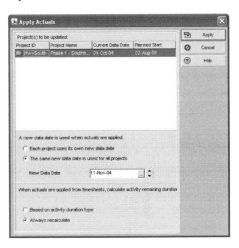 button.

- If more than one project is open a different data date may be selected for each project.

- The Activity requires the Task **Auto Compute Actuals** field checked for this function to apply to an Activity and all the Resources assigned to an activity.

- When the Task **Auto Compute Actuals** field is not checked only the resources that have the Resource **Auto Compute Actuals** field checked in the **Resource Window** will be updated. If one resource is checked and one not, then the checked resource will be updated and the unchecked resource work will be delayed until after the **Current Data Date**.

There are some important issues with using **Apply Actuals** that must be understood:

- This function uses the **Planned Dates** not the current schedule dates to progress a schedule so Actual Start Dates and the Early Finish dates may be changed by this function. This calculation process makes this function of little use to most schedulers.

- The Apply Actuals function does not work in the same way as the P3/SureTrak function "Update Progress" or the Microsoft Project function "Update Project" which both update all activities irrespective of resource assignment. The Apply Actuals function only updates resourced activities and unresourced activities such as milestones have to be updated manually when the task **Auto Compute Actuals** is not checked.

- With the introduction of **Progress Spotlight** there would appear to be no need to use **Apply Actuals** to automatically update a project and **Update Progress** and/or **Progress Spotlight** could be used. But as the **Update Progress** function also re sets **Actual Dates** to **Planned Dates** this make this function also of little use to many schedulers.

- A **Global Change** may be run first to set the **Planned** dates to the **Start** and **Finish** dates, but this results in a change to the Original Duration and therefore the % Duration will calculate incorrectly.

20.9   Updating Expenses

Expenses are updated in a similar way to resources and will not be covered.

20.10 Store Period Performance

This new function to Primavera Version 5.0 enables:

- The creation of user definable financial periods, say monthly or weekly, and
- The ability to record the actual and earned costs and quantities for each period.

Therefore, actual costs and quantities which span over more than one past period will be accurately reflected per period in all reports. If **Store Period Performance** is not used then the actuals are spread equally over the actual duration of an activity, which may not accurately reflect when the work performed and what was achieved in each period. These Periods apply to all projects in the database.

This function is similar to the **P3 Store Period Performance** function but will not Store Period Performance on Microsoft Project managed projects

The steps required to store period performance are:

- Ensure that the user has the necessary global privileges to **Edit Financial Period Dates**, **Store Period Performance** and **Edit Period Performance** when past actuals need to be edited.
- Open the appropriate project and ensure **Link Actual and Actual This Period Units and Cost** is enabled, select the **Calculations** tab in the lower pane of the **Projects** window and click the check box. This option is grayed out if the project is not open.
- Set the **Financial Periods** by selecting **Admin, Financial Periods….** Which will open the **Financial Periods** form:

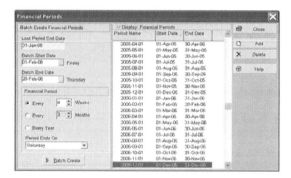

- To store the period performance select **Tools**, **Store Period Performance...** to open the **Store Period Performance** form, select the projects to have the period performance stored and click the ⊞ Store Now button.

Finally these results may be viewed and edited in the Past Period Actuals columns of the Resources Assignments Window, Activity Details Resources tab and the Activity Table.

20.11 Workshop 17 - Updating a Resourced Schedule

Background

We now need to update the activities and resources as at 12 Dec 11.

Assignment

1. If you did not complete the previous Leveling Workshop you will need create and assign a baseline and display the Baseline bar:

    ➢ Select **Project**, **Maintain Baselines...** and create a Baseline by saving a copy of the existing project,

    ➢ Select **Project**, **Assign Baselines...** and select this as both your **Project Baseline** and Primary **User Baseline**, thus ensuring and baseline bar will either be blank or display the Baseline and not the **Planned Dates**.

    ➢ Apply your **OzBuild Workshop 13 – Baseline** layout and the Baseline bar should be displayed.

2. In the **Project Window**, **Calculations** tab ensure your settings are as per the following picture, these are the standard settings:

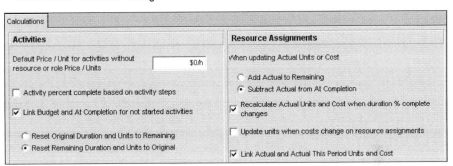

3. Assign the **Project Manager** to the **Create Technical Specification** task as this resource was missed out at the estimating stage and will give an immediate difference between the Current Schedule and the Baseline Units and Costs.

4. Save the Layout as **OzBuild Workshop 17 – Updating Resources** and format the columns as per the following picture, display the Primary Baseline bar.

5. Update this schedule manually by entering the following data in the **Activities**, **Status** tab or columns.

Activity ID	Activity Name	Actual Start	Actual Finish	Remaining Duration	Act % Comp
Bid for Facility Extension					
Technical Specification					
OZ1000	Approval to Bid	05-Dec-11 08		0d	100%
OZ1010	Determine Installation Requirements	05-Dec-11 08	07-Dec-11 16	0d	100%
OZ1020	Create Technical Specification	07-Dec-11 08		2d	40%

Continued.....

6. As you work through this workshop you should create several layouts, one for Actual Dates and Durations, one for Units, one for Costs and one for Percentages. The Costs layout would display costs in the Activity columns and the Resources tab. The Units layout would display units in the Activity columns and the Resources tab.

7. Schedule and move the **Data Date** to 12-Dec-11 08:00.

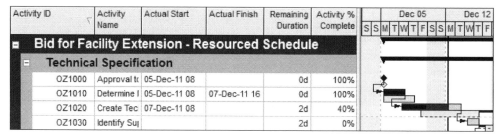

8. Create a **OzBuild Workshop 17 – Units** layout and display the columns shown in the Resources tab as shown below, see how the resources have been updated.

9. OZ1010 is complete so there are no costs or units to go and the Actuals have been set to equal the Budget, but may be manually adjusted.

Resources					
Activity	OZ1010		Determine Installation Requirements		
Resource ID Name	Remaining Units / Time	Budgeted Units	Actual Units	Remaining Units	At Completion Units
PM.Project Manager	0h/d	32h	32h	0h	32h
SE.Systems Engineer	0h/d	32h	32h	0h	32h

10. Now create a **OzBuild Workshop 17 – Costs** layout and check the costs:

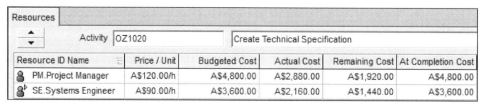

11. OZ1020 is in progress and the Remaining Units and Costs have been calculated from the Remaining Duration and the Remaining Units / Time, but may be manually adjusted.

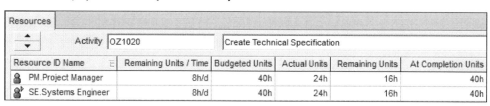

12. Now display the **Workshop 17 – Units** layout and check the costs:

Resources					
Activity	OZ1020		Create Technical Specification		
Resource ID Name	Remaining Units / Time	Budgeted Units	Actual Units	Remaining Units	At Completion Units
PM.Project Manager	8h/d	40h	24h	16h	40h
SE.Systems Engineer	8h/d	40h	24h	16h	40h

Continued.....

13. Check the expenses for the Specialist Consultant assigned to OZ1020. The Actual Costs could be updated manually at this time.

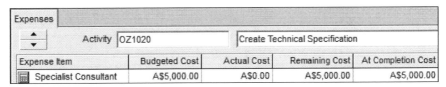

Expense Item	Budgeted Cost	Actual Cost	Remaining Cost	At Completion Cost
Specialist Consultant	A$5,000.00	A$0.00	A$5,000.00	A$5,000.00

Activity OZ1020 — Create Technical Specification

14. Now create a **OzBuild Workshop 17 – Percentages** layout and display the Percent Complete columns as per the following picture.

15. Enter 80% against the Physical % Complete of Create Technical Specification and see the Activity % Complete change to 80% as the activity % Complete Type is Physical:

Activity ID	Activity Name	Activity % Complete	Physical % Complete	Units % Complete	Duration % Complete
Bid for Facility Extension				20%	13.89%
Technical Specification				58.33%	45.45%
OZ1000	Approval to Bid	100%	100%	0%	100%
OZ1010	Determine Installation Requirements	100%	100%	100%	100%
OZ1020	Create Technical Specification	80%	80%	60%	60%

16. Select the Create Technical Specification activity, open the Status tab and change the Actual Labor Units from 48h to 24h in the box on the left side. Notice the Units % Complete change to 30% as less hours have been used, but the Remaining has increased to 56 hours:

Activity ID	Activity Name	Activity % Complete	Physical % Complete	Units % Complete	Duration % Complete
Bid for Facility Extension				15.71%	13.89%
Technical Specification				45.83%	45.45%
OZ1000	Approval to Bid	100%	100%	0%	100%
OZ1010	Determine Installation Requirements	100%	100%	100%	100%
OZ1020	Create Technical Specification	80%	80%	30%	60%

17. Now open the **OzBuild Workshop 17 – Units** layout and both resources now show 12h Actual and 28h remaining each. The **Remaining Units / Time** is now 14 hours/day because the **Activity Type** is **Fixed Duration**:

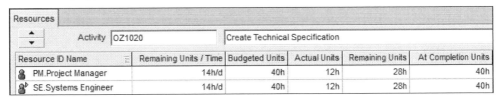

Resource ID Name	Remaining Units / Time	Budgeted Units	Actual Units	Remaining Units	At Completion Units
PM.Project Manager	14h/d	40h	12h	28h	40h
SE.Systems Engineer	14h/d	40h	12h	28h	40h

Activity OZ1020 — Create Technical Specification

18. Now open the **OzBuild Workshop 17 – Costs** layout and the Actual Costs and Remaining Costs should be recalculated:

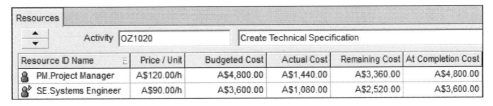

Resource ID Name	Price / Unit	Budgeted Cost	Actual Cost	Remaining Cost	At Completion Cost
PM.Project Manager	A$120.00/h	A$4,800.00	A$1,440.00	A$3,360.00	A$4,800.00
SE.Systems Engineer	A$90.00/h	A$3,600.00	A$1,080.00	A$2,520.00	A$3,600.00

Activity OZ1020 — Create Technical Specification

Continued.....

19. Now open the **OzBuild Workshop 17 – Units** layout and change the **Remaining Units** of **Create Technical Specification** to in the **Status** tab to 24. Note the change in the Units and Costs against the resources.

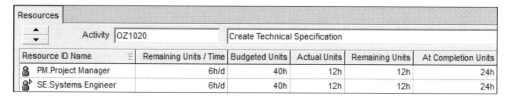

20. Now open the **OzBuild Workshop 17 – Costs** layout and the Actual Costs and Remaining Costs should be recalculated:

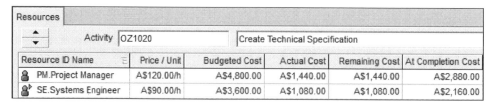

21. Create a new View titled **OzBuild Workshop 17 – Baseline Comparison** and edit the columns so you are able to see the **At Completion Variances** against activity OZ1020, the Technical Specification WBS Node and the Project:

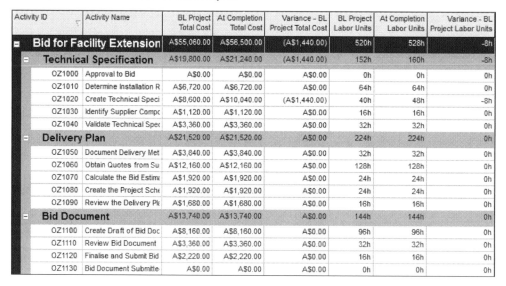

Activity ID	Activity Name	BL Project Total Cost	At Completion Total Cost	Variance – BL Project Total Cost	BL Project Labor Units	At Completion Labor Units	Variance – BL Project Labor Units
Bid for Facility Extension		A$55,060.00	A$56,500.00	(A$1,440.00)	520h	528h	-8h
Technical Specification		A$19,800.00	A$21,240.00	(A$1,440.00)	152h	160h	-8h
OZ1000	Approval to Bid	A$0.00	A$0.00	A$0.00	0h	0h	0h
OZ1010	Determine Installation R	A$6,720.00	A$6,720.00	A$0.00	64h	64h	0h
OZ1020	Create Technical Speci	A$8,600.00	A$10,040.00	(A$1,440.00)	40h	48h	-8h
OZ1030	Identify Supplier Compo	A$1,120.00	A$1,120.00	A$0.00	16h	16h	0h
OZ1040	Validate Technical Spec	A$3,360.00	A$3,360.00	A$0.00	32h	32h	0h
Delivery Plan		A$21,520.00	A$21,520.00	A$0.00	224h	224h	0h
OZ1050	Document Delivery Met	A$3,840.00	A$3,840.00	A$0.00	32h	32h	0h
OZ1060	Obtain Quotes from Su	A$12,160.00	A$12,160.00	A$0.00	128h	128h	0h
OZ1070	Calculate the Bid Estim	A$1,920.00	A$1,920.00	A$0.00	24h	24h	0h
OZ1080	Create the Project Sche	A$1,920.00	A$1,920.00	A$0.00	24h	24h	0h
OZ1090	Review the Delivery Pla	A$1,680.00	A$1,680.00	A$0.00	16h	16h	0h
Bid Document		A$13,740.00	A$13,740.00	A$0.00	144h	144h	0h
OZ1100	Create Draft of Bid Doc	A$8,160.00	A$8,160.00	A$0.00	96h	96h	0h
OZ1110	Review Bid Document	A$3,360.00	A$3,360.00	A$0.00	32h	32h	0h
OZ1120	Finalise and Submit Bid	A$2,220.00	A$2,220.00	A$0.00	16h	16h	0h
OZ1130	Bid Document Submitte	A$0.00	A$0.00	A$0.00	0h	0h	0h

22. At this point you may experiment with this activity. Uncheck **Auto Compute Actuals** will allow you to change the Costs and they are not recalculated for the Resource Rate.

23. You may also look at some of the other tabs such as the **Summary** tab.

21 OTHER METHODS OF ORGANIZING PROJECT DATA

The **Work Breakdown Structure – WBS** function was discussed earlier as a method of organizing projects and activities under hierarchical structures. There are alternative features available in Primavera for grouping, sorting and filtering activities, resources and project information:

- Activity Codes
- User Defined Fields (UDF)
- Project Phase or WBS Category
- Resource Codes
- Cost Accounts
- EPS Level Activity Codes

There are no Activity ID Codes in Primavera like the function found in P3 and SureTrak. In Primavera each project must have a unique Activity ID but no logical code system may be associated with the Activity ID. Some users double code activities so some Activity ID characters are the same as an Activity Code.

21.1 Understanding Project Breakdown Structures

A Project Breakdown Structure represents a hierarchical breakdown of a project into logical functional elements. Some organizations have highly organized and disciplined structures with "rules" for creating and coding the elements of the structure. Some clients also impose a WBS code on a contractor for reporting and/or claiming payments. The following are examples of such structures:

- WBS **Work Breakdown Structure**, breaks down the project into the elements of work required to deliver a project.

- COA **Code of Accounts**, also known as **Cost Breakdown Structure**. Often this contains costs that are not included in a schedule, such as insurances and overheads. The WBS would in this situation represent part of the COA.

- OBS **Organization Breakdown Structure**, shows the hierarchical management structure of a project. Primavera has a predefined field for this breakdown structure.

- CBS **Contract Breakdown Structure**, shows the breakdown of contracts into elements.

- SBS **System Breakdown Structure**, a **System Engineering** method of breaking down a complex system into elements.

- PBS **Product Breakdown Structure**, a **PRINCE2** term used for the breakdown of project deliverables under two headings of Project Management and Specialists products.

The following functions are available in Primavera to represent these structures in your schedule.

21.2   Activity Codes

Activity Codes may be used to Group, Sort and Filter activities from one or more open projects.

- **Activity Codes**, such as Phases, Trades or Disciplines, are often defined in the **Activity Codes Definition** form.

- **Activity Code Values** are defined in the **Activity Codes** form, such as:
  - ➢ Phases of Design, Procure, Install and Test,
  - ➢ Trades of Brickwork, Plumbing and Electrical, and
  - ➢ Disciplines of Concrete, Mechanical, Pipework.

- **Activity Codes** are assigned from the **Activities Window** using the **Codes** tab in the lower pane or displaying the Activity Code column.

P3 and SureTrak have one WBS Code Dictionary with a hierarchical structure of WBS Codes, effectively producing an unlimited number of WBS Codes with a maximum of 20 levels. Microsoft Project 2002 introduced Custom Outline Codes, which is a hierarchical coding structure that may be assigned to activities and enables the activities to be Grouped under these codes. There are 10 codes available with every project that may be renamed to suit the project requirement. The Primavera Activity Code function operates similarly to both the P3 and SureTrak WBS Code functions and the Microsoft Project Custom Outline Codes, yet enables an unlimited number of Code Dictionaries and Values for each Code Dictionary.

21.2.1   Creating Activity Codes

There are two types of Activity Codes:

- **Project Activity Codes** that may only be created when a project is opened and applied only to the project they were created for. These may be made Global by clicking the 🌐 Make Global button in the **Activity Codes Definition - Project** form.

- **Global Activity Codes** that may be created at any time and applied to any project.

Activity Codes may be added, deleted or modified:

- Select **Enterprise**, **Activity Codes...** to open the **Activity Codes** form,

- Select either **Global** or **Project** depending on whether the codes are for a specific project or are to be available to all projects,

- Select from the drop down box which code structure is to be operated on.

- The code structure is modified in a similar way to WBS codes.

- Each Activity Code has a Code and a Description. The length of the Code is defined when the code is created; see the next section.

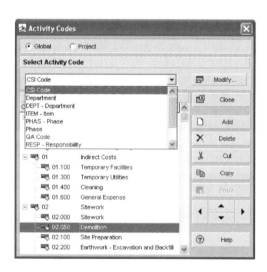

21.2.2 Defining an Activity Code

Defining an Activity Code is similar to creating a Code Dictionary in P3 and SureTrak or renaming a Microsoft Project Custom Outline Code:

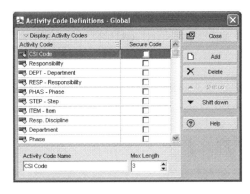

- From the **Activity Codes** form select **Project** or **Global**,

- Click the [Modify...] button to open the **Activity Codes Definition** form,

- The Activity Codes may be created, deleted, made Global and reordered in this form.

- The **Maximum Length** is the maximum number of characters a code may be assigned when it is created in the **Activity Codes form**.

The **Activity Codes Definition - Project** form has a button [Make Global] that makes a Project Activity Code a Global Activity Code.

21.2.3 Assigning Activity Codes to Activities

Activity Codes may be assigned to an activity:

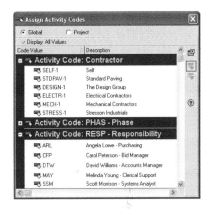

- Select the **Codes** tab in the lower pane by clicking the [Assign] button to open the **Assign Activity Codes** form.

- Display the appropriate activity code column and either:
  - ➢ Type in the code, or
  - ➢ Click twice on the Activity Code cell and open the **Select "Code"** form.

- Right-click in the top pane and select **Assign, Activity Codes...**.

21.3 Add Activity Codes When Assigning Codes

Activity Codes may be added on the fly, there is a new button title **New** on the **Assign Activity Codes** form that allows Activity Codes to be created as they are assigned:

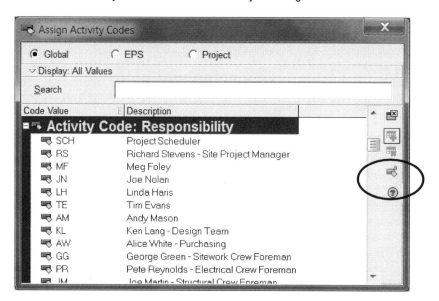

Click on the ![button] button to open the Add Code Value form and enter the new Code Value and Code Vale Description.

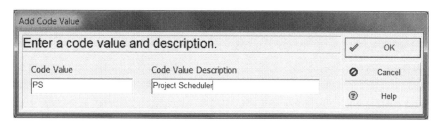

21.3.1 Grouping, Sorting and Filtering with Activity Codes

When more than one project is open an Activity Code may be used to group activities from all the open projects under one code structure.

Activity Codes are Grouped and Filtered in the same way as WBS codes.

21.3.2 Importing Activity Codes with Excel

If an Activity Code is to be imported with activities using the Primavera Excel Import function, it must exist in the database before it is imported; otherwise, the code will not be imported.

Activity Codes may be imported by loading the Software Developers Kit (SDK) and using a Excel spreadsheet available from the Oracle Primavera Knowledgebase. Instructions for loading the SDK are available from the Administration Guide.

21.4 User Defined Fields

User Defined Fields are similar to Custom Data Items in P3 or Custom Fields in Microsoft Project and provide the ability to assign additional information to database records. They may be used for recording information about the data field as an alternative to Activity Codes and other predefined Primavera fields. The type of data that may be assigned to User Defined Fields would be equipment number, order number, variation or scope number; road, railway or pipeline changes; address and additional costs data.

Activity data may be filtered, grouped and sorted using these User Defined Fields in a similar way to Activity Codes.

Data may be imported into the fields and, unlike Activity Codes, the data item does not have to exist in the database before importing.

There are a number of predefined fields that may be renamed and new ones may be created. User Defined Fields may be defined for:

- Activities
- Activity Resource Assignments
- Activity Steps
- Issues
- Project Expenses
- Projects
- Resources
- Risks
- WBS
- Work Products and Documents

The fields are assigned a **Data Type** from the following list:

- Text – maximum of 255 characters
- Start Date and Finish Date – which may be used to create bars
- Cost
- Indicator – select from ⊗ ⍦ ⊘ ★
- Integer
- Number

After some data has been entered against a field in any project, the **Data Type** may not be changed.

User Definable Field values may be imported with activities using Excel as long as the field has been created and the data is in the correct format.

 One advantage of **User Definable Fields** over **Notebook Topics** is that they may be also displayed in columns and be cut and pasted into other programs like Excel.

Select **Enterprise**, **User Defined Fields...** to open the **User Defined Fields** form:

- Select the **Subject Area** in the drop down box in the top right-hand side of the form.
- Use the [Add] and [X Delete] buttons to create and delete fields.
- Select the **Data Type** from the drop down list.

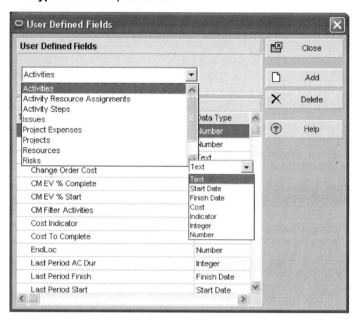

To display or edit data in a User Defined Field the column should be displayed in the appropriate window. For example, if a Risk User Defined Field has been created then the Risk window should be selected and the field will be displayed under **User Defined**.

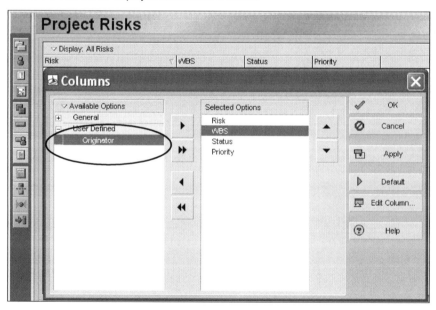

21.5 Project Phase or WBS Category

The **Project Phase** or **WBS Category** may be created, deleted and reordered in the **Project Phase** tab of the **Categories** form.

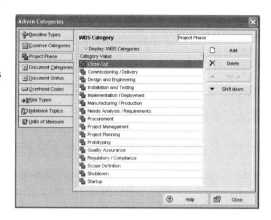

The **Project Phase** is assigned to **WBS Nodes** in the **WBS Window** and may be used to Group and Sort WBS Nodes under a different set of headings in a similar way to Project Codes in P3.

This would enable, for example, all design WBS Nodes that were distributed throughout a project WBS to be grouped together under one heading without assigning an Activity Code to each activity.

21.6 Resource Codes

Resource Codes are to resources as Activity Codes are to activities and allow resources to be Grouped, Sorted and Filtered by these codes. Resources may have codes such as Office, Location or Employment Status assigned to them.

To create a Resource Code:

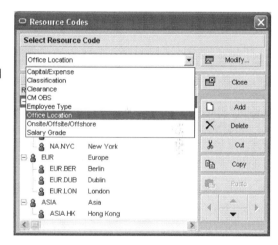

- Select **Enterprise**, **Resource Codes...** to open the **Resource Codes** form.
- The Resource Codes are created, edited and deleted in a similar way to Activity Codes.

Resource Codes may be Assigned to Resources in a similar way to Activity Codes by:

- Displaying the appropriate Code Column, or
- Opening the **Codes** tab in the **Resources Window**.

21.7   Cost Accounts

Cost Accounts are to resources as Activity Codes are to activities and are intended to reflect the accounting code structure of a project. As in P3, a Cost Account in Primavera is assigned to a resource. They enable the grouping of resource data into Cost Accounts which would allow budgets to be calculated and used to update Corporate Budgets.

Cost Accounts have additional functions that Activity Codes do not have:

- A default Cost Account for each new Resource or Expense may be specified in the **Projects Window**, **Defaults** tab. This is used for each new Resource or Expense and does not affect existing assignments. The **Project Default Cost Account** may be changed at any time:

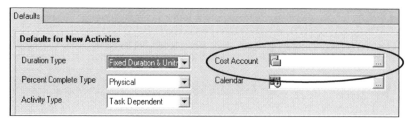

- Cost Accounts may be reassigned and merged.
- Cost Accounts may have descriptive fields when they are created.

Costs accounts are created in the **Cost Accounts** form by selecting **Enterprise**, **Cost Accounts...** and opening the **Cost Accounts** form.

Cost Accounts are assigned to Resources or Expenses by displaying the Cost Account column in the **Activities Window** lower pane **Resources** and **Expenses** tabs.

21.8   Owner Activity Attribute

"Owner," the new activity field in Primavera Version 6.0, enables a User who is not a resource to be assigned to an activity. This now enables the person responsible for an activity to be assigned from the list of users. This function may be used in combination with a Reflection project.

21.9   EPS Level Activity Codes

EPS Activity Codes may be created and assigned only to project activities that belong to the EPS Node for which the EPS Activity Codes have been created. This enables the display of all project activities under one or more EPS Nodes utilizing dedicated alternative hierarchical structure. There are also specific privileges for the management of these codes.

21.9.1   Create an EPS Level Activity Code Dictionary

- Select **Enterprise, Activity Codes...** to open the **Activity Code** form and click the **EPS** radio button,
- Select **Modify...** to open the **Activity Code Definition – EPS** form where the new code dictionary is created,
- Click **Add** to open the **Select EPS** form, select an EPS Node that the New Code will be used with and click to select the node,
- Type the EPS Activity Code Name and assign the Max Length of the code.
- The **Make Global** button converts the Activity Code to a Global Activity Code.
- The **Secure Code** box hides the code from people without the required access privileges.
- Select **Close** to return to the **Activity Code Definition – EPS** form.

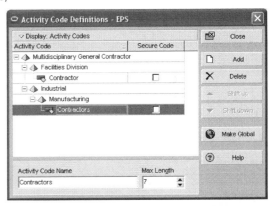

21.9.2   Create EPS Activity Codes

- Select the Code Dictionary to be modified from the drop down list under the heading **Select Activity Code** in the **Activity Codes** form, **EPS** tab.
- Click **Add** to add a hierarchical set of codes in the same method as other codes.

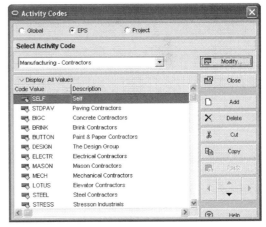

21.9.3   Assigning EPS Activity Codes to Activities

EPS Activity Codes may only be assigned to activities belonging to projects that are a member of the EPS Node and are assigned in the same way as Global and Project Activity Codes.

21.10 Workshop 18 - Activity Codes and User Defined Fields (UDF)

Background
This workshop will look at creating an Activity Code and some UDFs. In the next workshop you will populate the UDFs using a Global Change.

We will create an activity code to represent the departments' responsibilities for the Project,

Assignment – Activity Codes

1. Select **Enterprise, Activity Codes...** to open the **Activity Code** form,
2. Click on the **Project** radio button at the top of the form.
3. Select [Modify...] to open the **Activity Code Definitions – Project** form.
4. Select [Add] to create a new code titled **Department** and assign a **Max Length** of 3.
5. Click on [Close] to close the form and create the Activity Codes as per the picture on the right.
6. Apply the **OzBuild Workshop 11 – Without Float** layout.
7. Add the Department column as per the picture and save the layout as **OzBuild Workshop 18 – Assign Codes** layout.
8. Assign the Departments using all the methods available as per the following picture:

Activity ID	Activity Name	Department
Bid for Facility Extension		
Technical Specification		
0Z1000	Approval to Bid	OBM
0Z1010	Determine Installation Requirements	OBM.EN
0Z1020	Create Technical Specification	OBM.EN
0Z1030	Identify Supplier Components	OBM.PR
0Z1040	Validate Technical Specification	OBM.PS
Delivery Plan		
0Z1050	Document Delivery Methodology	OBM.EN
0Z1060	Obtain Quotes from Suppliers	OBM.PR
0Z1070	Calculate the Bid Estimate	OBM.PR
0Z1080	Create the Project Schedule	OBM.PS
0Z1090	Review the Delivery Plan	OBM.PS
Bid Document		
0Z1100	Create Draft of Bid Document	OBM.PS
0Z1110	Review Bid Document	OBM.PS
0Z1120	Finalise and Submit Bid Document	OBM.PS
0Z1130	Bid Document Submitted	OBM

Continued.....

9. Now organize by the **Activity Code Department**, sort by Start date, the Milestones are now at the top of the screen, display the Bars and Baseline Milestone (moving both o the bottom of the form to ensure the relationships would be displayed on the Current Schedule bars:

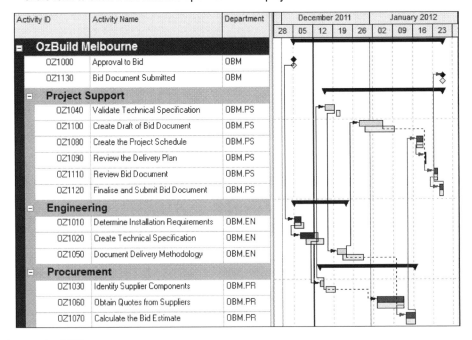

Assignment – UDFs

10. We will create some UDFs which we will populate using a Global Change,
11. Select **Enterprise**, **User Defined Fields…** to open the **Used Defined Fields** form,
12. Select **Activities** in the drop down box at the top of the form,
13. Add three UDFs titled
    - **Last Period Start** as a **Data Type** of **Start Date**
    - **Last Period Finish** as a **Data Type** of **Finish date**
    - **Last Period AC Dur** (Last Period At Completion Duration) as a **Data Type** of **Number**.
14. Display the columns and Group by WBS as per the following picture:

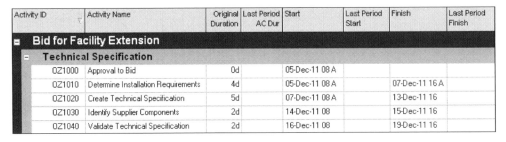

15. Save the Layout as **Workshop 18 – UDF**.

22 GLOBAL CHANGE

22.1 *Introducing Global Change*

Global Change is a facility for changing more than one data item in one step. Examples of uses of Global Change are:

- Assigning Resources to Roles

- Increasing or decreasing durations of selected activities by a factor

- Creating new activity descriptions by placing activity codes at the beginning or at the end of the original description

- Removing constraints

- Changing Calendars.

At the time of writing this publication, Global Change could not be used in the **Projects Window** as this data may not be accessed by Global Change.

This chapter is intended as an introduction to **Global Change** and covers the following topics:

- The Basic Concepts of Global Change

- Specifying the Change Statements

- Simple Examples of Global Change

- Selecting the Activities for the Global Change

- Temporary Values and Global Change Functions

- More Advanced Examples of Global Change.

After you understand the basics you will then develop some interesting ways of using Global Change.

It is very easy to specify a Global Change that will not change data in the way you intended. You must consider your Autocost rules when using Global Change on resources, percentages complete and durations. For example, changing Original Durations will have no effect on the Early Finish of activities that have commenced when Remaining Duration and Percent Complete are unlinked.

 Be careful when using Global Change, as the changes may not be undone. Consider copying your project or making a Reflection project if you are using Primavera before making Global Changes. Study the **Global Change Report** to review your changes before making permanent changes.

22.2   The Basic Concepts of Global Change

A Global Change may be created, saved, and used at a later date.

A Global Change may not be "Undone."

Select **Tools**, **Global Change...** to open the Global Change form:

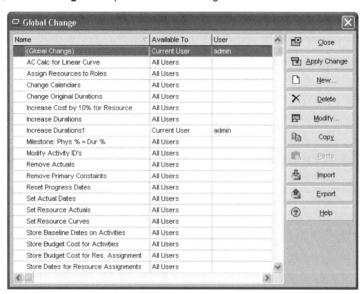

The **Global Change** form displays the list of Global Changes available in the project.

- [Apply Change] enables the effects of a Global Change in the **Global Change Report** before finalizing changes to the project data by selecting [Commit Changes] in the **Global Change Report.**

- [Close] closes the Global Change form.

- [New...] creates a new Global Change.

- [Modify...] enables you to modify the highlighted Global Change.

- [Delete] deletes the highlighted Global Change.

- [Copy] and [Paste] create a copy of an existing Global Change that may then be edited.

- [Import] and [Export] are used to import from or export to a Global Change from another database in the **Primavera Change File pcf** file format.

 It is **STRONGLY** recommended that you always review the **Global Change Report** to review your changes before making permanent changes by running a Global Change.

It is **STRONGLY** recommended that you consider making a copy of your project before using a Global Change: copy the project in the Enterprise Window, make a Baseline or use a Reflection Project.

After creating Global Change using the [New...] option or [Copy] and [Paste] or by selecting [Modify...], you will be presented with the second **Global Change** form.

This is where you select the data to be changed and where the operation to the data is specified.

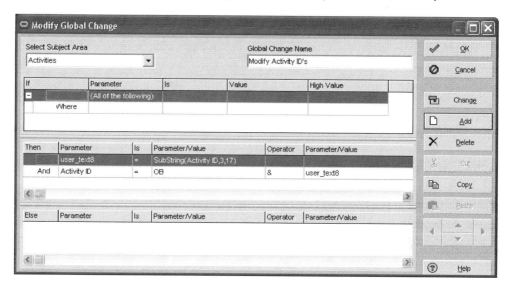

There are boxes at the top of the form:

- **Select Subject Area** enables the option of Activities, Activity Resource Assignments or Project Expenses, and

- **Global Change Name** is the name displayed in the **Global Change** form.

The form has three lower sections. You will need to click into each area and then use [Add] and [Delete] buttons to add or remove criteria or operation lines:

- **If** area is where you create a criteria for selecting the data on which to be operated. This is similar to the method of creating a filter.

- **Then** area is where you specify the operation to be applied to the selected data.

- **Else** area is where you have an option to specify an operation to data that has not been selected.

- [OK] accepts edits to the Change but does not execute it.

- [Cancel] cancels any edits to the Change.

- [Change] enables you to see the results of your action in a **Global Change Report** before changing the database.

- The other commands are self-explanatory and are used to create and edit lines in the Global Change, but you will need to click into the **If** or **Then** or **Else** sections that you wish to work on.

22.3 Specifying the Change Statements

The basic Global Change in the following picture will add 5 days to the Original Durations of activities, where the Original Duration is greater than or equal to 10 days, and increase all others by 20%.

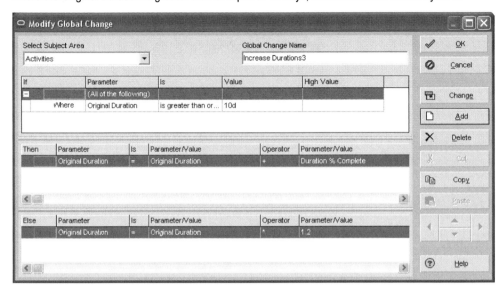

There are three areas in the **Modify Global Change** form:

- The **If** section has 5 fields and works in the same way as a Filter. It is used to select the data to be changed.

- The **Then** section has 5 fields:
  - ➢ **Parameter** – This is the data field(s) that is(are) to be modified when the **If** statement is satisfied.
  - ➢ **Is** – This is a statement.
  - ➢ **Parameter Value** – This is the source data for the change and may be the same field as the **Parameter** when it is intended to change the parameter value.
  - ➢ **Operator** – This is how the Parameter Value is to be changed.
  - ➢ **Parameter Value** – This is the value or other parameter that will be used to make the change.

- The **Else** section operates in the same way as the **If** section when the **If** statement is NOT satisfied.

22.4   Examples of Simple Global Changes

The following examples are very simple Global Changes.

Increase Original Durations

This Global Change will increase the Original Duration field value by 20% by multiplying the original duration by 1.2.

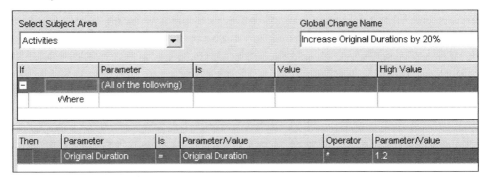

Copying Dates

This example will copy the Early Start (ES) and Early Finish (EF) into two custom data item fields: **user_start_date1** and **user_end_date1**.

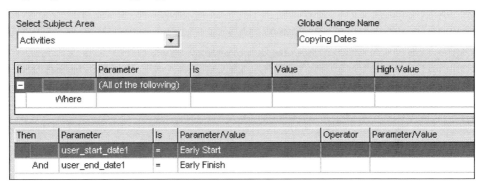

Removing Actual Dates

Setting a field to be blank will remove data in some situations:

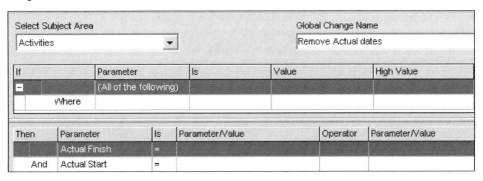

22.5 Selecting the Activities for the Global Change

Often you will want to make a Global Change to data that meets a specific criteria. The **If** statement lines are used to select the data. The operations defined in the **Then** lines will be executed. Data that does not meet the **Then** criteria may be changed with operations defined in the **Else** statement lines.

The following example will double Remaining Durations if the percent complete is greater than 50%.

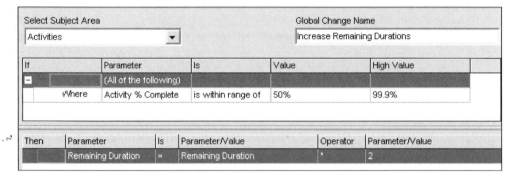

The following example will add 5 days to the Original Duration of activities over 10 days and increase by 20% those less than 10 days

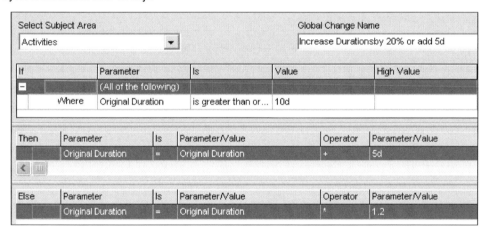

(Any of the following) and (All of the following)

There are two options under the **Parameter** title in the **If** section, **(Any of the following)** and **(All of the following)**. These are used with the **If** statements in the same way as with filters.

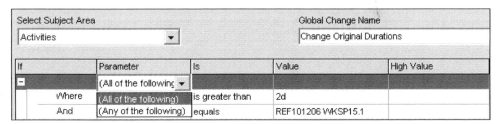

When **(Any of the following)** is selected, the Global Change will operate when any of your selection criteria is met. In the example following, any activity with the Original Duration greater than 2 days, or an activity that is assigned to the WBS Node REF101206WKSP15.1, will be doubled.

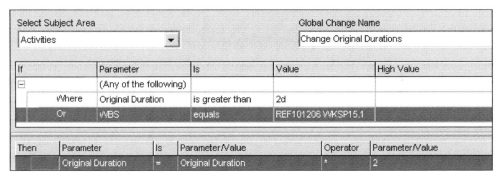

Every selection criteria has to be met when **(All of the following)** is selected for the Global Change to operate on the data. In the example following, only activities with the Original Duration greater than 2 days and an activity that is assigned to the WBS Node REF101206WKSP15.1, will be doubled.

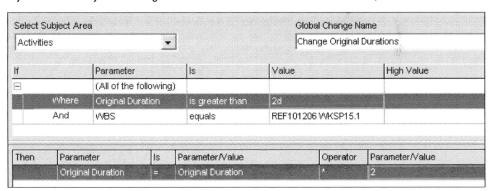

22.6   Temporary Values

Some calculations require more than one operation to achieve the required change. A **Temporary Value** is created on a **Then** or **Else** line. This **Temporary Value** may then be used on a subsequent line. Any **User Defined Field** may be used as a Temporary Value.

The following example is used to calculate Cost to Complete (CTC) based on a unit cost calculated from the Actual Cost divided by the Actual Quantity:

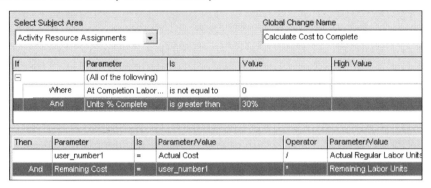

In this example, Actual Costs /Actual Regular Labor Units calculates the actual unit rate in the **user_number1** field, and the Remaining Cost is the unit rate x the Remaining Labor Units.

- The percent complete must be greater than 30%.

- The resource must have a quantity.

- **user_number1**, a temporary value, is cost per unit calculated by dividing Actual Cost by Actual Regular Labor Units and represents the resource actual unit rate.

- Remaining Cost is equal to Remaining Labor Units multiplied by the actual unit rate.

It is important that you consider the Autocost rules that you have assigned to the activities and resources, otherwise your Global Change may not work. In this situation you would not want **Cost Linked** or **Auto Compute Actuals** checked.

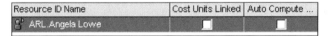

22.7   Global Change Functions

There are some functions that may be used with Global Change in the **Parameter/Value** field under **Then** and **Else** and that operate in a similar way to Excel or P3. These functions may be used to populate User Defined Fields from other data fields as part of the process of editing Activity Descriptions and Activity IDs.

Global Change Function	Function Operation
• DayOfWeek(Parameter)	Selects the weekday number of the date.
• LeftString(Parameter,*)	Selects * of characters from the start of a field.
• RightString(Parameter,*)	Selects * of characters from the end of a field.
• SubString(Parameter,a,b)	From character "a" selects "b" number of characters.

22.8   More Advanced Examples of Global Change

At the time of writing this publication, Global Change may be used to assign resources to roles, replace resources, but not assign resources to activities.

Changing Activity ID by Adding a Middle Character

The following Global Change adds a "C" after the second character of the Activity ID:

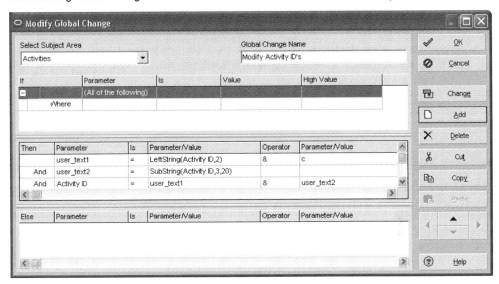

Adding Resources with Global Change

The following example assigns a resource, ARL Angela Lowe, to the Sales Engineer Role when the Start Date is greater than the Current Data Date.

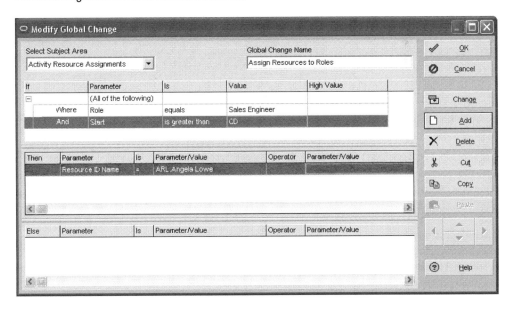

Other Global Change Uses

Global Changes may be used for the following purposes and you may wish to inspect some of the sample Global Changes provided in the sample database:

- Add a middle character in an Activity ID or other field by using two User Defined fields and the **Concatenation** operator, which is the **"&"** character.

- Add a prefix to an Activity ID.

- Replace a resource with another. Ensure that you check the **Assignment Staffing** setting in the **User Preferences**, **Calculations** tab.

- Update the **Remaining Duration** from a **Step Percent Complete** by setting the **Duration Percent Complete** equal to the **Physical Percent Complete**.

- Edit the Activity Name using Global Change Functions.

- To set the **Planned Dates** to equal the **Start** and **Finish** dates before applying **Progress Spotlight** so **Actual** dates are not changed by **Progress Spotlight**.

22.9   Workshop 19 - Global Change

Preamble
We wish to copy the current update information to the User Definable Fields created in the previous workshop.

Assignment
1. Apply the **Workshop 18 – UDF**.
2. Create a Global Change titled Set Last Period Data and add the following parameters:
   ➢ Last Period Start to equal Start
   ➢ Last Period Finish to equal Finish
   ➢ Last Period AC Dur to equal At Completion Duration divided by 8

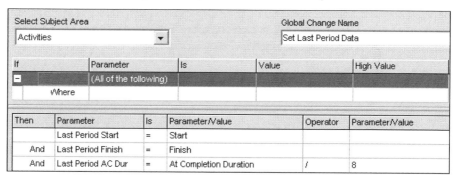

3.   Run the Global Change and commit the changes with the button at the bottom of the screen:

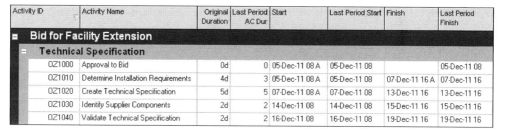

3. Create and display a gray bar showing from **Last Period Start** to **Last Period Finish** in position 3.

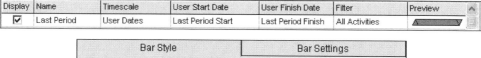

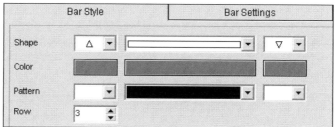

4. Adjust the row height as required and your schedule may look like the following picture with three bars.

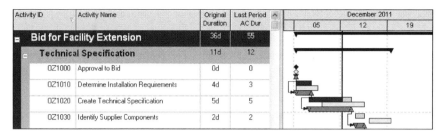

NOTE: The Last Period AC Dur Project displayed against the WBS bands are not correct as they are an addition of the Durations and not calculated from the dates. These may be hidden in Version 6.0 from the **Group and Sort** form.

5. Create and run a Global Change to multiply the Remaining Durations of tasks in the Delivery Plan Phase by 1.5 and then schedule.

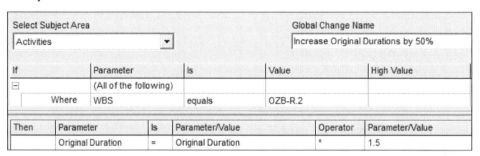

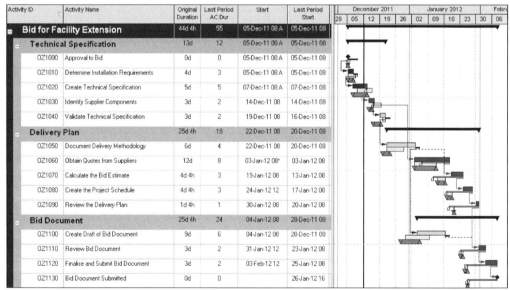

6. You will notice that:
   ➢ Negative Float has been created and the change in durations is observed in the bars and from the differences in the Duration values.
   ➢ The hours are now displayed and although the display was in days, the durations are not rounded up to whole days as in P3 with the application of a Global change.

23 MANAGING THE ENTERPRISE ENVIRONMENT

This section introduces the management of an Enterprise environment and discusses more thoroughly some subjects that have been addressed earlier.

For all databases that have more than one user, it is important to appoint a database manager who is responsible for security and maintenance of the database. A database will very quickly degenerate into a mess if it is not strictly controlled. Typical problems include multiple Resources representing the same person, excessive numbers of Layouts, Filters, Calendars and other codes, the deletion of important data and a misunderstanding or total ignorance of how the software works. The database manager should be responsible for maintaining the database, including but not limited to the following responsibilities:

- Users and Security Profiles
- Enterprise Breakdown Structure
- Organizational Breakdown Structure
- Project Codes
- User Defined Fields
- Global and Resource Calendars
- Roles and Resources
- Global Layouts and Filters
- Creating Projects including setting defaults
- Importing Projects and other data
- Maintaining Methodology Manager if in use.

Topic	Menu Commands
• Users	A **User** is created by selecting **Admin**, **User**....
• Security Profiles	**Security Profiles** are created by selecting **Admin**, **Security Profiles**....
• Enterprise Project Structure (EPS)	Select **Enterprise**, **Enterprise Project Structure...** to open the **Enterprise Project Structure (EPS)** form.
• Portfolios	To create, edit or delete a **Portfolio** select **Enterprise**, **Project Portfolios...** to open the **Portfolio** form. The **File**, **Open** (project) form also allows the selection of a **Portfolio.**
• Organizational Breakdown Structure – OBS	Select **Enterprise**, **OBS...** to open the **Organizational Breakdown Structure** form..
• Project Codes	Select **Enterprise**, **Project Codes...** to open the **Project Codes** form.
• Job Services	A Job Services may be set up by selecting **Tools**, **Job Services** to open the **Job Services** form.

23.1 Multiple User Data Display Issues

The following issues **MUST** be managed by the Database Administrator and have been covered in this publication in other sections:

- The author has found that each user, with access rights, may set a different database **Default Calendar** is set in the **Enterprise**, **Calendar** form, but using the **Refresh Data** option will reset all users to the same calendar. This calendar calculates EPS, Project and WBS Nodes durations in days in conjunction with the **Hours/Day** value. A project will display misleading EPS and WBS Node durations in days when the Default Calendar hours per day is not aligned with the project calendars hours per day. Therefore, if the EPS and WBS Nodes durations in days are important, then it may be best if all calendars in a one database have the same number of hours per day. This is often impractical in complex projects that demand different calendars. In that case, it may be best to display all durations in hours or create a database for each project.

- Users may, if they have been granted access, change their **Hours per Time Period** in their **Edit, User Preferences…**, **Time Units** tab. Thus, users with different **Hours/Day** settings will display different activity durations in days for the same project.

- By default more than one person may open a project unless the **File**, **Open**, **Read Only** option is used or access is limited through **Security Profiles**. Thus, two people may make changes and create two versions. Depending on who closes what and when, the final saved version may not be what it is thought to be. The **File, Refresh Data** option enables a user to refresh project data to see other users changed. Trials by the author indicate that only changed data is saved, thus the final version of the project may be a hybrid of both users' versions.

- When more than one project is opened at a time and each project has different **Scheduling Options**, then the **Scheduling Options** of all the projects is set to the same as the **Default Project** without warning. It you are intending to open multiple projects then it may be best to ensure all projects have the same scheduling options.

- **User Baselines** are not **Project Baselines**. When a second user opens a project which has a **Primary User Baseline** set by the first user, then this baseline will not be available to the second user. When the same layout is used to display the project, the **<Current Project> Baseline**, which displays the **Planned Dates**, will be displayed as the **Primary User Baseline**. Again, two users opening the same project and using the same Layout may display different data.

- It is possible to have two **Currencies** with the same symbol and if a User selects a different currency then all costs displayed by the user will be converted to a different value. This option must be carefully monitored and if you do not need multiple currencies then it is suggested that you should delete them all, to avoid any possible problems. If you are using multiple currencies then make sure that all currencies have a different sign so there is no confusion.

It is critical for contractors to appoint a database manager who understands these issues and keeps an eye on what is being sent to clients and makes sure that any display issues are either hidden or explained to the client in writing. Contractors may wish to consider making the system user the project as this resolves a number of issues. For example User Filters and Layouts including headers and footers are by default the projects, reducing the possibility of sending out a report with the incorrect header or footer. User defaults become project defaults resolving display issues. Access to the project may be easily restricted to the one user and therefore only one person may have the project open at one time.

23.2 Enterprise Project Structure (EPS)

It is likely that your organization has defined an EPS (unless you have a standalone load of Primavera) that is available for new projects to be assigned, but:

- You may need to add an additional EPS Node for your project, or
- If you are starting with a blank database and an EPS has not been defined, you will need to create at least one EPS Node to assign to your projects.

To add, delete or modify the EPS Node structure:

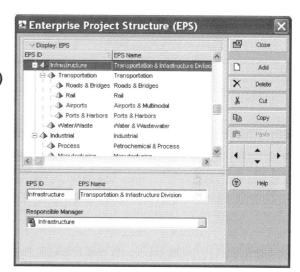

- Select **Enterprise**, **Enterprise Project Structure...** to open the **Enterprise Project Structure (EPS)** form.

- The picture shows the EPS of a demonstration database supplied with Primavera.

- The ⌐ Add ┘ button is used to create a new EPS Node.

- The node is then assigned an:
  - ➤ **EPS ID**,
  - ➤ **EPS Name**, and
  - ➤ **Responsible Manager**.

- The arrows under the [📋 Paste] button are used to reorganize the EPS Nodes.
- The remainder of the buttons are for modifying the structure, as you require.

23.3 Portfolios

The **Portfolio** function reduces the number of Projects that are viewed in the **Projects Window**:

- To create, edit or delete a **Portfolio** select **Enterprise**, **Project Portfolios...** to open the **Portfolio** form.
- Create a portfolio and add projects using this form. A **Portfolio** may be **Global** and all users have access or just be available to the assigned user.
- The **File**, **Open** (project) form also allows the selection of a **Portfolio**, which reduces the number of projects that are displayed in the **Open** (project) form.
- After a **Portfolio** has been selected using **File**, **Select Project Portfolio...**, only those projects in the Portfolio will be displayed in the **Projects Window**.

This feature is essential when you have a data base with a large number of projects.

23.4 Organizational Breakdown Structure – OBS

The OBS is an Enterprise hierarchical structure that represents the organization's hierarchy:

- People in the OBS may be assigned to projects or nodes in the EPS or to a WBS Node.
- A person assigned to an EPS is by default responsible for all projects associated with all elements of the EPS.
- The OBS may also be used to assign access by individual people to projects and WBS Nodes of a project.

23.4.1 Creating an OBS Structure

To create, edit or delete an OBS:

- Select **Enterprise, OBS...** to open the **Organizational Breakdown Structure** form.
- Add, delete and edit the OBS Nodes in a similar way to a WBS.

23.4.2 General Tab

The description of the OBS may be added in the **OBS General** tab.

23.4.3 Users Tab

The Login Name is assigned to the OBS in the OBS **Users** tab. Users should therefore be assigned:

- A resource for when they are assigned to work on an activity, and
- An OBS Node for the work they are responsible for or should have access to.

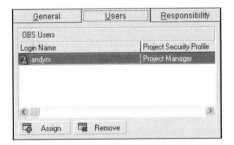

23.4.4 Responsibility Tab

The OBS **Responsibility** tab is used to indicate to which EPS or WBS Node a person has been assigned. The person is assigned to:

- A Project in the **General** tab of the **Projects** Window.
- An EPS in the **General** tab of the **Projects** Window.

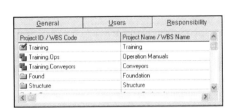

- A WBS in the **General** tab of the **WBS** Window. Assigning responsibility at the WBS Node controls access to the activities under the WBS Node, but does not prevent the user from seeing the entire project's data.

23.5   Users, Security Profiles and Organizational Breakdown Structure

This section is intended to introduce this topic. Please refer to the Primavera Administration Manual for full details.

Security Profiles are created by selecting **Admin**, **Security Profiles....** There are two types of profiles, **Global Profiles** and **Project Profiles**, which are assigned to Users allowing access such as Read Only, Create, Delete, etc:

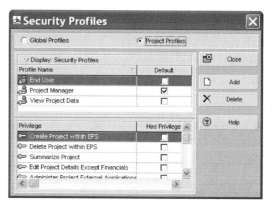

- Access to **Global Data** is controlled through **Global Profiles**, and
- Access to one or more **OBS Nodes** is controlled through **Project Profiles** by assigning **Users** to one or more **OBS Nodes** and assigning an applicable **Project Profile**.

A **User** is created by selecting **Admin**, **User...** and each User is assigned:

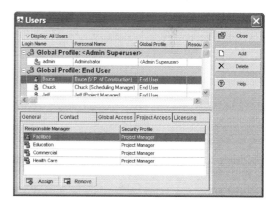

- A **Global Profile** that enables access to Global data,
- An optional **Resource Node** thus limiting access to an area of the **Resource Window**, and
- One or more **OBS Nodes** and an applicable **Project Profile** for each **OBS Node**.

Therefore, access to projects is controlled through the **OBS**. Each **OBS Node** that is assigned to a User may be assigned a different **Project Profile**.

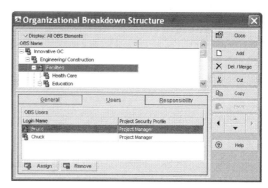

As a result, a User may have read-write access to some projects and read-only to others.

The OBS is edited by selecting **Enterprise**, **OBS....**

Projects are assigned to an OBS when they are created and the OBS Node must provide the required access rights to the project data.

WBS Nodes may be assigned to individual Users which, although does not prevent them from viewing all the project data, will limit their access to just the node they have been assigned to in the **WBS Window**.

23.6   Project Codes

Project Codes in Primavera work in a similar way to Project Codes in P3. The codes are assigned to projects and enable projects to be Grouped and Sorted under an alternative structure to the EPS.

For example, when an EPS represents the physical location of offices by country, state/county and city, the Project Codes enables projects to be given tags, such as Reason for the Project, Safety, Compliance, New Product, and Increase Production. The Projects may be grouped under these headings.

Therefore, project codes are used to Group and Sort Projects in a similar way that Activity Codes are used to Group and Sort Activities.

To create a Project Code:

- Select **Enterprise**, **Project Codes...** to open the **Project Codes** form.

- The Project Codes are created, edited and deleted in a similar way to Activity Codes.

Project Codes may be Assigned to Projects in the Projects Window in a similar way as Activity Codes are assigned to activities by:

- Displaying the appropriate Code Column, or

- Opening the **Codes** tab in the Project Window.

Projects may be Grouped, Sorted and Filtered in the **Projects Window** using the Group and Sort and the Filter functions.

23.7   Filtering, Grouping and Sorting Projects in the Projects Window

Projects are Grouped and Sorted and filtered in the **Projects Window** in the same way as activities are in the **Activities Window**. Layouts, Filters, columns and bar formatting works in the same way in both Windows.

Projects may be Grouped by fields such as **OBS**, **Responsibility**, **Project Codes** and many other fields. See the **Group, Sort and Layouts** chapter for more detail on this subject.

Projects may be filtered by similar fields, but some of the more useful fields to filter projects by are the **Status**, **Responsible Manager** and **Project Code** fields.

23.8 Project Durations in the Project Window

This topic has been mentioned several times before and repeated here for completeness of the chapter. WBS Node durations and the projects summary durations in days or weeks in the **Projects Window** are calculated from the user database **Default Calendar**, which is set using the **Enterprise, Calendars...**, **Global** radio button and the **Hours Per Time Period** option in **User Preferences**. The **Hours Per Time Period** option in **User Preferences** option may be disabled in the **Admin Preferences** and the **Default Calendar**. This situation may result in meaningless WBS Node durations and the projects durations in days being displayed when projects have calendars that are not aligned with the these database parameters.

The following example shows a project with one 30-day activity on an 8-hour per day calendar and the Default Calendar set to 24 hours per day, 7 days per week. The WBS and Project durations are misleading as the durations are clearly not 130 days.

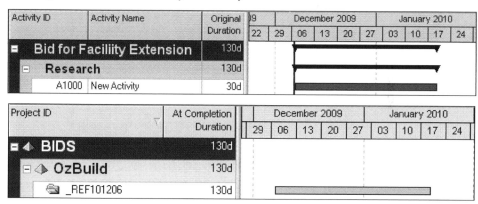

This issue may be overcome by:

- Ensuring all calendars have the same number of hours per day, although this is not always practical,
- Using a separate database for projects with a different number of hours per day.
- In P6 you may hide Group Totals form the **Group and Sort** form.

23.9 Why Are Some Data Fields Gray and Cannot Be Edited?

If you are unable to edit data then consider the following points:

- You may not have access. Discuss your access rights with your administrator.
- Some data, e.g. the project **Status**, needs the project open before the data may be edited.
- The field may be calculated, such as **Actual Duration**, and cannot be edited.

23.10 Summarizing Projects

The data displayed in the **Projects** and **Tracking Windows**, such as Durations, Dates, etc., may be incorrect unless the projects have been summarized by selecting **Tools**, **Summarize**. The **Settings** tab in the **Project Window** specifies to what level the data is summarized and indicates when it was last summarized.

A large database takes a significant amount of time to summarize and may be summarized automatically using Job Services.

23.11 Job Services

A Job Services may be set up by selecting **Tools**, **Job Services** to open the **Job Services** form, which can perform the following functions on one or more selected projects or EPS Nodes:

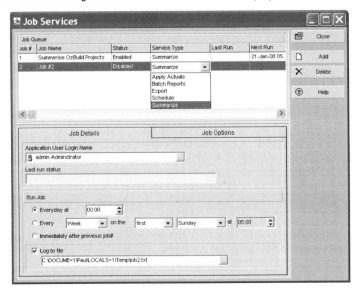

- **Apply Actuals** to projects when timesheets are used,
- **Batch Reports**. In the **Reports Window** a **Batch** may be created by selecting **Tools, Reports, Batch Reports…** to open the **Batch Reports** form. This creates one or more reports simultaneously A Batch may be run on a regular basis using a job service:

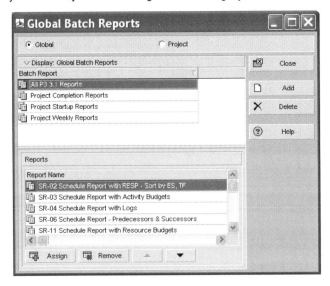

- **Export** one or more projects on a regular basis, or
- **Schedule** one or more projects on a regular basis.
- **Summarize** projects.

23.12 Tracking Window

Tracking Layouts are used for the resource, cost and schedule analysis of multiple projects. This section introduces the concepts but does not go into the detail of using this function. You should experiment with the Group, Sort and Filtering options available, which all function in a similar way to other Windows.

- These layouts typically display summarized data to EPS or OBS and WBS Node level. The data must be summarized using **Tools**, **Summarize** or using **Job Services** to display the latest current data.

- To see when a project was last summarized, select both the **Settings** tab in the lower **Projects Window** pane and the WBS level to which data is summarized.

There are four **Tracking Layout** types and a new layout is created by:

- Saving an existing layout, saving with a new name and editing it, or

- Selecting **View**, **Layout**, **New** which opens the **New Layout** form:

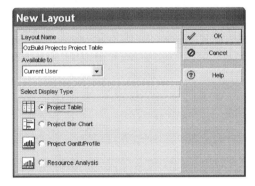

The following pictures indicate the type of data a **Tracking Layout** will display:

- **Project Tables** display columns of data for selected Projects or WBS Nodes:

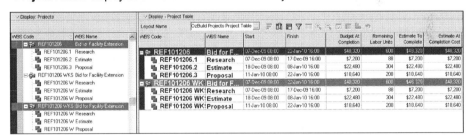

- **Project Bar Charts** display select projects of WBS Node data in horizontal bars:

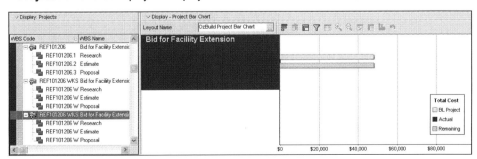

- **Project Gantt/Profiles** display three panes, with bars in the top right pane and either a spreadsheet or a profile in the bottom pane.

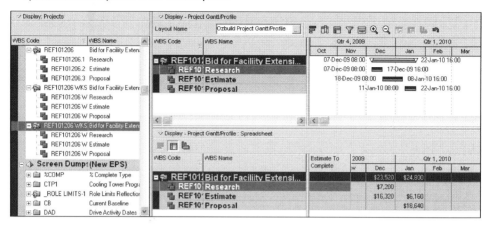

- **Resource Analyses** displays four panes:
  - ➤ The projects to be analyzed are selected in the top left-hand pane,
  - ➤ The resources to be analyzed are selected in the bottom left-hand pane,
  - ➤ Bars, a Resource Profiles or a Resource Table may be displayed in the top right-hand pane, and
  - ➤ The bottom right-hand pane may display either a Resource Profile or a Resource Table:

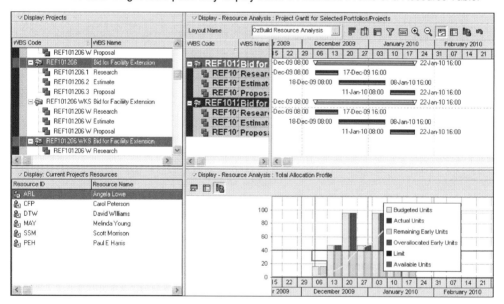

An existing layout may be seen by opening the **Open Layout** form. Select **View**, **Layout** or click the 📖 button in the top right-hand pane.

The bottom pane of a Tracking Layout may be hidden, as with other Windows.

You should experiment by right-clicking in all the panes to see all the display options.

24 MULTIPLE PROJECT SCHEDULING

24.1 Multiple Projects in One Primavera Project

When there are many small projects that need to be managed, it would be logical to create a Primavera Project for each project.

On the other hand, one should also consider putting a number of small projects in one Primavera Project and have the projects identified by the first level WBS Node or some other coding, such as Activity Codes or Project Phase/WBS Category. This is especially practical when there are many projects with a very small number of activities or when an organization only realizes benefits from a number of completed projects when they are all completed. This option is especially practical when one scheduler is managing all the small projects.

24.2 Multiple Primavera Projects Representing One Project

Normally, one Primavera Project would be created for each of an organization's projects. There may be a requirement to break a Project down into Sub-projects, these reasons include:

- The project is large enough to require a number of schedulers and therefore a Primavera Project could be created for each scheduler to delineate each scheduler's area of responsibility. **NOTE:** Remember two or more schedulers may open one project and access may be assigned down to WBS Node.

- There could be a requirement to keep individual organization's financial information confidential and as security and access is set at project level, information in one project may be hidden from specific users. This situation may exist when there are two or more contractors scheduling parts of a project and they require their cost to be kept confidential from other contractors.

- A project may have individual parts or multiple clients but it is necessary to report the project separately, yet allow resource management project-wide. Again, a Primavera project could be created for each separate part of the project. In this situation each user may be given access to only one **Resource Node** from the **Global Access** tab of the **Admin, Users** form.

- A sub-project could be created as a Primavera Project for the security of sensitive financial information. The cost may be assigned to resources in the financial sub-project with access given to specific individuals. Activities in the financial sub-project may be LOE (Level of Effort) activities, spanning activities in other non-cost sub-projects. This method is generally suitable for high level cost planning and management but allowing the detailed planning of project in a non-financial sub-project without the burden of managing costs.

When a Primavera Project is created for each sub-project, it would be logical to keep all the Primavera Projects located under one "project" EPS Node. All the Primavera Projects could be opened at one time for scheduling and reporting by selecting the EPS Node.

The decision to break a project into two or more Primavera Projects must have a sound basis and be well thought out. The environment chosen should be well piloted and tested to ensure the desired results are obtained from the software. Planning and scheduling software is hard enough to use without adding the burden of creating multiple projects. There is a large amount of analysis that may be completed without using multiple projects. Filters may be used to isolate parts of a project and sub-net critical paths may be generated a number of ways such as using the **Calculating Multiple Paths** function. You must ensure that the requirement to break a project into sub-projects using individual Primavera projects is well-founded.

Some people suggest that sub-contractors should run their own sub-projects within a master schedule. My experience is that smaller or new sub-contractors often are very inexperienced at scheduling and many do not know the basics of scheduling. It is therefore unreasonable and risky to expect sub-contractors to drive strange and complex scheduling software and get it right. Some industries are better equipped to manage complex software, with skills found more likely in industries such as IT, but less likely to be found in the construction-related sector.

It is also my experience that it is better to reduce the number of schedulers working on a project schedule to the absolute minimum required to manage a project. In large complex projects, these people need to be trained in the use of the software, be reasonably experienced running the software (or working under a person who is experienced), and run the schedule by an agreed and documented set of guidelines.

Managing the inclusion of sub-contractors' schedules always becomes an issue. Alliances tend to help resolve this problem as the schedules then become a joint responsibility.

24.3 Setting Up Primavera Projects as Sub-projects

There are a number of issues to be considered when moving to this environment. Be aware that Primavera does not have the sub-project options that are found in other products. Thus the Float Calculations for each Primavera Project is based on the end date of each individual Primavera Project and not on the last date of all the open Primavera Projects. There is no inbuilt "P3 Project Group" calculation option, which may result in some interesting float calculations that result from inter-project relationships. This section explains some workarounds.

24.3.1 Opening One or More Projects

Enterprise and Project data may be accessed in the **Projects Window**. To access Project activity information, such as activities, resources and relationships, a project must be opened and the **Activities Window** displayed. One or more projects may be opened at the same time by selecting one or more projects and/or selecting one or more EPS levels and then:

- Right-click and select **Open Project**,
- Select **Ctl+O**,
- Select **File**, **Open…** to open the **Open** form:

The **Open** form enables the options of opening as **Exclusive**, **Shared** or **Read Only**.

Note: A project may only be opened as **Exclusive** (meaning that only the current user may edit it) by using the **Open** form. All other methods will result in the project's being opened in the **Shared** mode and all users with access to the project may open and edit the project(s) at the same time. The **Shared** option may result in one user's edits overwriting another user's edits, depending on who saved what and when. In addition, opening in the **Shared** option may result in different users seeing different values for Activity, WBS Nodes and Project durations in days if the users have different **User Preferences Time Units**.

24.3.2 Default Project

When multiple projects are opened:

- The system selects the **Default Project** when two or more projects have been opened at the same time.

- The **Default Project Scheduling Options** are used to calculate all the open projects.

- Select **Project, Set Default Project...** to open the **Set Default Project** form where you may change the default project:

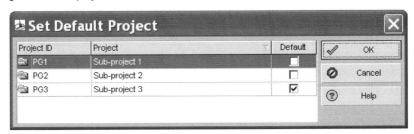

- All open projects **WILL** have their **Scheduling Options** set to the same as the **Default Project** after the projects have been scheduled.

The help file indicates that the **Default Projects** scheduling and leveling settings are used for scheduling. It is also the default project for new data such as activities or issues when the projects are not grouped by WBS.

 Note: When more than one Primavera project is opened at the same time and each project has different scheduling options, then the non-default project's scheduling options are changed to be the same as the default project, without warning. These non-default projects may calculate differently when opened with other projects. In addition, the next time a non-default project is opened in isolation it may calculate very differently from the previous time it was opened in isolation. To prevent this, either all projects in each database must have the same scheduling options, or access to projects carefully restricted, or ensure users only open one project at a time.

An example of changing the default project when each project has different options is demonstrated in the following picture. The first has retained logic and the second has progress override. Activity PG3-2 has moved forward in time as it is now being scheduled with Progress Override after initially being scheduled with Retained Logic. These types of unexpected changes may significantly affect your project and may occur when two or more projects, each with different scheduling options, are opened together.

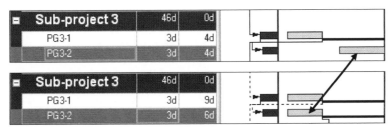

24.3.3 Setting the Projects Data Dates

The default project does not set the Data Date for all projects, in the example following:

- The default project is Sub-project 1, which has had the Data Date set to 7 Feb,
- Sub-project 2 Data Date is set to 3 Feb,
- Sub-project 3 has a Data Date of 1 Feb.

When scheduling, the following message is received:

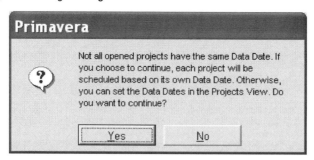

Unlinked activities, PG1-6, PG2-6 and PG3-4, has been added to each project and it may be seen in the following picture:

- All projects are scheduled according to their own Data Dates,
- The Data Date line is shown on the earliest project Data Date.

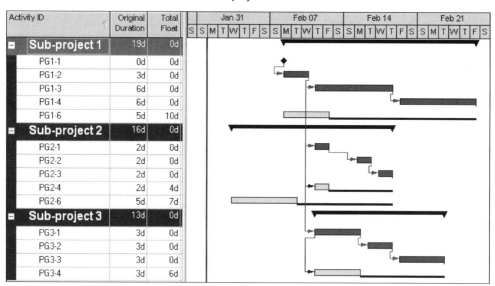

The **Data Date** of multiple projects may be set using A column in the **Projects Window** and the **Fill Down** function.

24.3.4 Total Float Calculation

In P6.1 and earlier versions the Total Float of each project is calculated to the last activity of each individual project schedule, but there are workarounds described next to make the Total Float calculate on the latest activity finish date from all the open projects.

In Primavera 6.2 a new function was create under **Tools**, **Schedule**, **Options**, **Calculate float based on either** which resolves this problem.

Therefore:

- There is no option like the P3 **Base float on end date of** either **project group** or **each project**; they are always calculated with the option of **each project**.

- There is no option like the Microsoft Project **Inserted projects are calculated like summary tasks**. When checked, an inserted project task's Total Float is calculated to the end of all Projects like a group of related projects. When unchecked, each Project's Total Float is calculated to the end of that Project only. Primavera calculates as if this option is always unchecked.

The Total Float for multiple projects in Primavera is correct per project only. This is demonstrated in the following picture. The Total Float for Sub-projects 2 and 3 is based on the last activity in each respective Primavera Project:

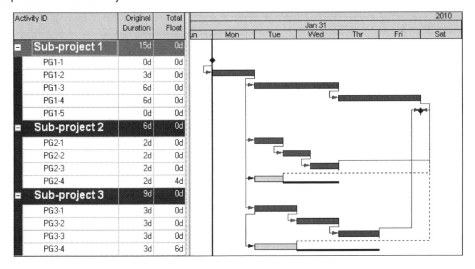

This may be resolved by placing a Finish Milestone against each project and linking them:

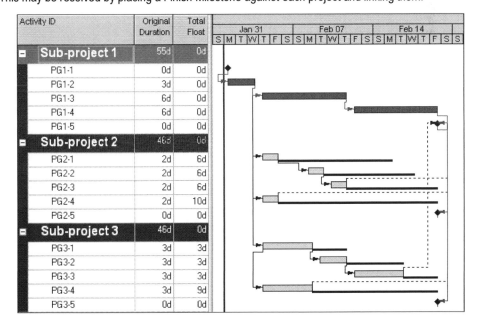

Another workaround to force the Total Float to calculate based on the last activity of multiple projects is:

- Identify the early finish of the last activity.
- Set a **Project Must Finish By** date in all projects to this date.
- Recalculate the projects.

Both options have weakness:

- In the first option the links between the Milestones may need to be changed, and
- The **Project Must Finish By** date may need to be changed in each project on a regular basis as the end date changes.

24.4   Refresh Data

The **File**, **Refresh Data** option is used when two people are working in the same project. It ensures that the latest data is displayed, which enables one user to see the latest edits made by another user. This includes resetting the Global Calendar if another user changes it.

24.5   Who Has the Project Open?

When a project is opened with Primavera using the **File**, **Open** option the **Open Project** form has Access Mode options to open the project as **Exclusive**, **Shared** or **Read Only**.

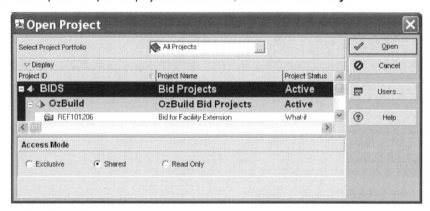

Select 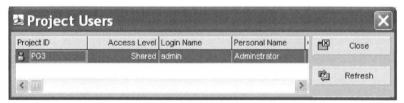 to open the **Project Users** form and see who else has the file open.

 The default option is **Shared** and that means any project that is not opened with the **Open Project** form will be opened as Shared. Anyone who has access may also open the project, calculate and display with their User Preferences, and report different data from the same project at the same time.

24.6 Setting Baselines for Multiple Projects

Baselines may be set for all the projects using the **Maintain Baselines** form (when multiple projects are open) and the **Assign Baselines** form. The following picture show the process of setting multiple project baselines:

- Open the **Maintain Baselines** form by selecting **Project**, **Maintain Baselines...**:
  - ➤ Either all projects may be selected and a copy of all projects set as the Baselines at one time, or
  - ➤ Other projects may be converted from the database one at a time.
- Select [☐ Add] to open the **Add New Baseline** form and create the new baselines,

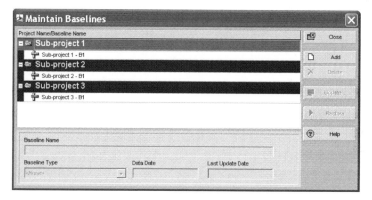

- Select **Project**, **Maintain Baselines...** to open the **Maintain Baselines** form and select one project at a time to assign the baselines.

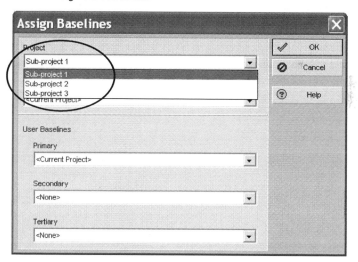

 Remember, a User Baseline set by one user will not be displayed when another user opens the project. The **<Current Schedule> Baseline** displays the **Planned Dates** from the current schedule, will be shown as a baseline.

One option to circumvent this problem is to create users that represent the "Project," allowing only the "Project User" to open or view the project. This resolves the Layouts, User Option, Printing and Baseline issues that are generated when different users open up the same project.

The process identified in the previous page results in one interesting issue in P6.2 and earlier versions when:

- The projects being baselined have relationships amongst each other and

- The option **Save a copy of the current project as a new baseline** option is used to set the baselines.

In this situation each baseline project does not maintain relationships to related baseline project but maintains a relationship to the original projects. Thus if two projects A and B have relationships between the projects and are baselined using the method outlined above :

- Project A Baseline will have relationships to project B

- Project B Baseline will have relationships to project A

- Project B Baseline will have no relationships to project A Baseline.

P7 operates slightly differently and the software maintains the relationship between the Baselined Projects but also developed relationships between both the Baseline Projects and the Projects being Baselined which is also not desirable.

Therefore if you wish your baseline projects to maintain the relationships to other baseline projects that are baselined at the same time then you must:

- Open the Projects Window,

- Copy the multiple projects in this view

- Then set the baselines using the **Convert another project to a new baseline of the current project**.

Now if the baselined projects are restored then their relationships will be related to the correct other baseline.

25 UTILITIES

25.1 Reflection Projects

Primavera Version 6.0 created a Reflection project function. A Reflection is a "What-if" copy of a project that may be edited and then merged back into the original project, as the changes made are required to be kept.

To create a Reflection:

- Open the project,
- Highlight the project and right-click,
- Select **Create Reflection**.

The Reflection project is created with a new ID and the term Reflection added to the Project Name.

To merge an edited Reflection project:

- Open the Reflection project,
- Highlight the Reflection project and right-click,
- Select **Merge Reflection into source project...**,
- This opens a form that will allow a choice to be made about which changes should be kept, if a backup XER file should be made and if the Reflection project is to be kept or deleted:

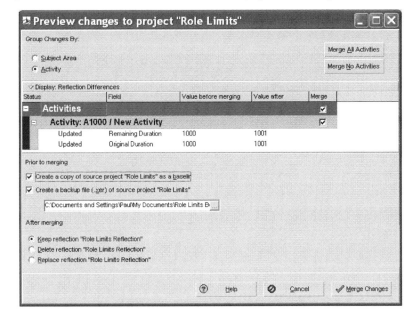

25.2 Advanced Scheduling Options

Primavera Version 5.0 has a new option that enables individual critical paths to be banded as per the following picture and is useful when analyzing larger projects that have more than one critical path. This is similar to Grouping by Total Float but Numbers the Paths and each path contains activities that are linked and banding by Total Float may group unlinked activities.

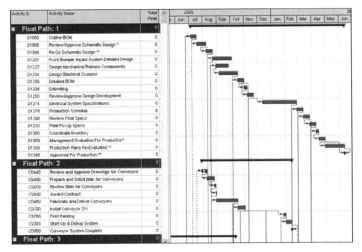

There are two steps involved, firstly calculating the multiple paths and secondly displaying the multiple paths:

25.2.1 Calculating Multiple Paths

To calculate multiple critical paths:

- Select **Tools**, **Schedule**, **Options**, **Advanced** tab,
- Click on **Calculate multiple float paths**,
- Select if your wish to the software to use the **Total Float** or **Free Float** to calculate the multiple paths.
- The **Display multiple float paths ending with activity** is used to select an activity that is in the middle of a schedule and the driving paths top this activity are calculated.
- Select the number of paths for the software to calculate in the **Specify the number of paths to calculate** box.
- Select [⊠ Close] and schedule the project.

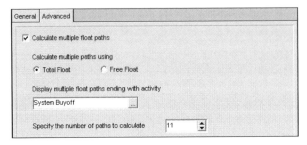

25.2.2 Displaying Multiple Paths

There are two fields that are populated in this process:

- **Float Path** and
- **Float Path Order**

Either select multiple path Layout or create a Layout that Groups by **Float Path** and Sorts by **Float Path Order** as per the following examples which show a before and after grouping:

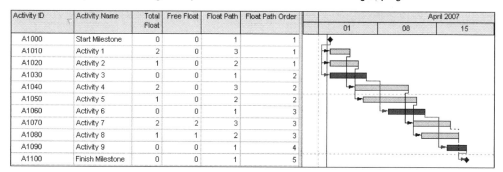

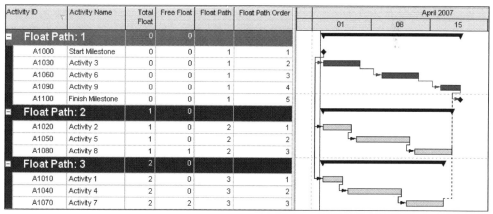

The reader may wish to read the help file or experiment with the software to see the results.

25.3 Audit Trail Columns

Primavera Version 5.0 introduced four basic audit trail columns that may be displayed in the Activities window which display the date user that added the activity when and by whom it was modified:

- Added By - the user that added the activity,
- Added Date - the date the activity was added,
- Modified By - the user that last modified the activity and
- Modified Date - the date the activity was last modified.

Primavera Version 6.0 introduced two new resource assignment fields available in the **Activities Window**, **Activity Details**, **Resources** tab:

- **Assigned by**, and
- **Assigned Date**

25.4   Excel Import and Export Tool

Primavera has a built in tool for importing to and exporting from Excel the following data when the user is assigned a Superuser security profile:

- Activities
- Relationships
- Resources
- Resources Assignments and
- Expenses

To import or export data to Excel select **File**, **Import...** or **Export...** and follow the instructions in the Wizards. **Export Templates** may be created and re-used at a later date with this tool.

When attempting to import data using this type of tool there are some guidelines that apply to many applications, not just to this Primavera tool:

- Create a test project and experiment with this function before using it on a live project.
- Export some data first as this exports the correct column headings and sheet names.
- Change or add data to the exported spreadsheet and import new data into the test environment. Then review the data is importing correctly and that the schedule is calculating as expected.
- Back up or take a copy of your project before importing into a live project.
- Usually is better not to try to import calculated fields, as these are normally recalculated after the data has been imported and the schedule recalculated.
- When only exporting some data on a one off basis then it may be easier just to copy and paste the data into a spreadsheet.

A few points to understand when using the Primavera Excel import function:

- The following sheets are created on export and these sheet names must not be changed:
  - ➢ **TASK** containing Activity data
  - ➢ **TASKPRED** containing Activity Relationships data
  - ➢ **PROJCOST** containing Expenses data
  - ➢ **RSRC** containing Resources data
  - ➢ **TASKRSRC** containing Resource Assignments data
  - ➢ **USERDATA** containing user data that should not be changed.
- Do not change the language between importing and exporting.
- The first row of data in each sheet that is exported contains the database field name. The first row must not be changed otherwise the data will not be imported.
- The second row in the spreadsheet contains **Captions** that may be changed.
- Dictionary data such as Activity Codes being imported must exist before the data is imported.
- Only a maximum of 200 columns of data may be exported.
- **Sub-units** of time are not supported and the Sub-unit checkboxes in the **Edit**, **User Preferences**, **Time Units** tab and should be unchecked.
- **Percent Completes** must be must have a value of between 0 and 100.

There is more information in the Help file under **Reference**, **Importing and Exporting**.

 Activity Codes and other data may be imported by loading the Software Developers Kit (SDK) and using a spreadsheet available from the Oracle Primavera Knowledgebase. You will need to create a Support Login at the Oracle website.

25.5 Project Import and Export

Projects may be imported and exported from and to the following formats:

- **XER**, which is a Primavera proprietary format, used to exchange projects between Primavera Version 6.0 databases regardless of the database type in which it was created.

- **Project (*.mpp)**. This is the default file format that Microsoft Project 2000 and 2002 uses to create and save files.

- **MPX (*.mpx)**. This is a text format data file created by Microsoft Project 98 and earlier versions. MPX is a format that may be imported and exported by many other project scheduling software packages.

- **Primavera Project Planner P3** and **SureTrak** files saved in **P3** format. A SureTrak project should be saved in Concentric (P3) format before importing.

- With Primavera Version 6.0 the importation of P3 files has been improved:
  - ➤ One or more individual subprojects may now be imported, and
  - ➤ The import EPS locations specified, which may be different for each subproject
  Select **File**, **Import...** or **Export...** to open the appropriate form.

- New to Version 4.1, Microsoft Project formats such as **Project Database (*.mpd)**, **Microsoft Access Database (*.mdb)** and **(*.mpt)** can be imported, however **Microsoft Project** is require to be installed on the computer.

- **Primavera PM – (XML)** is a new format introduced with Primavera Version 6.0 which is industry standard and enables the export of most data for single projects only.

- Primavera Version 6.0 projects that are open may be exported in XER format that may be imported into **Primavera Contractor**, but there are some issues with backward compatibility.
  - ➤ Select **File**, **Export...** to open the **Export** form.

The installation of **Microsoft Project 2007** disables the Microsoft Project import function.

It is recommended that you read the notes carefully in the user manual before importing a schedule from a non - Primavera format and even consider importing it into a blank database to clearly understand how the data is imported.

25.6 Check In and Check Out

Check In and Check Out function is similar to the P3 and SureTrak function of the same name, which enables a project to be copied from a database, worked on in a remote location, and then be checked in to the original database at a later date and update the original schedule.

 External Dates. Be sure to check the **External Early Start** and **External Late Finish** date settings on import as these act as constraints that represent the lost relationships and will affect how your schedule calculates.
Also ensure you check what has happened to any external relationships.

The project may be checked into another installation of Primavera P6 or Primavera Contractor irrespective of the database format, edited, checked out and then checked back into its original database at a later date.

26 WHAT IS NEW IN P6 VERSION 7

26.1 Calendars - Hours per Time Period

In earlier version of P6 the calculation of the durations in hours for all calendars was set either by the Administrator in **Admin**, **Admin Preferences...**, **Time Periods** tab or by the User in the **Edit**, **User Preferences...**, **Time Units** tab.

These options calculated the duration in days correctly when all database calendars were assigned the same number of work hours per day. When tasks are scheduled with calendars that do not conform to the **Edit**, **User Preferences...**, **Time Units** tab settings (e.g. when settings are set for 8 hours per day but there are tasks scheduled on a 24 hour/day calendar), then the Activity durations in days or weeks will be displayed incorrectly. These results often create confusion for new users and people reviewing the schedule.

This issue has been resolved in Release 7 by the removal of the two options above and the creation of a new calendar function titled **Hours per Time Period**.

When creating or editing a calendar there is a new [Workweek...] button in the **Enterprise**, **Calendars**, **Modify** form that allows the definition of the number of hours per day, which in turn will enable the duration in days to be calculated and displayed correctly as long as the number of hours per day is the same for each work day in the calendar.

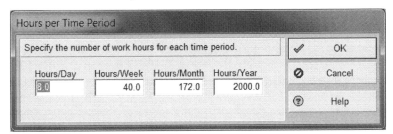

26.2 Calendars for Calculating WBS and Other Summary Durations

The calculation of the duration in days for WBS and other summary durations such as Project and Activity Code bands in Version P6.2 and earlier was calculated by a combination of the User or Administrator Hours/Day and the Global Calendar. These options calculate correctly when all database calendars are have the same number of work hours per day and days per week. When tasks are scheduled with calendars that do not conform to the **Edit**, **User Preferences...**, **Time Units** tab settings (e.g. when settings are set for 8 hours per day but there are tasks scheduled on a 24 hour/day calendar), the Activity durations in days or weeks will be incorrect. These results often create confusion for new users and people reviewing the schedule.

In Version 7 these summary durations are calculated in a similar way as SureTrak:
- When all the activities in a band share the same calendar then the summary duration is calculated on the calendar of the activities in the band and
- When they are different then the summary duration is calculated on the Project Default calendar.

The picture below has the Project Default Calendar set as the 8hr/d & 5d/w and the picture shows that when the calendars are different this calendar is used to calculate the summary duration:

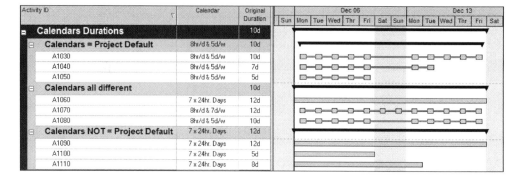

26.3 Renumbering of Activity IDs with Copy and Paste Copy

The new function allows the renumbering of pasted activities, the options are self explanatory:

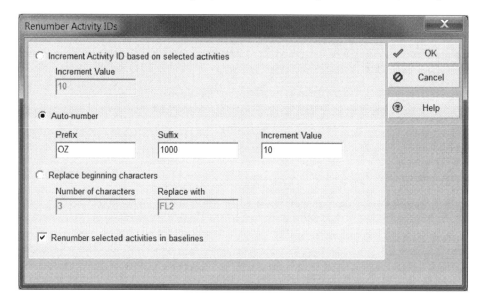

Should you attempt to renumber to Activity IDs that exist then a further form is presented to allow manual renumbering:

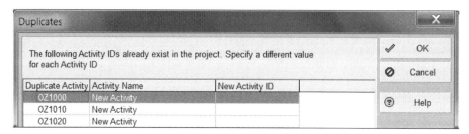

26.4 Renumbering Activity IDs

There is a new function allowing the renumbering of activities, to use this function:
- Select the activities that are to be renumbered,
- Select from the menu **Edit**, **Renumber Activity IDs** or right click in the columns area and select **Renumber Activity IDs**,
- This opens the **Renumber Activity IDs**, as per the earlier picture, allowing renumbering of the activity IDs.

26.5 Progress Line Display on the Gantt Chart

A progress line displays how far ahead or behind activities are in relation to the Baseline. Either the Project Baseline or the Primary User Baseline may be used and there are four options:
- Difference between the Baseline Start Date and Activity Start Date,
- Difference between the Baseline Finish Date and Activity Finish Date,
- Connecting the progress points based on the Activity % Complete,
- Connecting the progress points based on the Activity Remaining Duration.

There are several main components of displaying a Progress Line in P7:
- Firstly the progress line is formatted using the **View**, **Bar Chart Options** form, **Progress Line** tab, which may also be opened by right clicking in the Gant Chart area:

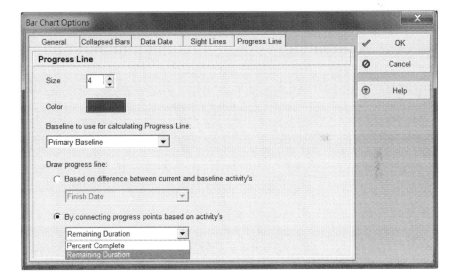

- Selecting **View**, **Progress Line** to hide or display the **Progress Line**.
- If you use either of the options of Percent Complete or Remaining Duration then you must display the appropriate Baseline Bar that has been selected as the **Baseline to use for calculating Progress Line:**.

- The picture below shows the option highlighted above of **Percent Complete**:

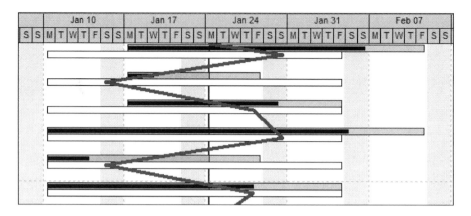

26.6 Add Activity Codes When Assigning Codes

Activity Codes may be added on the fly, there is a new button title **New** on the **Assign Activity Codes** form that allows Activity Codes to be created as they are assigned:

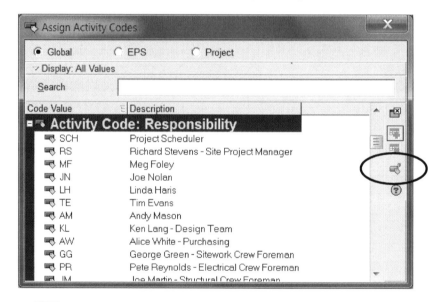

Click on the 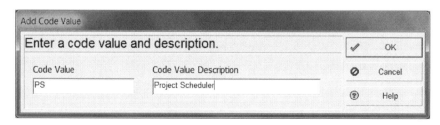 button to open the Add Code Value form and enter the new Code Value and Code Vale Description.

26.7 Copy Baseline When Creating a Baseline

A new baseline may be created by copying an existing baseline in the **Project**, **Maintain Baselines** form:

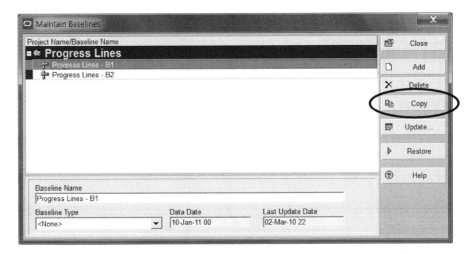

This new baseline may then be updated using the **Update** function.

26.8 License Maintenance Changes

The **Module Access** have been changed and the Current and Named Licensing options removed and replaced by a single access option:

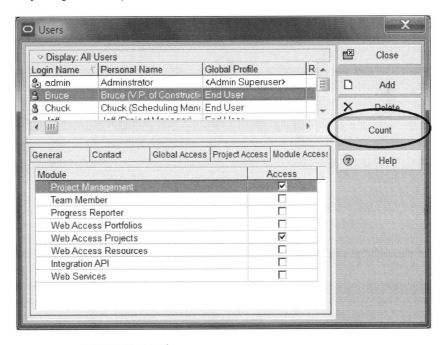

There is also a new [Count] button which allow the administrator to easily count how many licenses have been assigned.

26.9 Recently Opened File List

When opening a file one can select a file from the recently opened list at the bottom of the **File** menu:

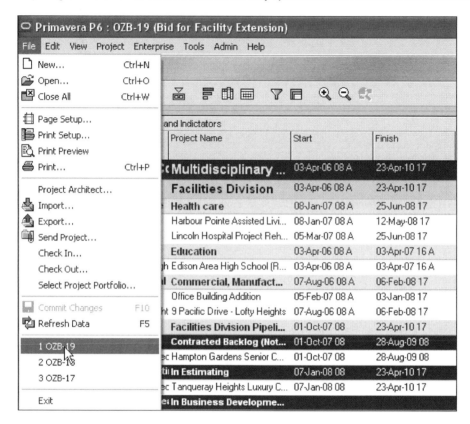

27   WHAT IS NEW IN VERSION 6.0

27.1   XML File Format for Import and Export

Primavera PM – (XML) is a new format introduced with Primavera Version 6.0 which is industry standard and enables the export of most data for single projects only.

27.2   Copy a Project with High Level Resource Assignments

Primavera Version 6.0 added the ability to copy **High Level Resource Planning Assignments** assigned in **Primavera Web** (earlier versions were called myPrimavera) when copying a project.

27.3   Role Limits

In Primavera Version 6.0, a Role limit may now be defined the same way as a Resource by selecting **Enterprise**, **Roles** and selecting the **Limits** tab.

- The **Edit**, **User Preferences...**
  Resources, **Analysis**, **Time-Distributed Data**, **Display the Role Limit Based on** option must be set to **Custom role limit** for the Role limits to display:

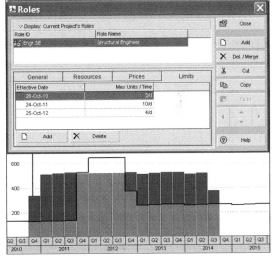

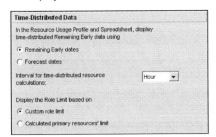

This option may be used with histograms, charts and spreadsheets.

27.4   Reflection Projects

Primavera Version 6.0 created a Reflection project function. A Reflection is a "What-if" copy of a project that may be edited and then merged back into the original project, as the changes made are required to be kept.

To create a Reflection:

- Open the project,
- Highlight the project and right-click,
- Select **Create Reflection**.

The Reflection project is created with a new ID and the term Reflection added to the Project Name.

To merge an edited Reflection project:

- Open the Reflection project,
- Highlight the Reflection project and right-click,
- Select **Merge Reflection into source project...**,

- This opens a form that will allow a choice to be made about which changes should be kept, if a backup XER file should be made and if the Reflection project is to be kept or deleted:

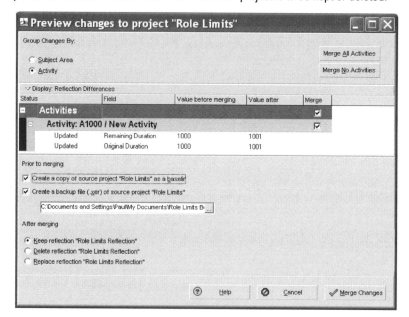

27.5   Editing the Resource Usage Spreadsheet – Bucket Planning

This new option in Primavera Version 6.0 enables resources assignments values to be manually edited. This enables more control over the assignment of resources that are working intermittently on an activity.

This is similar to editing a Microsoft Project Resource Usage table and making a resource assignment "Contoured."

The following picture shows the values edited in the **Resource Usage Spreadsheet**.

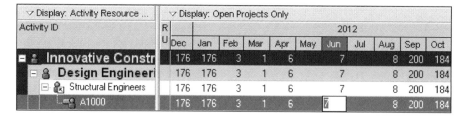

27.6   Owner Activity Attribute

"Owner," the new activity field in Primavera Version 6.0, enables a User who is not a resource to be assigned to an activity. This now enables the person responsible for an activity to be assigned from the list of users. This function may be used in combination with a Reflection project.

27.7 Resource Assignment Audit Trail

There are two new resource assignment fields available in the **Activities Window**, **Activity Details**, **Resources** tab:

- **Assigned by**, and
- **Assigned Date**.

27.8 Project Layouts

Primavera Version 6.0 introduced the option to create and save **Project Layouts**. When **View Layout**, **Save As** is used there is the additional option of **Project**.

Project Layouts are exported with a project.

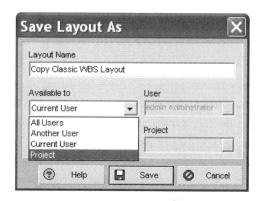

When multiple projects are open, the project that the layout is associated with may be selected by clicking on the **Project** cell in the **Save Layout As** form to open the **Select Project** form.

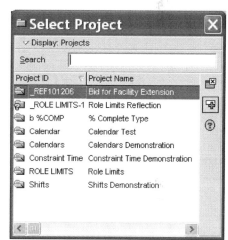

27.9 Curtains and Spotlights

In Primavera Version 6.0 these are now assigned to layouts, whereas in earlier versions they were associated with all Layouts after they were applied.

27.10 Group and Sort

The Group and Sort function has two extra options:

- **Show Group Totals**, which when unchecked hides the summary data in the bands. This may be the best option to use when you have a database with multiple calendars that have different hours per day and the WBS Summary Durations are not displaying the correct value. They may now be hidden.

The first following picture is with both options checked and the second with both unchecked. This feature also prevents the truncating of Band titles.

Summary Data Displayed

Activity ID	Original Duration	Start	Finish	Total Float
■ **Bid for Fac**	139d	08-Dec-09 A	22-Jan-10	0d
⊟ **Research**	31d	08-Dec-09 A	21-Dec-09	6d
0Z1000	0d	08-Dec-09 A		
0Z1010	1d	08-Dec-09 A	08-Dec-09 A	
0Z1020	8d	09-Dec-09 A	21-Dec-09	2d
⊟ **Estimate**	52d	22-Dec-09	08-Jan-10	3d
0Z1070	2d	07-Jan-10	08-Jan-10	0d

Summary Data Hidden

Activity ID	Original Duration	Start	Finish	Total Float
■ **Bid for Faciiity Extension**				
⊟ **Research**				
0Z1000	0d	08-Dec-09 A		
0Z1010	1d	08-Dec-09 A	08-Dec-09 A	
0Z1020	8d	09-Dec-09 A	21-Dec-09	2d
⊟ **Estimate**				
0Z1070	2d	07-Jan-10	08-Jan-10	0d

- **Shrink vertical grouping bands** is a function that narrows the Vertical Bands. This is useful in projects with a number of levels in the WBS as this provides more usable screen space and paper width for printing.

Option Unchecked   **Option Checked**

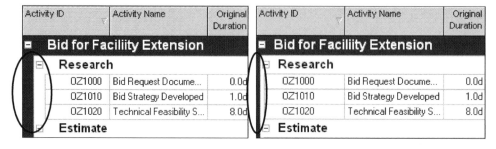

27.11 Planning Resources

Planning Resources may be assigned to a Project or a WBS Node using **Primavera Web** (earlier versions were called myPrimavera), the web interface. These may be viewed in Primavera Version 6.0.

27.12 Copying a Project with Baselines

Primavera Version 6.0 introduced the option of copying baselines when a project is copied in the **Projects Window**.

NOTE: You must manually reassign the baseline after the project has been copied.

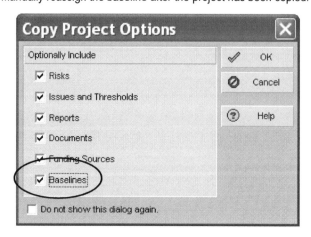

28 WHAT IS NEW IN VERSION 5.0

28.1 MSDE Database for Standalone Installations

Primavera Version 5.0 now uses the Microsoft SQL Server Desktop Engine (MSDE) for standalone installations, Version 4.1 used Interbase.

28.2 Undo

Primavera Version 5.0 has a new multiple **Undo** function that operates on Resources, Resource Assignments, and Activities windows, but no **Redo** function.

There are many functions will erase the Undo memory such as scheduling, summarizing, importing, opening a project, opening Code forms, opening User and Admin Preferences and closing the application.

28.3 WBS Summary Activity

The new Primavera Version5.0 **WBS Summary Activity** is an activity that spans the duration of all activities which are assigned exactly the same WBS Code and unlike a Level of Effort Activity it does not have any predecessors or successors.

Activity ID	Activity Name	Activity Type		Qtr 2, 2005				Qtr 3, 200	
			Mar	Apr	May	Jun	Jul	Aug
⊟ **Hardware**									
AS-H	Hardware Summary	WBS Summary							
AS310	Site Preparation	Task Dependent							
AS240	Installation Begins	Start Milestone							
AS315	Install Electrical Pow...	Task Dependent							
AS109	Test & Debug Line A	Task Dependent							
AS110	Test & Debug Line B	Task Dependent							
AS111	Pilot Start Line A	Task Dependent							
AS112	Start-Up Line B	Task Dependent							
AS275	Path Refinement an...	Task Dependent							
AS265	Path Refinement an...	Task Dependent							

Therefore a WBS activity will change duration when either the earliest start or latest finish of activities that it spans is changed. This may happen as the project progresses and activities do not meet their original scheduled dates, or the duration of an activity is changed, or logic is changed, or the schedule is leveled.

This function calculates the WBS Activity Duration in the same way as WBS activities in P3 or SureTrak, Topic activities in SureTrak. It is similar to the way Summary activity durations are calculated in Microsoft Project, except the activities do not need to be demoted below the detailed activities in as in Microsoft Project.

WBS activities may be used for:

- Reporting at summary level by filtering on WBS activities,
- Entering estimated costs at summary level for producing cash flow tables while the detailed activities are used for calculating the overall duration for the WBS and day to day management of the project and
- Recording costs and hours at WBS level when it is not desirable or practicable to record at activity level, especially when the detailed activities are liable to change.

28.4 EPS Level Activity Codes

EPS Activity Codes may be created and assigned only to project activities that belong to EPS Node for which the EPS Activity Codes have been created. This enables the display all project activities under one or more EPS Node utilizing dedicated alternative hierarchical structure. There are also specific privileges for the management of these codes.

28.4.1 Create an EPS Level Activity Code Dictionary

- Select **Enterprise, Activity Codes...** to open the **Activity Code** form and click the **EPS** radio button,
- Select ▨ Modify... to open the **Activity Code Definition – EPS** form where the new code dictionary is created,
- Click on ▯ Add to open the **Select EPS** form and select an EPS Node that the New Code will be used with and click ⊞ to select the node,
- Type in the EPS Activity Code Name and assign the length of the code

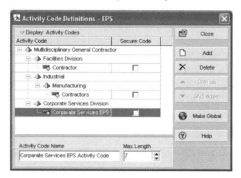

- The ⊛ Make Global button converts the Activity Code to a Global Activity Code.
- The **Secure Code** box is used to hide the code from people without the required access privileges.
- Select ▨ Close to return to the **Activity Code Definition – EPS** form.

28.4.2 Create EPS Activity Codes

- Select the code dictionary to be modified from the drop down list under the heading **Select Activity Code** in the **Activity Codes** form, **EPS** tab.

- Click on the ▯ Add to add a hierarchical set of codes in the same method as other codes

28.4.3 Assigning EPS Activity Codes to Activities

EPS Activity Codes may only be assigned to activities belonging to projects that are a member of the EPS Node and are assigned in the same way as Global and Project Activity Codes

28.5 Activity Step Templates

The new Primavera Version5.0 function enables Templates to be created for Steps and then the Steps assigned to other activities. Existing Steps may be also converted into Step Templates. Select **Enterprise, Activity Step Templates…** to open the **Activity Step Template** form:

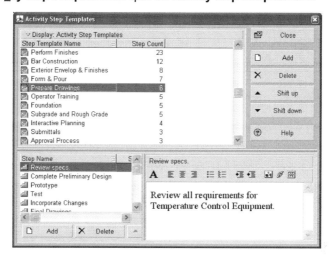

- The Step Template name is added in the upper pane,
- The Steps are added in the lower left pane and
- Comments on the Step may be added in the bottom left pane.

Steps may be assigned to activities from the **Activities Details** form **Steps Details** tab by clicking on the [Add from Template] button and selecting the Step Template required:

Existing Steps may be converted to a Step Template by:

- Selecting the required Steps to be made into a Step Template, and
- Right-clicking and selecting **Create Template…**.

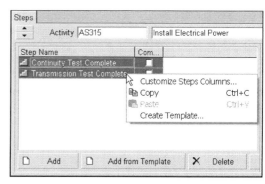

28.6 Assignment Staffing

There are new Version 5.0 options available on the **Calculations** tab of the **User Options** form allowing the user to set the defaults for:

- Selecting the Units per Time when assigning a substitute resource to an existing resource assignment.

- Selecting the Price per Unit for a resource which is being assigned to a Role.

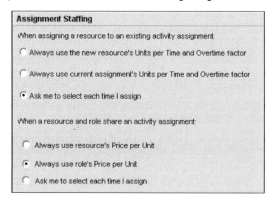

The options are to select the existing resource, the new resource or to be prompted each time a resource/role is substituted.

28.7 Resource Security

The Primavera Version 5.0 **Resource Security** has the ability to restrict access to resources. The security may be established at a resource Node level allowing the user access to all the children of that Resource Node.

- Select **Admin**, **Users**, **Global Access** tab to open the **Users** form,

- Uncheck the **All Resources Access** check box,

- Click on the right side of the **Resources Access** bar to open the **Select Resource Access** form and

- Select the resources from the list:

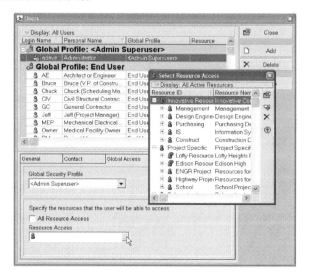

28.8   Baseline Functionality

28.8.1   Update Baselines

The new Primavera Version 5.0 **Update Baseline** function is similar to the P3 function and enables the Baseline schedule to be updated with data from the current schedule or activities deleting that are no longer in the current schedule without restoring the Baseline schedule:

- Select **Project**, **Maintain Baselines…** and select the [🖳 Update…] button to open the **Update Baseline** form:

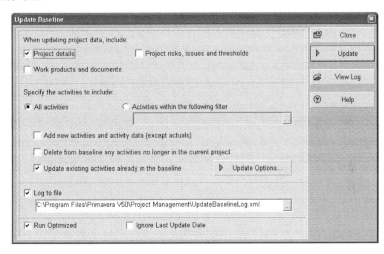

- When **Run Optimized** is not checked then an error log is kept during the updating process.
- **Ignore Last Update Date** may be used when a project has project is updated at different times and the last Baseline Update may not be valid for the current schedule although the Baseline has been updated with more recent data..
- Select [▷ Update Options…] to open the **Update Baseline Options** form to select which data items are updated.

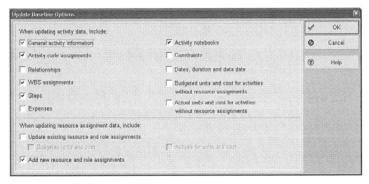

There is a new project privilege allowing a user to run Update Project Baselines.

28.8.2 Assign Baselines

The new Primavera Version 5.0 **Assign Baselines** form is used to assign up to three project baseline schedules: primary, secondary, and tertiary.

The **Project Baseline** may be used for calculating **Earned Value**. See the next para for more options. Also see **Admin**, **Admin Preferences...**, **Earned Value** tab for other Earned Value options.

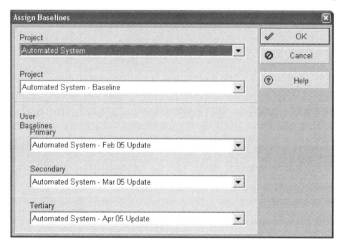

28.8.3 Baseline Used for Earned Value Calculations

Earned Value calculations may be performed using either the **Primary Baseline** values or the **Baseline** values, the values from the current project. Select the **Settings** tab in the **Projects Window**. This is similar to the P3 option **Tools**, **Options**, **Earned Value**.

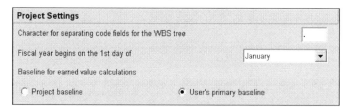

28.9 Progress Spotlight and Update Progress

Primavera Version 5.0 introduced a new function for highlighting the activities that should have progressed in the update period. The user then has the option of selecting some or all of the activities that should have progressed and updating (progressing) them as if they progressed exactly as they were **Planned**.

It is sometimes easier to **Automatically update** a project with functions like **Progress Spotlight** and then adjust the Actual dates and remaining Duration as a second step in the updating process, especially if the project is going to plan.

This function is similar to the P3 Progress Spotlight function however does not have the additional SureTrak features of reversing progress and not updating the resources.

The Spotlight may be moved to reflect the new Data Date by either:

- Dragging the Data Date, or
- Using the Spotlight Icon -

 Unlike P3 and SureTrak this facility uses the **Planned Start** and **Planned Finish** dates for setting the **Actual Start** and **Actual Finish** dates of in-progress activities. Thus when the **Planned Dates** are of an in-progress activity are different to the **Actual Start** and **Early Finish** dates and the task is Automatically updated to be complete then both these dates are set to the **Planned** dates and the **Actual Start** may be changed and the **Actual Finish** not set to the **Early Finish**.

The following picture display the Early bar and the Baseline:

Activity Name	Original Duration	Start	Finish	February 2010		
				31	07	14
Activity 1	5d	02-Feb-10 A	04-Feb-10 A			
Activity 2	5d	05-Feb-10 A	11-Feb-10			
Activity 3	5d	12-Feb-10	18-Feb-10			

The following picture show the effect of applying **Update Progress** to the schedule above. The Actual Start of Activity 2 has been changed and the Actual Finish of Activity 2 is not the same as the original Early Finish.

Activity Name	Original Duration	Start	Finish	February 2010		
				31	07	14
Activity 1	5d	02-Feb-10 A	04-Feb-10 A			
Activity 2	5d	08-Feb-10 A	12-Feb-10 A			
Activity 3	5d	12-Feb-10 A	18-Feb-10			

NOTE: You should not use this facility when you wish your activities to be Automatically updated to the Early dates (as in P3, SureTrak and Microsoft Project) and not the Planned dates. You may consider using a Global Change to set the Planned Dates to the Start and Finish dates before running Progress Spotlight, but this will change the Original Duration and the % Duration will not calculate correctly.

28.9.1 Highlighting Activities for Updating by Dragging the Data Date

To highlight activities that should have been progressed in the last period by dragging the Data Date:

- Hold the mouse arrow on the Data Date line and display the double-headed arrow ↔,
- Press the left mouse button and drag the Data Date line to the required date.
- All the activities that should have been worked in the time period are highlighted.

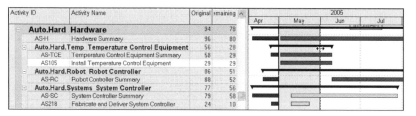

28.9.2 Spotlighting Activities Using Spotlight Icon

The Spotlight facility highlights all activities that should have progressed in one minor time period of the timescale settings. To use **Progress Spotlight**:

- Set the Timescale to be the same as your Update Periods. If you are updating weekly then set the time period to weeks in the **Timescale** form.
- Select **View**, **Progress**, **Spotlight** or click the 🔳 icon and the next period of time (one week if your scale is set to one week) will be highlighted.
- Click on the **Progress Spotlight** 🔳 icon a second time to return the Spotlight back to the Data Date.

You are now ready to update progress.

28.9.3 Updating Using Update Progress

To update a schedule using the **Update Progress** form select **Tools**, **Update Progress**.

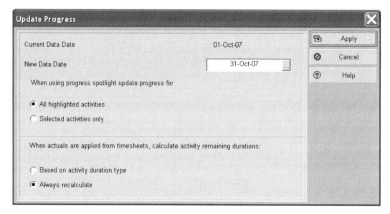

There are two options for setting the New Data Date:

- You may use the highlight facility before opening the Update Progress form and the New data date will be set to the highlighted Data Date; or
- You may select the New Data Date when opening the form.

Either all the activities that are Spotlighted may be updated or if some were selected before opening the form then just the selected ones may be updated.

- To update all the activities select **All highlighted activities** radio button, or
- To update selected activities highlight the activities (hold the Ctrl key and click the ones you wish to status) before selecting **Tools, Update Progress...** and the click the **Selected activities only** radio button.

The option **When actuals are applied from timesheets, calculate activity remaining durations:** decides how the Remaining Duration is calculated:

- **Based on the activity duration type** will take into account activity type and hours to date and reschedule the Remaining Duration in accordance with the activity Duration Type, or
- **Always recalculate** will override the activity Duration Type and calculate the activity Remaining Durations and Hours as if the activity was a Fixed Units and Fixed Units/Time activity.
- Click on [📅 Apply] and the schedule will be updated as if all activities were completed according to the schedule.

28.10 Suspend and Resume

The new Primavera Version5.0 Suspend and Resume function enables the work to be suspended and the activity resumed at a later date. Open the **Activity Details** form **Status Details** tab and enter the **Suspend** and **Resume** dates. This function works in a similar way to the P3 and SureTrak function and enables only one break in an activity.

The following example shows an activity suspended from 30 Apr 05 to the 10 May 05.

- This feature works when a task has commenced and normally the Suspend date is in the past and the Resume date in the future.
- The activity must have an actual start date before you can record a suspend date.
- Only Resource Dependent and Task Dependent activities may be Suspended and resumed.
- The suspended period is not calculated as part of the task duration and resources are not scheduled in this period.

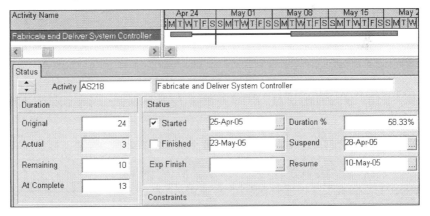

 The Suspend and Resume time are set at midnight when set without the time being displayed therefore there will be work on 28 Apr 05. Therefore you may wish to display the time when setting Suspend and Resume dates.

28.11 Store Period Performance

This new function to Primavera Version 5.0 enables:

- The creation of user definable financial periods, say monthly or weekly, and
- The ability to record the actual and earned costs and quantities for each period.

Therefore, actual costs and quantities which span over more than one past period will be accurately reflected per period in all reports. If **Store Period Performance** is not used then the actuals are spread equally over the actual duration of an activity, which may not accurately reflect when the work performed and what was achieved in each period. These Periods apply to all projects in the database.

This function is similar to the P3 **Store Period Performance** function but will not Store Period Performance on Microsoft Project managed projects

The steps required to store period performance are:

- Ensure that the user has the necessary global privileges to Edit Financial Period Dates, Store Period Performance and Edit Period Performance when past actuals need to be edited.
- Open the appropriate project and ensure **Link Actual and Actual This Period Units and Cost** is enabled, select the **Calculations** tab in the lower pane of the **Projects** window and click the check box. This option is grayed out if the project is not open.
- Set the **Financial Periods** by selecting **Admin, Financial Periods....** Which will open the **Financial Periods** form:

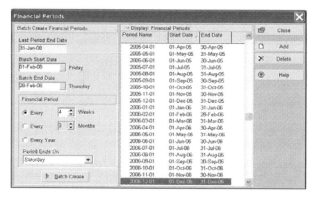

- To store the period performance select **Tools, Store Period Performance...** to open the **Store Period Performance** form, select the projects to have the period performance stored and click the ⬚ Store Now button.

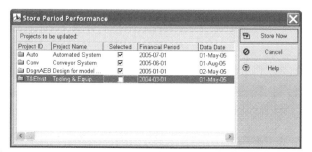

Finally these results may be viewed and edited in the Past Period Actuals columns of the Resources Assignments Window, Activity Details Resources tab and the Activity Table.

28.12 Advanced Scheduling Options

Primavera Version 5.0 has a new option that enables individual critical paths to be banded as per the following picture and is useful when analyzing larger projects that have more than one critical path. This is similar to Grouping by Total Float but Numbers the Paths and each path contains activities that are linked and banding by Total Float may group unlinked activities.

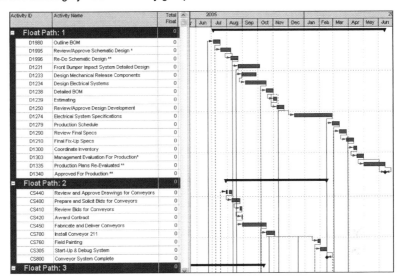

There are two steps involved, firstly calculating the multiple paths and secondly displaying the multiple paths:

Calculating Multiple Paths

- Select **Tools**, **Schedule**, **Options**, **Advanced** tab,
- Click on **Calculate multiple float paths**
- Select if your wish to the software to use the **Total Float** or **Free Float** to calculate the multiple paths.
- The **Display multiple float paths ending with activity** is used to select an activity that is in the middle of a schedule and the driving paths top this activity are calculated.
- Select the number of paths for the software to calculate in the **Specify the number of paths to calculate** box.
- Select ⊞ Close and schedule the project.

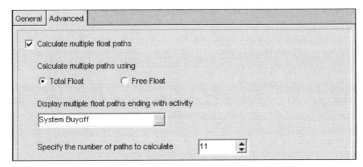

Displaying Multiple Paths

There are two fields that are populated in this process:

- **Float Path** and

- **Float Path Order**

Either select multiple path Layout or create a Layout that Groups by **Float Path** and Sorts by **Float Path Order** as per the following examples which show a before and after grouping:

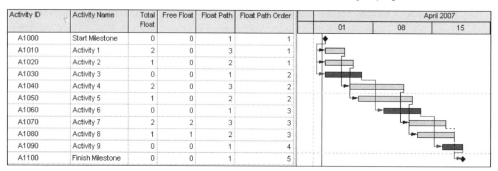

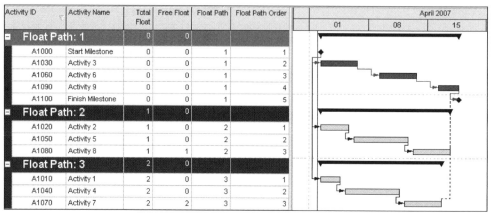

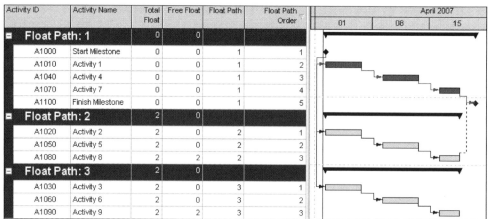

The reader may wish to read the help file or experiment with the software to see the results.

28.13 Rates for Roles

Primavera Version 5.0 supports rates with Roles. Up to five rates (the same number of rates as resources) may be assigned to roles which may be used for estimating and cash flow forecasting of projects before the actual resource completing the work is assigned to the activity. Select **Enterprise**, **Roles...** to open the **Roles** form:

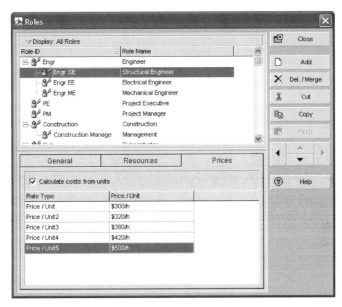

Different rates may be required for different clients such as an internal project rates and rates for different types of external clients.

28.14 Excel Import and Export Tool

Primavera Version 5.0 has a built in tool for importing to and exporting from Excel the following data when the user is assigned a Superuser security profile:

- Activities
- Relationships
- Resources
- Resources Assignments and
- Expenses

To import or export data to Excel select **File**, **Import...** or **Export...** and follow the instructions in the Wizards. **Export Templates** may be created and re-used at a later date with this tool.

When attempting to import data using this type of tool there are some guidelines that apply to many applications, not just to this Primavera tool:

- Create a test project and experiment with this function before using it on a live project.
- Export some data first as this exports the correct column headings and sheet names.
- Change or add data to the exported spreadsheet and import new data into the test environment. Then check that the data is importing correctly and that the schedule is calculating as expected.
- Back up or take a copy of your project before importing into a live project.
- Usually is better not to try to import calculated fields as these are normally recalculated after the data has been imported and the schedule recalculated.
- When only exporting some data on a one off basis then it may be easier just to copy and paste the data into a spreadsheet.

A few points to understand when using the Primavera Version 5.0 function:

- The following sheets are created on export and these sheet names must not be changed:
  - ➢ **TASK** containing Activity data
  - ➢ **TASKPRED** containing Activity Relationships data
  - ➢ **PROJCOST** containing Expenses data
  - ➢ **RSRC** containing Resources data
  - ➢ **TASKRSRC** containing Resource Assignments data
  - ➢ **USERDATA** containing user data that should not be changed.
- Do not change the language between importing and exporting.
- The first row of data in each sheet that is exported contains the database field name. The first row must not be changed otherwise the data will not be imported.
- The second row in the spreadsheet contains **Captions** that may be changed.
- Dictionary data that is being imported must exist before the data is imported.
- Only a maximum of 200 columns of data may be exported.
- **Sub-units** of time are not supported and the Sub-unit checkboxes in the **Edit**, **User Preferences**, **Time Units** tab and should be unchecked.
- **Percent Completes** must be must have a value of between 0 and 100.

There is substantially more information in the Help file under **Reference**, **Importing and Exporting**.

28.15 P3 Subproject Import

With Primavera Version 5.0 the importation of P3 files has been improved:

- One or more individual subprojects may now be imported, and
- The import EPS locations specified, which may be different for each subproject

Select **File**, **Import...** or **Export...** to open the appropriate form.

28.16 Export to Primavera Contractor

Primavera Version 5.0 projects that are open may be exported in XER format that may be imported into Primavera Contractor 4.1 and Primavera Version 6.0 projects that are open may be exported in XER format that may be imported into Primavera Contractor 5.0.

Select **File**, **Export...** to open the **Export** form.

28.17 Audit Trail Columns

Primavera Version 5.0 introduced four basic audit trail columns that may be displayed in the Activities window which display the date user that added the activity when and by whom it was modified:

- Added By - the user that added the activity,
- Added Date - the date the activity was added,
- Modified By - the user that last modified the activity and
- Modified Date - the date the activity was last modified.

28.18 Enhanced or New Graphics Functions

The following are a list of the new graphics functions in Primavera Version 5.0:

28.18.1 Bar Label Placement

Primavera Version 5.0 introduced two more positions for bar labels titled Top and Bottom.

28.18.2 Three Timescale Units

Primavera Version 5.0 introduced the option of two or three timescale lines in the Gantt Chart Timescale and may be used to show ordinal and/or calendar dates.

Ordinal dates display the time scale by counting in the selected units starting from a user definable start date. This option works in a similar way to the P3 function where the Ordinal start date may be selected.

When 3 lines are displayed the ordinal dates and calendar dates may displayed

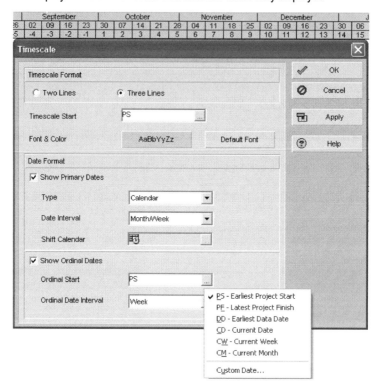

28.18.3 Vertical Sight Lines

Primavera Version 5.0 introduced a new **Bar Chart Options** form **Sight Lines** tab bar which now enables the specification of both vertical and horizontal Sight Lines, which brings the functionality up to match P3, SureTrak and Microsoft Project:

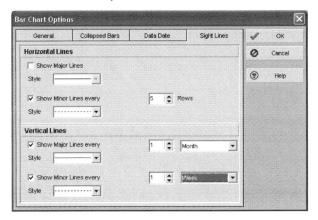

28.18.4 Reorganize Automatically

Primavera Version 5.0 introduced a function titled Reorganize Automatically, which is similar to the P3 and SureTrak function but applies to all Layouts, not just the selected Layout. Select **Edit, User Preferences…** to open the **User Preferences** form and click the **Application** tab.

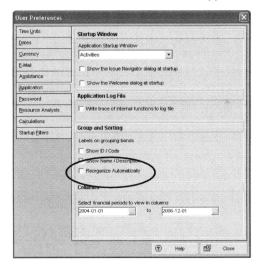

When the **Reorganize Automatically** box is checked, all views will reorganize automatically when data fields are changed that are used in the layout such as Grouping and Sorting.

It is often better to disable **Reorganize Automatically** when data is being edited that is used in the grouping of data in a Layout which will prevent the activities moving to their new position in the Layout until all data has been edited.

To reorganize a view, select **Tools, Reorganize Now** or **Shift+F2**.

28.18.5 Gantt Chart Curtains

Primavera Version 5.0 introduced a function allowing the placing of multiple curtains on the Gantt Chart which may be all hidden or displayed.

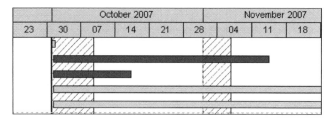

Select **Vie̲w**, **A̲ttachments** to display the **C̲urtain** menu:

- **A̲dd Curtain** opens the **Curtain Attachment** form used to create a curtain:

- **S̲how All** shows all the curtains,
- **Hi̲de All** hides all the curtains and
- Clicking on a curtain in the Gantt Chart also opens the **Curtain Attachment** form where individual curtains may be deleted or hidden.

28.19 Improved Report Wizard Functionality

The Primavera Version5.0 **Report Wizard** has been enhanced with the following additional features:

- Enhanced column formatting and
- Multiple subject area selection.

29 TOPICS NOT COVERED IN THIS PUBLICATION

The following topics are not covered in this publication:

- Budgets, including
  - ➢ Budget Summary
  - ➢ Budget Log
  - ➢ Funding
  - ➢ Spending Plan
- Resource Assignments Window
- Work Products and Documents
- Thresholds
- Issues
- Risks and Risk Calculation
- Top-Down Estimation
- External Applications
- Earned Value Calculations
- Timesheets
- Timesheet Date Administration
- Claim Digger
- Project Web Site Publisher

30 INDEX

Made in the USA
Lexington, KY
12 April 2011